The United States in Cuba

1898-1902 *Generals, Politicians, and the Search for Policy*

The United States in Cuba

1898–1902

Generals,
Politicians,
and the Search
for
Policy

David F. Healy

THE UNIVERSITY OF WISCONSIN PRESS

Madison, 1963

Published by
The University of Wisconsin Press
430 Sterling Court, Madison 6, Wisconsin

Copyright © 1963 by the
Regents of the University of Wisconsin

Printed in the United States of America by
George Banta Company, Inc.
Menasha, Wisconsin

Library of Congress Catalog Card Number 63–13742

To Manley B. Healy,
who first interested me
in American history

Acknowledgments

This study has grown out of an interest in late nineteenth-century American expansionism and has been both stimulated and guided by the sympathetic interest of Professor (now President) Fred Harvey Harrington of the University of Wisconsin, to whom grateful acknowledgment is here made. Acknowledgment should also be made of the courtesy and efficiency with which the staffs of the Library of the State Historical Society of Wisconsin, the University of Wisconsin Library, the Manuscripts Division of the Library of Congress, and the National Archives, Interior Department Branch, helped the author to find his materials. Special thanks are due Professor Joe Patterson Smith of Illinois College for his painstaking reading of the manuscript and his valuable suggestions for improving it. It goes without saying that none of the above are responsible for the shortcomings of this work, which are mine alone.

Finally, I would like to express my deep gratitude to my wife, whose sound historical judgment, keen critical analysis, and plain good sense have helped me through the hard places.

DAVID F. HEALY

Jacksonville, Illinois
December, 1962

Contents

Introduction

Hawaii is ours; Porto Rico is to be ours; at the prayer of her people Cuba finally will be ours; in the islands of the East, even to the gates of Asia, coaling stations are to be ours at the very least; the flag of a liberal government is to float over the Philippines, and may it be the banner that Taylor unfurled in Texas and Fremont carried to the coast.
Albert J. Beveridge, 1898.

Although territorial expansion was a commonplace of United States development long before 1898, the Spanish-American War brought in its wake a new kind of expansion, which lay largely outside the American experience. The acquisition or control of large, populous dependencies not contiguous to the home land and inhabited by alien peoples with their own cultures, values, and institutions, posed problems for the United States to which it could bring no ready-made answers. American leaders had to decide whether such areas should occupy the traditional territorial status through which most of the states of the Union had at some time passed, whether they should be permanent colonies in a new American Empire, or whether some other, less formal relationship should be devised. They had to determine how the new acquisitions should be governed, and to what extent these "subject peoples" could share in their own government. Finally, they were faced with the problem of reconciling one theory of government at home with another abroad.

The nation's policymakers worked out the answers to these these questions chiefly in the twin laboratories of Cuba and the Philippine Islands, where they applied two different approaches. In the Philippines, formal annexation and direct colonial government brought insurrection by the Filipinos and discord in the United States. In Cuba, where circumstances prevented quick annexation, American leaders had time to learn from experience and to develop methods of indirect control which avoided many of the burdens and pitfalls of traditional colonial rule.

In the long run, it was the Cuban solution to the problem of overseas expansion which the United States chose to adopt for general use. This solution involved at least three elements, which could be applied either singly or in combination. The first of these, basic to the others, was the establishment of informal protectorates which left a large degree of internal self-government. When necessary, these could involve military occupation by United States forces, but never the assumption of formal sovereignty. The second element was the establishment, through trade treaties or financial arrangements, of strong economic ties with the United States. The third was economic penetration through United States investment and development.

The United States utilized these techniques for at least three decades to spread American influence over the Caribbean. At first they were transferred to other areas almost unchanged, as in the case of Panama. Later on, and further afield, the application often came in a variety of modified forms. Thus the study of the formation of America's Cuban policy from 1898 to 1902 has an interest transcending the immediate case at hand, for the Spanish-American War and the first Cuban occupation led to decisions which were soon applied in many other areas.

The United States in Cuba

1898-1902 *Generals,*
Politicians,
and the Search
for
Policy

Cuban Rebellion and United States Reaction

It was New Year's Day, 1899, and the morning was sunny. Cuban and American flags and bunting gleamed from the buildings of Havana. Crowds of Cubans, in which mingled a few Americans, thronged the streets, hoping to witness a part of the day's ceremonies. Troops, too, swelled the crowds—Spanish troops, marching in long columns toward the water front to board transports for the voyage back to Spain, and American troops, gathering in the center of the city. As the morning wore on, a double file of Spanish soldiers formed in front of the old Governor's Palace and a body of United States infantry drew up in the Plaza de Armas, immediately facing them. By half-past eleven the American generals began to arrive, splendid in dress uniforms and swords. Shortly before noon General John R. Brooke, about to become the first United States Military Governor of Cuba, led the group into the Palace and up the stairs to the Salón de Sesiones, a large, bare-looking room on the second floor.

Inside this chamber waited General Adolfo Jiménez Castellanos, the last Spanish Governor General of Cuba, and his staff. A few minutes were devoted to introductions; then General Jiménez indicated that the formalities should begin. The officers present quickly took their places in an orderly semicircle, the American generals in the gold braid of full dress, the Spanish in plain fatigue uniforms. A little knot of Cuban insurgent commanders, standing apart, wore sober dark blue, with only tiny silver stars to denote their rank.

General Jiménez, a small, bullet-headed man with a military goatee, stepped forward, handed a copy of his speech to an American interpreter, and addressed himself in Spanish to General James Wade, head of the American Evacuation Commission. In brief, dry phrases, the Spanish general began the formal transfer of the sovereignty of Cuba from Spain to the custody of the United States. His words were partly obscured by the noise of an American regimental band which was playing patriotic airs on the plaza just outside. An aide left the room and the music ceased abruptly, but the booming of saluting cannon continued to disturb the quiet of the big room. When Jiménez had finished, General Wade turned to General Brooke and, in a single sentence, invested him with the military command of Cuba.

Outside, the masses of people gathered along the Punta and at the foot of the Prado saw the flag of Spain rise slowly over Morro Castle. It hung there long enough to be saluted by the guns of the United States warships in the harbor before it came down for the last time. For better or for worse, the United States government was now responsible for the government of the island of Cuba.[1]

This new responsibility would bring with it a host of problems and perplexities. It would be necessary to resolve the basic ambiguities of United States policy in Cuba, which so far were largely unrecognized. Had the nation gone to war with Spain to secure Cuban liberty, to stop human suffering, to protect American business interests, or to acquire new territory? Was Cuba to be made an independent nation, to become an American protectorate, or to be annexed to the United States? The beginning of American rule in Cuba made it imperative that the United States define her objectives there, and this was to be the greatest single task of the next three years.

The island of Cuba sprawls beyond the mouth of the Gulf of Mexico like a great hammerhead shark swimming lazily out to sea. It dominates by its position both the Gulf and the Caribbean; it is the largest of the West Indies and one of the nearest to the United States. Seven hundred and thirty miles long, and reaching a maximum breadth of over 150 miles, it is big enough to hold a variety of contrasts. The broad, rolling fields of western Cuba's Havana and Matanzas provinces differ sharply from the rugged mountains of the eastern end of the island, where the Sierra Maestre rises at one point to over 8,000 feet above sea level, just as the upland tobacco farms of Pinar del Río differ from the low-lying swamps of the south coast. Similarly, in the 1890's, the two halves of the island contrasted in their levels of development, with the bulk of the wealth, agriculture, and population concentrated in the western portion.

This rich and varied island has attracted the interest of the United States in almost every period of the nation's history. The reasons for this are to be found, not only in the great intrinsic value of the place, but in other factors as well. Its location, less than 100 miles from the Florida keys and under 600 miles from the mouths of the Mississippi, has made it seem to some American statesmen a natural appendage of the United States, while to all it has appeared a strategic key to the nation's Gulf coast. During the sectional controversy of the 1850's, Southern leaders sought to add Cuba to the union by purchase or filibuster, in order to redress the failing balance between slave and free states. After the Civil War, there appeared an increased commerce between Cuba and the United States, followed in time by a substantial and growing United States investment in the island. While annexationist dreams came and went with the years, it was the nation's fixed policy to oppose the acquisition of Cuba from Spain by any other power. To this was added in time a dawning realization that American interests were bound to be involved in almost any drastic change in Cuba's status or condition.

The 1890's were a period of such drastic change. Cuba was a land in transition, undergoing basic shifts in her society, economy, and political orientations. What had once been a sleepily prosperous colony of large cattle estates and diversified agriculture was being transformed by the rise of an ever more dominant sugar industry. This metamorphosis was complicated by accompanying cross currents: the reorganization of the labor system was made necessary by the progressive abolition of slavery, beginning in 1868 and reaching completion in the 1880's, while the growing impact of the industrial revolution called for constant change in the organization and techniques of sugar production.

There were political complications, too. Cuba, with Puerto Rico, constituted the last remnant of Spanish empire in the western hemisphere. The nineteenth century saw a slow alienation of the native creole leaders from the privileged newcomers who came out from Spain in an endless succession to rule the island. In 1865 the local leaders formed an Autonomist Party to work for the peaceful reform of their government within the Spanish empire. Along with a voice in their own government, the Cubans hoped to secure the modification of the economic controls exercised over them by Spain. The Spanish colonial authorities had long imposed a restrictive tariff policy designed to protect the interests of monopolistic Spanish merchants and shippers in the Cuban trade. To the resulting higher prices for Cuban consumers and an added difficulty in marketing Cuban exports abroad, was added a high local tax burden and an inefficient bureaucracy. This Spanish effort to maintain an ancient mercantilist policy in a new era of world exchange was to cost both Spain and Cuba dearly.

Most of these issues relate to the so-called Ten Years' War, a period of intermittent turmoil in Cuba which lasted from 1868 to 1878. Born in creole discontent with Spanish rule, it never got far beyond a desultory guerrilla warfare, centered in the wilder parts of eastern Cuba. As the upper classes gradually lost interest in the movement, its leaders appealed to the large Negro population by proclaiming the immediate abolition of slavery and urging the slaves to fight for their freedom. A widespread destruction of property by the *insurrectos* and a good deal of indiscriminate killing on both sides, government and rebel, brought numerous protests from the United States. Spanish-American friction was increased by the activities of a swarm of gun-runners of Cuban extraction and United States citizenship. After ten years, however, peace was negotiated in 1878 between the Spanish government and the rebels.

This rude struggle, though militarily unimpressive, was to have lasting results for Cuba. The only real reform won by the revolutionists was the final liquidation of slavery. One effect of this was to raise the cost of labor on the sugar estates, thus forcing on the planters an increased mechanization of production. But many planters had been hard hit by the wartime destruction of property and were in no position to make large new capital investments. Others, who annually purchased their necessities on credit from mercantile houses in Spain or New England, were unable to pay their debts. The resulting foreclosures and dearth of local capital brought large American business interests for the first time into direct control of Cuban sugar properties.

During this same period Cuban cane sugar was hard pressed in the world market by the competition of European beet sugar, whose production was subsidized by the governments of most of the great continental powers. The only salvation for the Cubans was to cut their own production costs through mechanization of production and centralization of control, and to seek to capture the United States market, in which their geographical nearness gave them an advantage over their rivals. But Cuban planters, hard hit by the effects of the Ten Years' War, a mounting debt burden, a shortage of local capital, and oppressive Spanish regulations, found it increasingly difficult to make these necessary adjustments, and a perceptible increase in foreign ownership appeared in the sugar industry.

Other segments of society also faced serious problems. With the end of slavery a quarter of Cuba's working population attained legal citizenship and became free wage laborers. But employees, unlike slaves, could be dispensed with when they were not needed. The highly seasonal nature of both sugar and tobacco production made for wide variations in the number of workers needed in different parts of the year. With their former slaves now mere employees, planters were able to cut their costs by laying off a large fraction of the labor force during the several months of the slack season. The resulting seasonal unemployment became a permanent social problem and added to the difficulties of the freedmen in finding a satisfactory place for themselves in Cuban life.

By the 1890's these currents had already run far in Cuban life. The island was increasingly dominated by a one-crop economy, rapidly centralizing in the hands of large investors, some of them American, and selling its product chiefly in the United States. In the early years of the decade these new conditions brought with them a short-lived prosperity, which soon gave way to depression and upheaval.[2]

On February 24, 1895, an insurrection against Spanish rule began in the island of Cuba. Organized by a Cuban revolutionary junta with headquarters in New York City (originally the headquarters of José Martí's Cuban Revolutionary Party), the revolt spread rapidly among a population full of discontent, in an economy crippled by depression. A three-year boom in the Cuban sugar industry had collapsed. This circumstance was chiefly due to the abrogation by the United States of a reciprocity treaty which had given Cuban sugar a favored position in the American market, and to a world-wide fall in sugar prices resulting from the intensive competition of European beet sugar. Cuban prosperity was at an end, and the old, festering resentment at Spanish rule was reinforced by a new indignation at Spain's backward colonial economic policies, which now bore the more heavily on the island. The countryside swarmed with unemployed sugar workers who were ripe for revolt, and the 1895 revolution came at the right time to win their allegiance.

The government of Spain was quick to see the threat posed by this revolt, and in a short time a large Spanish army began operations in Cuba. The insurrection, however, proved curiously hard to quell. Led by a tough old Santo Domingan named Máximo Gómez, who had been an *insurrecto* leader in the Ten Years' War, the motley insurgent forces repeated the tactics of the former struggle, but with greater success. Rarely did they attempt to face the Spanish armies in pitched battle. Instead, they sought to disrupt the economic life of Cuba through the skillful use of guerrilla tactics. While the exploits of leaders like Gómez and Antonio Maceo, a dashing mulatto general, filled newspaper headlines, dozens of small local bands carried the revolution through the countryside. By terrorizing planters and workers and by burning cane fields, these bands rapidly wrecked the island's sugar industry. This in turn made the economic situation more hopeless, swelled the ranks of the indigent workers from whom the rebels were chiefly recruited, and crippled the operations and revenues of the insular government.[3]

In an attempt to cope with Gómez's tactics, the Madrid government sent General Valeriano Weyler to Cuba in 1896 with instructions to put down the rebellion through harsh measures. Máximo Gómez had hoped that his constant raiding would force the civil population either into the revolutionary ranks or into the garrisoned towns, where they would starve. Weyler seized this strategy and, through what came to be known as the Reconcentration Policy, turned it to his own purposes. The new Governor General ordered the entire populace to leave the countryside and move into the garrison towns. Supplies left in the country were destroyed; anyone found there was presumed to be an *insurrecto* and thus fair game for the army. The export of food from the towns was forbidden. Deprived of supplies and recruits, the Cuban army was to be harried through the land.

These measures, added to the actions of Gómez, virtually ended the normal economic life of Cuba. The refugees who huddled in the towns could not begin to feed themselves from the inadequate garden plots set aside for them, and sickness and starvation took a heavy toll. Those who did not join the miserable crowds in the towns fell prey to Spaniards and *insurrectos* alike. By 1897 Cuba was reduced to misery, while the struggle there showed little sign of abating.[4]

In the meantime, the situation in Cuba had grown into a major public issue in the United States. The American press and people were sympathetic from the first toward the Cuban independence movement, and had tended to blame the distress in Cuba wholly on the harsh measures of Weyler. This tendency was fostered by the Cuban junta in New York, whose agents flooded the desks of editors across the nation with circumstantial accounts of Cuban victories and Spanish outrages. In an era when few newspapers could afford foreign correspondents of their own, the junta's stories were the only easily accessible source of copy on the Cuban Revolution. Since these stories were hard-hitting, lively, and readable, hundreds of editors took to running them as straight news, often without even identifying their source.

As the revolt continued, the national imagination was daily inflamed by highly colored accounts of bloody struggles for freedom, of terrible human suffering, and of horrifying Spanish atrocities, all occurring, not at the ends of the earth, but virtually on the nation's doorstep. Supplied to an uncritical public by an increasingly sensational press, such accounts fanned the traditional American sympathy for the underdog into a formidable mass emotionalism oriented on Cuba.[5]

This attitude was strongly reflected in Congress, and every session after 1895 saw the introduction of numerous resolutions providing for the recognition of Cuban independence, the recognition of Cuban belligerency, or some kind of United States intervention in aid of the Cubans. As early as the spring of 1896, the Senate and the House of Representatives had passed a concurrent resolution declaring that, in the opinion of Congress, the United States government should extend belligerent rights to the so-called Cuban Republic.[6] This the executive refused to do, but a similar resolution was passed by the Senate alone in May of 1897.[7] Both in and out of Congress, sentiment in favor of the Cubans appeared to grow steadily, even after the adoption of a less severe policy by the Spanish government late in 1897.

President Grover Cleveland did not see the situation in the same light as did the pro-Cuban congressmen. To the President's strong aversion to involvement in a war with Spain was added an intense distrust of the Cuban rebels, who threatened the security of valuable American properties in Cuba. More interested in American interests than in Cuban independence, Cleveland held to a strict neutrality in the Cuban struggle and refused to allow any official recognition of the insurgent government.

For one thing, such recognition would automatically stop the collection of indemnities from the Spanish Government for damage done to American-owned property in Cuba. An official admission that Cuba suffered, not from mere internal disorders, but from a legal state of war, would relieve Spain from any responsibility for international obligations in territory under insurgent control. And the penniless and struggling insurgents, who would assume such responsibility, did not appear a very sound business risk to the cautious men who steered the ship of state. American businessmen expected someone to repay them for the damage done to their Cuban property, and the Spanish government still seemed the best candidate for that unhappy task.[8]

The administration feared Cuban success, however, for even more basic reasons. To Secretary of State Richard Olney it was clear that the restoration of Spanish control was the best way to bring back stability and order to Cuba, thus permitting the resumption of normal business operations there. A Cuban victory, he thought, meant an inevitable decline into anarchy, and therefore the permanent loss of the entire American economic interest in the island. If Spain were driven from Cuba, Olney wrote the Spanish Minister early in 1896, the end result must be a war of the races, black against white, among the insurgents themselves.[9]

Olney's opinions were probably influenced by Edwin F. Atkins, a prominent Boston businessman who owned large sugar properties in Cuba and who had pioneered in the penetration of American investment there. Atkins was in Washington at this time, working to prevent the recognition of the insurgents for the very reasons now urged by the Secretary of State. He claimed to represent not only himself, but the other American property owners in Cuba as well, and had conferred with Olney a number of times about the Cuban situation.[10]

Grover Cleveland summarized the Cuban policy of his administration in his annual message to Congress of December 7, 1896. The President began by disqualifying the rebel government from recognition by the United States. Its functions were shadowy, he reported, and the real direction of the insurgents came from the generals in the field and from the Cuban junta in New York. The Cuban Republic was "a government merely on paper," and unworthy of American aid.

But, as the blunt-spoken Cleveland stated, the nation's concern with Cuba was "by no means of a wholly sentimental or philanthropic character," since "our actual pecuniary interest in it is second only to that of the people and government of Spain." The President estimated the total United States investment in Cuba at between $30,000,000 and $50,000,000, and he placed the annual value of trade between Cuba and the United States at the time the revolution began at around $100,000,000.

Condemning both the Cubans and the Spanish for their indifference to property rights, Cleveland suggested that the war in Cuba could be ended with satisfaction to both sides by a Spanish offer of autonomous rule for the Cubans under the Spanish crown. He offered the good offices of the United States in reaching such a solution, and reiterated the American desire for peace and the nation's disinterest in conquest. At the end of the President's statement, however, was a threat. It should not be assumed, he said, that the "hitherto expectant attitude of the United States will be indefinitely maintained." If it became obvious that Spain was unable to deal successfully with the insurrection in Cuba, the obligation of the United States to respect Spain's sovereignty would be superseded by "higher obligations." Cleveland reminded Congress that the time might come when "a correct policy and care for our interests," as well as broad humanitarian motives, would demand United States intervention in the Cuban war in order to stop the fighting and prevent further destruction.[11] In short, if Spain could restore order in Cuba, well and good, but if not, the United States might have to do so. The President did not speak of the possibility of peace and order under the insurgents.

Thus the talk of intervention in Cuba soon implied different objects to different groups. A large group in Congress continued to speak in terms of helping the Cubans gain independence, while Cleveland feared Cuban independence as the plague, and considered the possibility of intervening, if at all, purely for the protection of American interests.

But by now the days of Cleveland's presidency were numbered. The great election campaign of 1896 had drawn to its climax, and culminated in the victory of William McKinley of Ohio, ex-Senator, ex-Governor, and triumphant apostle of protection for American industry. Through the year 1897 Republicans streamed into Washington to replace Democratic officeholders, and White House routines were altered to meet the desires of still another occupant. A new group now manned the executive branch of the government; and yet, as far as Cuba was concerned, surprisingly little had changed. When William McKinley succeeded Grover Cleveland as president, he took a position essentially similar to that of his predecessor.

In his annual message to Congress of December 6, 1897, President McKinley reviewed the Cuban situation at length. He named, and dismissed in turn, three possible new policies which the United States might adopt. The first alternative, United States recognition of Cuban belligerency, he deemed "now unwise," but promised to reconsider it should it ever thereafter appear proper. The second step, recognition of Cuban independence, he considered even more premature. The third possibility would be either a "neutral intervention" by the United States to impose a "rational compromise" on the two parties, or an intervention in favor of one or the other party. This approach McKinley alo rejected for the present, recommending that the recently formed Sagasta ministry in Madrid be given a chance to try out its policies and see what they could accomplish. But the President, like Cleveland before him, included a veiled threat that, if the new ministry failed to make headway in Cuba, United States intervention might become necessary.

On one point McKinley was definite. "I speak not of forcible annexation," he said, "for that cannot be thought of. That, by our code of morality, would be criminal aggression."[12]

In the meantime, the continued failure of Spaniards and Cubans to progress toward a compromise settlement of the Cuban fighting led some Americans to advocate the purchase of Cuba by the United States. President Cleveland had mentioned this as a theoretical solution of the problem in his annual message for 1896, but he pointed out that Spain had never indicated that she was willing to sell the island.[13] However, General Stewart L. Woodford, McKinley's newly appointed Minister to Spain, became hopeful that Spain could be persuaded to sell as a way out of her difficulties. In March of 1898, Woodford requested authority from McKinley to raise the question with the Spanish government as soon as conditions should appear favorable.[14] But time was already running out, and Woodford's efforts to arrange the purchase of Cuba came to nothing.

While the United States government remained an acutely interested observer of events in Cuba, a group of American financiers had evolved an astonishing scheme for solving everything through an exuberant application of private enterprise. Their object was no less than the purchase of Cuba from Spain by the Cuban insurgents themselves. This purchase would be financed and negotiated by a New York financial syndicate, at a profit to itself which could only be conjectured but which might prove very large. The ostensible head of this syndicate was Samuel M. Janney, of the Wall Street banking firm of Christy and Janney, but the central figure in the group was really Colonel John J. McCook, a prominent New York corporation lawyer. McCook, a leading New York Republican, had close contacts with President McKinley and had been offered the post of Secretary of the Interior in McKinley's first cabinet.[15]

As early as the spring of 1897 there were persistent press reports that McCook had submitted a plan to McKinley providing for the purchase of Cuba from Spain by the insurgents, with money borrowed from an American banking syndicate acting under the supervision of the United States government.[16] McCook denied the reports, but he was in fact actually working toward just such an arrangement. A formal agreement with the Cubans was concluded in New York City on August 5, 1897, signed by Tomás Estrada Palma, the Cuban Republic's delegate to the United States, and Samuel M. Janney, representing the American syndicate.

According to this contract, Janney and his associates would offer to pay a part of the huge debt incurred by Spain in Cuba, in return for the complete withdrawal of Spain and her formal recognition of Cuban independence. The syndicate was to receive bonds of the Cuban Republic to the amount of one hundred and fifty million Cuban dollars (worth somewhat less than United States dollars),[17] paying interest at 4 per cent per annum, the principal to be paid off within fifty years. These bonds were to be secured by a lien on Cuban customs receipts, and their servicing and collection was to be under the supervision of the United States government, which was to act as financial trustee. More important, the United States was to use its official influence to induce Spain to accept the whole arrangement and was also to act as guarantor for the fulfillment of the terms by all parties.

The contract named Colonel McCook as the man who was to persuade the United States government to fulfill its part of the plan. If McCook failed to enlist the support of the McKinley administration by October 1, 1897, the contract would be voided. The Mercantile Trust Company of New York was named as fiscal agent for the transaction. Nowhere was there specified the amount to be paid by the syndicate to Spain. It would make the best bargain it could with the Spaniards, while receiving a fixed amount of bonds from the Cubans, so that the profit margin depended on the outcome of the negotiations.[18]

Although the contract contained an October 1 deadline, later extended to November 1, it was not until December, 1897, that the Cuban Council of Government approved it with minor modifications.[19] But in November Janney and Estrada Palma had signed a second contract, with essential changes in the terms. This time the New York group was to receive Cuban bonds worth thirty-seven and a half million Cuban dollars, in return for securing the evacuation of Cuba by Spain and the formal recognition of Cuban independence by both Spain and the United States. This was to be done *without* paying anything at all to Spain. The war tide was rising in America; the syndicate now meant to buy influence in Washington rather than Madrid and let the United States government handle Spain. The first Janney contract remained in force, however, and the second contract was to be voided if the first were ever implemented.[20] The Council of Government approved this second Janney contract on January 27, 1898.[21]

In spite of the syndicate's attempts to keep them secret, some of these schemes eventually became public. An article in William Randolph Hearst's *New York Journal* described the broad outlines of the first Janney contract on March 12, 1898, and charged that McKinley had been willing to support the plan until the *Maine* disaster made it hopeless.[22] In subsequent editions the *Journal* assailed the scheme as an attempt to "transfer the Cuban question into a commercial transaction."[23] But on March 18, the Hearst newspaper reversed its stand and appropriated the now futile idea for its own. A front-page box headed: "Cuba, through the *Journal,* offers to buy her freedom," contained an announcement by Bartolomé Masó, President of the Cuban Republic, that his "government" was ready to pay Spain a large indemnity in return for independence.[24]

By this time, however, events had begun to outrun both the careful explorations of the McKinley administration and the intricate machinations of promoters. The nation was catapulting toward a war over Cuba, and all peaceful and conventional approaches to the problem became increasingly irrelevant.

McKinley's War Message
Arouses Congressional Debate

Early in 1898 conditions grew worse in Cuba, and Spanish-American relations were subjected to an increasing strain. In February the Cuban junta published a personal letter written by Enrique Dupuy de Lôme, the Spanish Minister to the United States, which had fallen into its hands. In it Dupuy had spoken slightingly of McKinley and made other injudicious statements, including a hint that current negotiations for a commercial treaty with the United States were only for effect, and not in entire good faith.

The sensation this caused was short-lived, for it was followed a week later by a second event which dwarfed it into comparative insignificance. On February 15, 1898, the United States battleship *Maine* was mysteriously blown up in Havana harbor with a loss of over 250 American lives, and a wave of feeling swept the United States which seemed to make war inevitable.

It appeared in Washington that the only way to save the situation was through the negotiation of an immediate end to the fighting in Cuba. Under heavy pressure from the United States, the Spanish government agreed to grant an armistice on condition that the Cubans should ask for it, but this the *insurrectos* refused to do. On the contrary, they saw a chance to win their war with the aid of American intervention; all they need do was to keep it going.[1]

As war with Spain approached, there was an increase in serious newspaper discussion about Cuba's future. Up to now most interventionist editors had simply favored the withdrawal of Spain from Cuba and the establishment of Cuban independence. Annexation talk was rare, and usually looked to some future voluntary action of the Cubans themselves.[2] This viewpoint was still common in the spring of 1898. An editorial in Pulitzer's *New York World* noted in March that "here and there in the country there is a voice raised for the capture and annexation of Cuba," and stamped the idea "an unworthy suggestion."[3] Nevertheless, the proximity of actual intervention led some editors to look at the future more closely.

Anti-war newspapers like the New York *Evening Post* warned that "the Cuban trouble would not end with the expulsion of the Spanish." If the United States forced Spain out of Cuba, a *Post* editorial warned, "We should then find ourselves in possession of an island, desolated by war, and inhabited by a mongrel race, unused to self-government, and grossly ignorant and superstitious."[4] If Cuba became an American dependency, the editorial asked, how was it to be governed? Would the Cubans be allowed popular suffrage? Would the island eventually be admitted to the Union as one or more states, and if so, what kind of an addition to the nation would these states make? If not, what was to be the alternative?

A similar uneasiness was expressed by Senator Redfield Proctor of Vermont in a famous speech to the Senate describing the appalling conditions he had observed on a personal inspection trip through Cuba. While Proctor considered some kind of intervention unavoidable, he declared himself opposed to annexation "because it is not wise policy to take in any people of foreign tongue and training, and without any strong guiding American element."[5]

Others, however, were not bothered by such questions. One well-publicized report on the Cuban question was made by a "Congressional Commission" which went to Cuba early in 1898 under the auspices of William Randolph Hearst. This "Commission" consisted of Senators Jacob H. Gallinger of New Hampshire, Hernando de Soto Money of Mississippi, and John M.

Thurston of Nebraska, and Representatives Amos J. Cummings of New York and William A. Smith of Michigan. Money and Cummings were Democrats, while Gallinger, Thurston, and Smith were Republicans, but the entire group held interventionist views, and their findings were sensationally displayed on the entire front page of Hearst's war-mongering *Journal.*

"The future of Cuba is American," the Commission's report stated confidently. Cuba, it declared, was already lost to Spain. Under an independent and stable Cuban government, immigration and capital would pour into the island from the United States, and the "Americanization" of Cuba would be accomplished within twenty years. "The exploration of Cuba by American capital is the certainty of the future when peace and stable government are assured," the legislators concluded, and investments, if made quickly, would yield "enormous profits" in the future. While the report spoke of an independent Cuba, it hinted strongly that independence would be a transitory stage, leading in time to annexation or a United States protectorate.[6]

Of all the major metropolitan dailies, Whitelaw Reid's *New York Tribune* was generally considered closest to the McKinley administration. On April 10, as the war crisis drew to a climax, a *Tribune* editorial examined the consequences of intervention in Cuba. In such a case, the editorialist found, "the responsibility of the United States is greater than most men realize," for if the Americans drove Spain from the island, they would become directly responsible for the establishment of better government there. "This does not mean annexation, nor military government, nor any other definite thing or form, of necessity, [the conclusion ran] but in some manner the United States must take care that decent government is provided for in Cuba." And if, as the *Tribune* hinted, the insurgents were unable to provide such government, then it would fall upon the United States to do so.[7]

The discussion of the future government of Cuba was not limited to the pages of newspapers, for the question was bound to be a central one in formulating a program of intervention. McKinley, like Cleveland, opposed the recognition of the Cuban revolutionary government, and wanted as free a hand as possible in the future. This brought him into conflict with the widespread

"Now, Little Man, I'll see what I can do for you."
—*New York Evening Journal*
Reprinted in *Literary Digest*, April 30, 1898.

American sympathy toward the *insurrectos'* fight for Cuban independence and with the Congressional bloc which favored recognition of the Cuban Republic.

As the diplomatic crisis heightened, McKinley worked on a message to Congress which would establish the position of his government. At the same time, conservative Senate Republican leaders were reported to be conferring on strategy to block the passage of any resolutions recognizing Cuban independence.[8]

Senator Orville H. Platt of Connecticut wrote a friend that "the President and those who sustain him do not want a recognition of independence" but a simple resolution allowing the government "to terminate hostilities in Cuba, to form a stable government there, and to this end to employ the land and naval forces of the United States." According to Platt, "Jingoes want independence and intervention."[9]

On April 11, 1898, President McKinley sent to Congress what amounted to a war message, in which he asked for power to intervene forcibly in Cuba. In the message the President reconsidered the advisability of recognizing the belligerency of the Cuban insurgents, and again rejected such an action. After challenging the stability and genuineness of the Cuban Republic, McKinley went on to question the expediency of recognizing it in any case. Recognition of any particular government in Cuba at present could "subject us to embarrassing conditions of international obligation toward the organization so recognized," he said. And during the intervention, "our conduct would be subject to the approval or disapproval of such government." We would have to submit to its direction, and to assume toward it "the mere relation of a friendly ally."

There were two forms of intervention which the United States could choose in its effort to end the war: intervention as an impartial neutral, or as an active ally of one party or the other. The United States had been acting so far, the President said, virtually as an impartial neutral, and should intervene as one. This, he was careful to state, would involve "hostile constraint" on both parties.[10]

McKinley's steadfast refusal to recognize the Cuban Republic was reinforced by the dispatches which he had been receiving during the preceding month from General Stewart L. Woodford, the United States Minister to Spain. Woodford had become entirely converted to a policy of American annexation of Cuba and repeatedly urged the necessity of this step on McKinley. He had written McKinley that "we shall probably have to accept the ownership and the responsible management of Cuba in order to establish permanent peace in the island,"[11] for in Woodford's opinion, "the rebel flag cannot give peace."[12]

McKinley based his justification of forcible intervention upon four general grounds: first, to end misery and death; second, to protect the lives and property of United States citizens in Cuba; third, to end the injury done to United States trade and commerce by the Cuban struggle; and fourth, to end the expense to the United States government resulting from the enforcement of the neutrality laws and the protection of its citizens in the danger area. He used the explosion of the *Maine* rather as an illustration of the dangers of the situation than as a cause of intervention in itself. Then came the peroration: "In the name of humanity, in the name of civilization, in behalf of endangered American interests which give us the right and the duty to speak and to act, the war in Cuba must stop."

To the main body of his message the President appended a brief statement that the Spanish government had just agreed to suspend hostilities in Cuba unilaterally. This meant Spain's virtual surrender to American demands and would seem to change the situation materially, but McKinley apparently attached little importance to the Spanish action.[13] Perhaps the insurgents' refusal to bargain had robbed it of meaning.

In this message the President's views of Cuban policy came through clearly. First of all, Cuba must be pacified and made politically stable, largely in order to protect American lives, property, and commerce, and "in behalf of endangered American interests which give us the right . . . to act." For this purpose forcible intervention was necessary, with "hostile constraint" on both Spanish and Cubans. The intervention stamped the seal of disapproval on Spanish rule in Cuba, but McKinley refused to endorse the Cuban revolutionaries either. In fact, it was the United States alone which was to determine the future of the island, not in the "mere relation of a friendly ally," but with such a degree of control as to be not "subject to the approval or disapproval" of any other government, nor "required to submit to its direction."

As the President had said, the issue was now with Congress.

The President sent his message to Congress on April 11, and the appropriate committees of the House and Senate went into action. The House was first to act, its Committee on Foreign Affairs reporting out its resolutions on April 13. The Democrats on the committee presented a minority resolution calling for the recognition of the Cuban Republic, but the administration forces quickly mustered the strength to reject it by a vote of 190 to 150.[14] The resolutions actually adopted by the House authorized the President to intervene forcibly in Cuba to stop the war, and to establish there "by the free action of the people thereof a stable and independent government of their own in the Island."[15]

After heated debate, the Senate adopted three resolutions on April 16. Two of them were in harmony with those passed by the House, since they called on Spain to relinquish her authority and withdraw from Cuba, and authorized the President to use the nation's armed forces to insure that this was done. In the first article of its resolutions, however, the Senate diverged sharply from the course followed by both the President and the House of Representatives. It not only declared that the people of Cuba "are, and of right ought to be, free and independent," but recognized the Cuban Republic as the "true and lawful government of that island."[16]

The second part of this article was adopted at the insistence of what the pro-McKinley *New York Tribune* called a "Democratic-Populist-Silverite and radical pro-Cuban coalition."[17] It originated in the minority report of the Foreign Relations Committee and was modeled on the wording of a previous resolution introduced by Senator Joseph B. Foraker of Ohio, the minority report's only Republican signer. It was introduced as an amendment to the Committee's majority report by a Democrat, Senator David Turpie of Indiana, and was hence known as the Turpie Amendment.[18]

The major speeches on the Turpie Amendment were given by Senator Foraker and by Senator Orville Platt of Connecticut. Foraker denied that Congress had any right to empower the President to create a "stable government," or any other kind of government, for the Cubans. He pointed out the inconsistency of saying both that the people of Cuba ought to be free and independent and that an external agency should establish a government for them. A free and independent people, he insisted, must establish their own government. In Foraker's judgment, "this intervention is to be deliberately turned from intervention on the ground of humanity into an aggressive conquest of territory."[19]

Foraker's powerful speech was most effectively countered by that of Platt, who reversed the argument of the Ohio Senator. The administration, Platt said, had placed its intervention in Cuba on irreproachably high grounds, which its opponents would actually lower. Instead of acting in the name of humanity and civilization, the Turpie Amendment, according to Platt, substituted action "in the name of Máximo Gómez, in the name of the Cuban junta in New York."[20]

The loyal administration Republicans supported Platt, but enough Republican senators defected to the opposition to carry the Turpie Amendment on April 16, by a vote of 51 to 37. Voting for the amendment were eighteen Republicans and thirty-three Democrats and Populists, while thirty-two Republicans and five conservative Democrats voted against it.[21]

After the other resolutions had been adopted, but on the same day, a fourth article was added to them by the Senate. It was adopted in the form of an amendment written by Senator Henry M. Teller of Colorado and was passed in the excitement with neither debate nor a roll call. This, the famous "self-denying ordinance," stated "That the United States hereby disclaims any disposition or intention to exercise sovereignty, jurisdiction, or control over said island except for the pacification thereof, and asserts its determination when that is accomplished to leave the government and control of the island to its people."[22]

Teller, a moderate expansionist, had said back in 1894 that "I am in favor of the annexation of Cuba," and had long worked for the annexation of Hawaii.[23] Once a leading western Republican and a member of President Chester Arthur's cabinet, he became a spokesman for western silverites in 1896, and bolted the Republican party to support the candidacy of William Jennings Bryan. Since then he had voted with the Democrats, although still calling himself a "Silver Republican." He had supported United States recognition of Cuban belligerency since 1896, but opposed the drift toward war with Spain.[24]

Horatio S. Rubens, chief legal counsel for the Cuban junta in New York, afterwards claimed that it was at his suggestion that

Senator Teller wrote his resolution and that its purpose was to block the annexation of Cuba by the United States, which Rubens believed to be the goal of the McKinley administration.[25] Since the Senate had already voted to recognize the Cuban Republic as the only lawful government in Cuba, the extra guarantee contained in the Teller Resolution appeared to make little change at the time it was adopted; this may explain the almost casual manner in which the Senate accepted it.

There were rumors of another factor in the easy passage of the amendment. The second Janney contract between the Cuban insurgents and the McCook group had provided for payment to the syndicate of Cuban bonds to the amount of thirty-seven and a half million Cuban dollars, on condition that the syndicate could secure the evacuation of Cuba by Spain and the recognition of Cuban independence by both Spain and the United States. The syndicate was to pay no money to Spain for this purpose and how it was to be achieved was not specified.

Although this contract remained secret, the existence of the syndicate gradually became public, as did the terms of the first Janney contract and the role played in it by John J. McCook. Only a week before the Senate adopted the Teller Amendment, Charles H. Grosvenor of Ohio dramatically warned of McCook's machinations in a statement before the House of Representatives: "Who is John J. McCook? He is the legal representative of the Cuban Junta, of New York, behind which stands four hundred million dollars, more or less, of bonds that can be validated by the recognition of the independence of Cuba by the United States, and they will be destroyed by a policy that drives Spain out of Cuba in the interest of the American people. . . ."[26]

After the United States had declared war, the Council of Government of the Cuban Republic wrote its delegate, Estrada Palma, inquiring about the two Janney contracts: "We need to know the present state of both negotiations, what you have done by virtue of them and the favorable or adverse effects that in your judgment they have produced or could produce, in order that we can take the proper steps."[27] At the same time the Council announced its intention to send to New York a special envoy, Dr. Domingo

Méndez Capote, who was instructed to check on the status of the Janney contracts, determine to what extent, if any, they had been fulfilled, and examine Estrada Palma's expenditures.[28]

The sequel became known some years later. In August, 1904, American newspapers carried a story from Havana which told of the payment by the Cuban government of $2,000,000 to influential Americans who had aided the cause of Cuban independence. The source of the story was a pamphlet printed by the Cuban government for free distribution from the Cuban pavilion at the St. Louis Exposition, which was then in progress. This pamphlet, prepared as an advertisement for Cuba's economic development, alluded to the second Janney contract and stated that influential Americans involved in it did important work for the Cuban cause. In return, the pamphlet said, the Americans received $2,000,000 in Cuban bonds in May, 1898. The bonds were delivered by Estrada Palma with the approval of the Council of Government, and redeemed by the Cubans after they received their independence.[29]

Estrada Palma, who had in the meantime become the first President of Cuba, promptly and vigorously denied this story.[30] But Herbert G. Squiers, United States Minister to Cuba, investigated it and concluded that the Cuban president's denial was for diplomatic purposes only. "I am told that at a Cabinet meeting soon after Mr. Palma explained his action stating that any other reply might have offended Washington," Squiers reported. "I understand that at the time the payment of the interest on the $2,000,000 was discussed in Congress, the President made representations quite to the contrary and he now fears that some radical member may embarrass him with a demand for an explanation."

To his report, Squiers attached a memorandum from an unnamed "reliable source" which claimed to tell the true story. According to this, Samuel Janney, representing the New York syndicate, had come to Estrada Palma after the passage of the Joint Resolutions which contained the Teller Amendment. Janney asked for compensation for the partial fulfillment of the second Janney contract and claimed to have promised the delivery of large amounts of Cuban bonds to persons who had played a part in smoothing the course of the "self-denying ordinance." Estrada Palma, said the anonymous account, objected that the Joint Resolutions did not give the form of recognition stipulated in the contract. Janney insisted that "it was practically the same thing and that his friends in Washington understood it so." The upshot was that the Cubans held a conference and decided to pay Janney two million dollars in bonds to withdraw his claims. The bonds were redeemed after the establishment of an independent Cuban government.[31]

Whatever it owed to such schemes, the Teller Amendment represented a sweeping and categorical commitment by the United States to forego either annexing Cuba or making a protectorate of it. The Senate now confronted the House of Representatives with a program differing essentially from that outlined by the President in his message. According to the Senate version the United States, far from becoming the supreme arbiter of Cuba's destinies, was merely to deliver power to the Cuban Republic and withdraw, promising to interfere no more.

In the face of this threatened reversal by Congress, McKinley held firmly to his own position. He actually prepared a veto message to be used in case the House adopted the Senate's resolutions, while using all the influence of his position to keep the restive House from bolting.[32] On April 18 the House adopted the Senate resolutions, including the Teller Amendment, but only after striking out the section which gave recognition to the Cuban insurgent government. The Senate refused to accept this compromise, and the resolutions went to conference committee.

In the course of the furious debate on the resolutions in the Senate, several members of the Democratic opposition raised searching questions about the refusal to recognize the Cuban Republic. On April 14, Senator William Lindsay of Kentucky asked Senator George Gray of Delaware just what government would eventually assume power in Cuba: "If we are to retain control until a government is formed which meets with our approval, will that government be the act of the people or the act of the United States?" Senator Donelson Caffery of Louisiana followed this with another poser for Gray: Would not "the making of such a government as we approve of" in itself constitute a protectorate? To both of whom Senator Gray, a conservative Democrat who had voted with the Republicans, replied that he was "not here to answer metaphysical conundrums."[33]

Two days later Senator Lindsay returned to the attack:

> Who are we to pacify? We refuse to recognize the republican government; we are to break down the Spanish government; we are to leave the people without any government at all; and then we propose to pacify the people who are thus left absolutely in a state of nature.
>
> Pacify them how? Pacify them through our Army, pacify them by military reconstruction, pacify them by setting up an American government which these people shall accept or remain without government?[34]

And the redoubtable Senator Benjamin R. ("Pitchfork Ben") Tillman of South Carolina cried that his state had lived through a policy of military reconstruction, and that he would not vote to fix a similar policy on the Cubans.[35]

This sniping, however, was not sufficient to hold the Senate to its original purpose under the mounting pressure from the White House. After sending the resolutions twice to conference committee, the Senate gave in to the House terms on April 18, with twenty-eight Democrats and Populists and seven Republicans fighting to the end for the recognition of the Cuban Republic. President McKinley signed these Joint Resolutions on April 20, 1898.[36]

While the public had shown considerable interest in the fight in Congress over the recognition of the Cuban insurgents, few observers paid much attention to the Teller Amendment. What comments were made tended to be favorable, with some notable exceptions. Whitelaw Reid, publisher of the *New York Tribune* and friend of McKinley, saw a basic inconsistency in intervening to end the chaos in Cuba while at the same time foreswearing the exercise of "sovereignty, jurisdiction, and control" there.

> I deeply regret the fourth paragraph in the resolutions as passed [he wrote the President]. We are making ourselves morally responsible for decent government in Cuba, and we can't wash our hands of it after turning Spain out, by merely telling them to set up for themselves. . . . If the result of our efforts is merely to establish a second Hayti nearer our own coast, it will be so pitiful an outcome from a great opportunity as to make Mr. Gladstone's pledge to "scuttle out of Egypt" respectable by comparison.[37]

In a similar vein, Senator Orville Platt complained that the resolutions meant either too little or too much. "If they do not mean that there is now in the island of Cuba a free and independent government, then to whom is Spain to relinquish its authority and government?" the Senator inquired. And if there were such a government, it could only be that Cuban Republic which was so little trusted by Platt and other administration spokesmen. The unhappy Senator feared that the Teller Resolution could only result in the recognition of the insurgents. "What else can the resolutions mean?" he asked himself in genuine perplexity, but there was no one to give him an answer.[38]

War and a New View of Cuba

The war that followed brought the nation into somewhat closer contact with the Cuban revolutionary movement. Although the United States government refused to recognize the insurgent government, United States military commanders were eager to take advantage of insurgent cooperation during their operations in Cuba. The only land campaign fought by the American Army in Cuba was that which centered about the city of Santiago, in the eastern end of the island. The Cuban commander here was General Calixto García, who was theoretically subordinate to Máximo Gómez but actually had a good deal of local independence. As García's forces included about half of the total insurgent strength, it became a matter of some importance to secure his cooperation in the coming operations.

This proved easy to do, and Cuban-American military relations opened on a note of warm cordiality. The revolutionary Council of Government had ordered both Gómez and García to put themselves under the orders of the American generals whenever the occasion presented itself,[1] and García promptly did so. Early in June he sent a message to General Nelson A. Miles, Commanding General of the United States Army, pledging his full cooperation. García said that he regarded Miles's wishes as his orders and had instructed his subordinates to do likewise.[2]

When General William R. Shafter appeared in Cuba at the

30

head of an American expeditionary army of eighteen thousand men, he lost no time in consulting with García and his staff. Before the American troops were disembarked, Shafter went ashore and met the Cubans on June 20 to discuss the best location for landing his army. The actual landing was made in an area recommended by the Cubans. García had previously promised to protect the American landings, and he was as good as his word. The United States forces went ashore on beaches covered by fifteen hundred insurgent troops, while other Cuban units hampered Spanish troop movements in the interior.[3]

At this time, García took a highly favorable view of the United States intervention, partly because he was thoroughly disgusted with his own revolutionary political leaders. While the American army gathered itself on the beaches of Daiquirí and Siboney, García expressed his views in a letter to Estrada Palma. It was no wonder, he said, that the McKinley administration had refused to recognize the Cuban Republic, for its Council of Government was weak, vicious, and oligarchic. He had hoped that a better revolutionary body would replace it, but this had not happened. Now it was too late. If the Cubans accepted the American intervention, they must also accept the fact that they had no government of their own, because the Council of Government was "incapable of fulfilling the most elementary duties" and because McKinley had killed it anyway when he intervened in Cuba without recognizing it.

This being the case, it was up to the Cuban army to prove the mettle of the people in the coming campaign. The Cubans must "fight at the side of the Americans in the first line" and share their sacrifices, in order to prove their worthiness for self-government.

"My only pre-occupation," the General said, "is to draw tighter our good relations with this allied army, and I have no doubt that before the campaign ends, all the people of the United States will be convinced that we do not lack the conditions to govern ourselves." Then it would be time to call together a great national assembly, to erect such a government as would satisfy the purposes of the American war resolutions.[4]

The campaign that followed must have seemed like a cruel

parody of the dreams of the idealistic general, for it saw the growth of a bitter hostility between the two armies. At first all was harmony. With the aid of the United States Navy, García brought between three and four thousand of his own men down the coast to operate with the American forces. But almost immediately friction developed with the Americans over the role to be assigned the Cubans in the joint operations. Many of the *insurrectos* were used as scouts and guides throughout the campaign. García was dismayed to learn, however, that Shafter saw the Cubans essentially as labor troops, and wished them to carry supplies and dig trenches for the Americans. Refusing to make his men into "pack-mules," the dignified old Cuban demanded a worthier task for them.[5]

General Shafter, too, was soon disgruntled with his allies. On July 1 his army attacked the outer defenses east of Santiago in a major engagement afterwards known as the Battle of San Juan Hill. In the attack almost half of his army was sent under General Lawton to carry a fortified outlying village named El Caney which the Spanish occupied in force. Lawton's troops were reinforced with a contingent of twelve hundred Cubans, who were to reconnoiter for the main forces and guide them to their objective. This the Cubans did satisfactorily, after which they considered their mission accomplished. While Lawton's men spent the rest of the day in heavy fighting to take the village, the Cubans sat on a high hill well to the rear, keeping up an ineffective long-range fire. They had fulfilled their orders, but the American soldiers present never forgave them for not coming down to join the attack.[6]

When Santiago was fully invested, García's troops were given a section of the lines to occupy. According to Shafter, the Cuban forces were responsible for blocking off the railroad which ran into Santiago from the north, and for preventing the reinforcement of the city's garrison from that direction. But on the night of July 3, a body of several thousand Spanish troops entered the city without opposition through the sector held by García and joined the defenders within. Dismayed by this complication of his problem, Shafter bitterly blamed García and the Cubans, rapidly losing all confidence in them. General García, he claimed, could not be compelled to obey his instructions. He concluded that "the Cuban forces are not to be depended upon for severe fighting," and that "we will have to depend alone upon our own troops." Soon Shafter extended his own lines in front of those of García and thenceforth virtually ignored the latter.[7]

All this friction, however, was as nothing compared to the open break which followed the surrender of Santiago by the Spanish on July 17. As the senior Cuban commander present, García had expected to participate in the surrender negotiations, and to share in the control of the city after its surrender. But Shafter was under strict instructions to avoid the recognition of the Cuban Republic in any form, and was in a mood to snub the Cubans anyway. The result was that the American general did not permit the Cubans to take part in the conference leading to the city's surrender, and after it, forbade all armed *insurrectos* to enter Santiago. To make the dose even less palatable, Shafter told the outraged García that the Spanish civil authorities in the city would remain in charge until it was convenient to change them for others. "I explained to him fully," Shafter reported, "that we were at war with Spain, and that the question of Cuban independence could not be considered by me."[8] General García angrily parted with Shafter and withdrew his forces into the interior, for a time entirely breaking off contact with the American commander.

The campaign, then, saw the original quarrels over military matters grow into a more serious political clash between the allies. By the time hostilities with Spain ended in August, both Shafter and General H. W. Lawton, the newly appointed military commander of Santiago Province, were beginning to see García's insurgents as a serious threat to United States control of the area. "Definite instructions as to policy to be observed toward the Cuban Army should be given [Lawton wired the War Department on August 16]. These people still maintain their organization, are scattered through the country in vicinity of city, are threatening in their attitude, and keep the inhabitants stirred up and panicky by threats and acts of violence."[9]

In his own despatch of the same date, General Shafter found the attitude of the "pronounced Cubans" hostile; what was worse, they would not disband and go to work, and therefore would have to live by robbery. Shafter did not shrink from his conclusions: "A dual government can't exist here; we have got to have full sway of the Cubans." He hoped, he said, that "wise councils [sic]" would prevail among the Cubans, "as war is no longer possible to them except with ourselves."[10]

The government's reply to these appeals reached Lawton on the same day. It came from the President, who reminded the generals that the United States was responsible for peace and order in the surrendered territory. The Cuban insurgents should be fairly treated, but they must recognize the military authority of the United States and the cessation of hostilities which had been proclaimed. Lawton should see the insurgent leaders and tell them this. The real point of the message was contained in a single line: "Interference from any quarter will not be permitted."[11]

Lawton was shortly afterward succeeded in command of Santiago Province by General Leonard Wood, and the latter lost no time in asserting the authority of the United States. García, Wood said later, came to him and demanded work and rations for his men. "I told him they could have neither, while they remained under arms." García threatened war, and Wood declared that the sooner he began it, the better, "because, as we had taken a mean job on our hands, that might be the best way out of it." According to Wood, García changed his tone, and the crisis passed.[12] Nevertheless, the whole affair had left a distinctly bad taste on both sides.

While the American commanders were embroiled in growing frictions with the Cubans, the rest of the American army had been developing an anti-Cuban bias of astonishing intensity. Early in the campaign, an English war correspondent in Cuba noted the Americans' "sudden, open disavowal of friendliness toward the Cubans."[13] After the Battle of San Juan Hill, Stephen Crane, the *New York World*'s correspondent with the army, reported that "both officers and privates have the most lively contempt for the Cubans. They despise them." Crane charged that the insurgents would not fight, but stayed in the rear to eat up rations and steal the belongings of the American soldiers.[14] The quarrels between the allied commanders had not remained unknown, and had strengthened the prejudices of the American troops. It soon became a commonplace in the army at Santiago that the Cubans would neither fight nor work, and had served no useful function in the campaign.

This was grossly unfair to the Cubans, whose help had actually been of great value. Not only had they covered the American landings, but they had been invaluable as scouts and guides, a fact witnessed by letters of appreciation to García from the American Generals Lawton and Ludlow. And in spite of García's refusal to convert his army into full-time "pack-mules," they had done substantial amounts of carrying and trench digging at crucial times. Furthermore, Cuban forces in the interior had played a role of great importance which was unknown to most Americans. The Spanish Army had a force of over eight thousand regulars at Holguín, some seventy miles northwest of Santiago, which was contained there throughout the campaign by a large body of *insurrectos.* Another thousand Cubans helped American Marines bottle up six thousand Spanish troops at Guantánamo, forty miles to the east. The fact is that the Cuban Army, cooperating with the Americans loyally and to the best of its ability, made a substantial contribution which was largely ignored at the time.[15]

The reasons for its being ignored are not hard to find. In the first place, to the American soldier the war in Cuba consisted chiefly of the Battle of San Juan Hill, where only a fraction of the Cubans served, and those with no great distinction in American eyes. Even more fundamental was the initial disillusionment which met the Americans after their first contacts in Cuba. The colorful newspaper accounts of dashing rebel exploits had done nothing to prepare them for the ugly realities of guerrilla warfare and civil conflict. The ragged, barefoot Cubans were not inspiring to look at, though the Cubans declared with some justice that George Washington's army had been similarly viewed by its scornful British antagonists. And it did not escape the many Southerners and Westerners in the army that the Cuban forces were composed of a large minority of Negroes and of a majority of persons whom they immediately categorized as "dagoes."

Furthermore, the half-famished Cubans, like veteran troops everywhere, took food where they found it, including the many supply dumps which the American army had not yet learned to guard in the early days of the campaign. To the American units whose food thus disappeared, the Cubans seemed ungrateful thieves. They seemed beggars as well. One correspondent reported that "whenever one lighted a fire a Cuban presented himself . . . and asked for food."[16] Yet to men who had been fighting for three years on short rations, it must have seemed natural that their wealthy new allies should share their supplies with them.

"The fact is," wrote the *Manchester Guardian*'s reporter, "that the United States Army made the very old mistake of judging its allies by its own standards." The Cubans were excellent at quick concentrations and hit-and-run attacks, and at the kind of guerrilla warfare with which they had tied down over 200,000 Spanish regulars in Cuba, operating as irregulars in small, mobile bands. The Americans expected them to act like a formal, drilled army, and were disillusioned whenever they failed to do so. Their reaction was to use the Cubans as scapegoats for the errors and ills of the campaign.[17]

By the end of the campaign, the army had made up its mind about the Cubans. On December 19, 1898, the Eastern newspapers contained an account of a conversation between some reporters and General Shafter in Savannah, Georgia.

"How about self-government for the Cubans?" Shafter was asked.

"Self-government!" he replied. "Why, these people are no more fit for self-government than gun-powder is for hell."[18]

The army in Cuba was accompanied by swarms of newspaper correspondents, and the army's view of the Cuban *insurrectos* was soon shared with the American public. A revolution in public opinion occurred during the summer of 1898, and the nation's editors suddenly discovered that the heroic and victimized Cubans were actually a base rabble unfit for freedom. The *New York World,* which had long whipped up feeling for an intervention to save the Cubans, now asserted that "we are not spending our blood and treasure in putting down one anarchy in Cuba for the sake of setting up another."[19] The *New York Tribune* similarly declared that "this Nation is not minded to accept anarchy in place of tyranny." The pledge of "Cuba for the Cubans" was no longer binding, the *Tribune* said, for it was based on the supposition that the Cubans were ready for self-government, an assumption which the *Tribune* declared "false and unsubstantial."[20]

The *Detroit Tribune* decided that the Cubans were unworthy of confidence as allies and incapable of erecting a stable government. It suggested that the United States, "for a long time at least," would have to administer the government itself, and if the Cuban attitude did not change, "a necessary preliminary . . . may be the military subjugation of the people we went to war to save." The *Hartford Post,* published by McKinley's private secretary, John Addison Porter, hailed the President's foresight, for "had it not been for our chief magistrate, these good-for-nothing allies of ours would have been established as an independent nation." And the Cleveland *Leader* rejoiced that "the Cubans have displayed their worthlessness thus early in the struggle. Their conduct may furnish an easy solution to the Cuban problem. While our Government disavowed a purpose of conquest, it may be absolutely necessary for us to keep Cuba and make it a part of the United States."[21]

This new view of the Cubans furnished ammunition to anti-imperialists as well as expansionists. To Carl Schurz, the aging professional liberal, it proved that the Cubans were not worth taking into the Union. Schurz pictured the dangers of annexation in a speech at Saratoga, New York, to a "National Conference on Foreign Policy." If the former Spanish colonies were annexed, he said, they must either be made territories, and eventually states of the union, or forever governed as "subject provinces." If the latter course were chosen, the nation endangered self-government at home by violating its principles abroad. If the new areas were to be assimilated by the nation, were they fit to be a part of the United States?

The answer to this last question, Schurz thought, was a decided "No." The Cuban population consisted of Spanish creoles and of people of Negro blood. There was little hope of submerging the native stock in a wave of Anglo-Saxon immigration, as some Americans had begun to hope, for Anglo-Saxons never went to the tropics in large numbers. Thus the present Cubans, "another lot of . . . Spanish-Americans and negroes," would some day expect to send numerous Senators and Representatives to Congress, perhaps enough to hold the balance of power on some issues. This prospect was not pleasing to the speaker: "There are multitudes of Americans who say now that if they had known what a sorry lot the Cubans are, we would never have gone to war on their behalf. However that may be, the same Americans should at least not permit those same Cubans to take part in governing us."[22]

In all the uproar of press and platform, however, the note which best harmonized with the public mind was probably that struck by Joseph H. Choate, the new president of the American Bar Association. In an oblique reference to the war resolutions, Choate declared that "the Government must not be held too rigidly to purposes and expectations declared before the commencement of the war, and in utter ignorance of its possible results." The noted New York lawyer reminded his audience that "in war, events change the situation very rapidly."[23] The current war, at least, seemed to prove him right.

_____

Moving Toward a New Role

The Spanish-American War had actually ended on August 12, 1898, with the signing of a preliminary protocol by representatives of the two nations. Its terms as to Cuba were decisive for the Spaniards: Spain would relinquish all claim of sovereignty over or title to Cuba, and evacuate the island immediately. Spain also agreed to cede to the United States the island of Puerto Rico, and an island in the Ladrones to be selected by the United States. The status of the Philippine Islands was left to be settled by the peace conference.[1]

Incidental to the ending of hostilities was some peculiar maneuvering between the United States government and the Cuban junta. Obviously it was necessary to inform the insurgent forces of the protocol ending the fighting, but the administration wished to shun all official intercourse with the Cubans for fear of seeming to recognize them. McKinley therefore sent an agent, Charles E. Magoon, to New York to arrange the matter with the Cuban junta there. Magoon met with Tomás Estrada Palma, the Cuban Republic's "Minister" to the United States, and Horatio S. Rubens, the young New York lawyer who was the junta's legal adviser and contact man. The President's agent wanted Estrada Palma to notify the Cuban commanders of the cease fire in a purely personal message, but Rubens insisted that such notification must be transmitted by Estrada Palma in his official capacity. After a series of telephone conversations with the White House, Magoon reluctantly agreed to the transmission of the message in the form demanded: that is, Estrada Palma directed it to the President of the Cuban Republic, and signed it as "Minister and Delegate Plenipotentiary to the United States."[2]

Such incidents served to emphasize the complexity of the Cuban situation. By now, the Administration had at least a threefold problem in connection with Cuba. First, it must arrive at a final peace settlement with Spain. Secondly, it must come to some kind of terms with the Cuban rebels, which might prove more difficult. And finally, necessary preparations must be made for the United States occupation which was to commence as soon as the Spanish forces left the island. In the closing months of 1898 the government attempted to cope with all three of these issues.

The peace conference with Spain opened at Paris on October 1, 1898. It soon became clear that the two great issues would be the disposition of the Philippine Islands and the settlement of the so-called Cuban debt. This last was a group of financial obligations of the Spanish government which had been carried as charges on the Cuban treasury and secured, at least nominally, by Cuban revenues. The total face value of the debt was reputed to be near $400,000,000 in American dollars. The Spanish peace commissioners insisted that this huge debt represented expenses and obligations springing from Spain's government of Cuba and pertaining solely to that island, and that it should therefore pass from Spain along with Cuba. The Spaniards said, in other words, that the debt was inseparable from Cuban sovereignty and should be transferred with it.

This issue had been anticipated by the United States Senate. Back in April, when Congress was hammering out the War Resolutions, Senator Foraker of Ohio had seized on the Cuban debt as an argument for the immediate recognition of the Cuban Republic. Such recognition, Foraker said, would leave the Cubans as the responsible authority in the island, and the question of the debt would lie solely between them and the government of Spain. A policy of non-recognition and United States occupation, however, would leave the United States as the responsible authority, and therefore liable for the debt. "If one country absorb another,"

Foraker argued, "it takes not only the legal rights and advantages of that country, but it takes also the obligations of that country."

The Ohio Senator also pointed out that much of the debt was held by bondholders in France and Germany, who would look to the United States for repayment, whatever the legal technicalities, once an American government ruled in Cuba. These people, he warned, could create grave international incidents if they were not repaid.[3]

The administration spokesmen in the Senate had admitted none of this. They held that American authority in Cuba was to be merely a temporary trust, which involved no permanent obligations of any kind. The United States would not "absorb" Cuba at all, they declared, and Foraker's reasoning was therefore invalid.

The United States commissioners at the peace conference took a similar position, and flatly refused to recognize the Spanish claims. Furthermore, they contended that a large part of the total debt represented the cost of putting down rebellions which embodied the true aspirations of the Cuban people, and that other items in it were not Cuban at all.

Seeking to minimize their losses, the Spaniards tried various expedients to get rid of the Cuban debt. They suggested that sovereignty over Cuba should be transferred directly from Spain to the United States, and that the latter should assume the obligations of Spain in Cuba at the same time. Then, if sovereignty were later transferred to the Cuban people, it should be on the same terms, but with the United States remaining a guarantor of the debt. The Spanish commissioners urged this scheme repeatedly in different forms, but the Americans refused either to assume sovereignty over Cuba or to recognize the Cuban debt. The Spaniards finally proposed that Cuba retain responsibility for "all debt not peninsular but properly and peculiarly Cuban," the amount to be determined by a mixed commission. The Americans, however, showed as little enthusiasm for assuming part of the debt as for assuming all of it.

In desperation the Spanish Ambassador to France called privately on Whitelaw Reid, now one of the United States commissioners, pleading that Spanish public opinion would not stand for a complete surrender of both the Philippines and the debt. He warned that the peace conference must fail if some concession were not forthcoming from the United States. Senator William P. Frye, another of the United States commissioners, suggested paying the Spaniards $20,000,000 on general principles in order to make the treaty more palatable. This was eventually done, but the basic American position regarding Cuba remained unchanged.[4]

The treaty of peace between Spain and the United States went into effect on April 11, 1899. Article One of the treaty stated that "Spain relinquishes all claim of sovereignty over and title to Cuba," and made the United States responsible for Cuba's international obligations during the period of her occupation of Cuba. The last article, Article Sixteen, stated: "It is understood that any obligations assumed in this treaty by the United States with respect to Cuba are limited to the time of its occupancy thereof; but it will upon the termination of such occupancy, advise any Government established in the island to assume the same obligations."[5]

Even before the peace conference began its sessions in Paris, President McKinley had sent a personal agent to Cuba in search of information. The man selected for this sensitive mission was Robert P. Porter, who was already well known to McKinley. Porter was an Englishman who had come to America in his youth and made a successful career in journalism, working on newspapers in Chicago, New York, and Philadelphia, and spending much time abroad as a writer on world trade and economic conditions. President Chester Arthur had appointed him to the Tariff Commission in 1882, while from 1889 to 1893 he was Director of the Eleventh Census, the memorable census which proclaimed the passing of the American frontier. Porter was a personal acquaintance of William McKinley, and a prominent publicist for McKinley's favorite cause of tariff protection. He wrote a campaign biography of McKinley for the presidential campaign of 1896,[6] and in 1898 he held a position in the Treasury Department, from which McKinley chose him to be "Special Commissioner of the United States to Cuba and Porto Rico." In addition to gathering information for McKinley's guidance, Porter was to make a special study of the Cuban currency and tariff.

Porter went to Cuba in the autumn of 1898, and for two weeks held public hearings in Havana in which he recorded the statements of witnesses regarding Cuban trade, currency, banking, or tariffs. Next he travelled about the island picking up general impressions. Eventually he returned to hold more hearings, in New York and Washington, at which interested parties in the United States could give their views on future fiscal policies in Cuba.[7]

Porter's first concern was to make recommendations for a new Cuban tariff. A schedule known as the "Santiago Tariff" had been adopted in July for use in the port of Santiago and in the lesser ports which fell under United States control in Santiago Province. This had consisted simply of adopting, with minor modifications, the existing schedules for Spanish products, to be applied without discrimination to imports from the United States and all other nations. Porter regarded this emergency tariff as unsuitable for permanent use, while the original Spanish tariff he found even worse. Starting from the beginning, he supervised the preparation of an entirely new tariff schedule.[8]

Porter intended that the new duties should bear lightest where the people could least afford taxation and heaviest on luxury goods and the things required by large enterprises. Only the tax and revenue features needed to be considered, he held, because Cuba had almost no local industry requiring protection. The new schedules were written in terms of United States currency rather than Spanish pesos, and they slashed an average of sixty per cent from the old Spanish rates. This would still yield sufficient revenue for the expenses of governing Cuba, Porter believed, because the new duties would actually be collected, while under the old system fraudulent classification and outright smuggling had kept most of the potential revenue from ever being realized.[9]

Perhaps the most important decision regarding the new tariff was that it was not to discriminate in favor of the United States. Porter said that his official instructions opposed such tariff favors for the United States, which was to take its chances with the rest of the world in securing Cuban trade (the unwritten corollary to this was that neither did Cuba receive any tariff favors from the United States). The administration had indicated to him, he said, that the object to be sought in readjusting the tariff was "the lowest possible rates on all commodities of general consumption consistent with sufficient revenue to meet the expenditures of the Government."[10]

Porter also discussed the possibility of a reciprocal trade agreement between the United States and Cuba. The making of such an agreement, he found, was supported by "a very strong feeling" in all parts of the island, but his conclusion for the present was a cautious negative: "However wise or desirable the recommendation of these [reciprocal] rates may be . . . the necessity of raising revenue sufficient for the immediate needs of Cuba precluded the possibility of seriously considering such a plan under existing or present circumstances."[11]

In the meantime, Porter was forming conclusions on subjects other than the tariff, and presumably he made his views known to McKinley in their many personal interviews. In the winter of 1898–99 he wrote a book entitled *Industrial Cuba,* in which he quoted at length from the statements of Cuban annexationists and concluded that the most promising future for Cuba could only be attained by "complete union with the greater Republic." Officially, he wrote, he had no opinion to express on the political future of Cuba, but personally he looked forward to the day when it should become a State of the Union.[12]

He expanded these views in an article in the *North American Review* for April, 1899. The closer and stronger the ties which bound Cuba to the United States, Porter wrote, the greater would be the prosperity of Cuba. The outside world already regarded Cuba as a part of the United States, while commercially and industrially the two countries complemented each other perfectly. The more intelligent Cubans must be aware of the "golden possibilities" of free trade between the two countries. Porter conceded that sentiment for a Cuban flag and nation was natural, but added that "in the final and mutual coming together of Cuba and the United States, the single star becomes not less bright by reason of association or companionship with the other stars."[13]

The development of Cuban policy moved into a new phase late in 1898, when the McKinley administration at last began direct negotiations with the Cuban revolutionaries. In November, a committee of Cubans came to Washington to explore, among other things, the possibility of obtaining funds to pay off the Cuban army, and for servicing some other debts contracted by the insurgent government. This group was headed by the elderly General Calixto García, who had commanded the Cuban troops in Santiago Province. It included, besides García and several other prominent soldiers, Gonzalo de Quesada, the Cuban "chargé d'affaires" in Washington, and Horatio Rubens, the lawyer for the Cuban junta.[14]

The precise legal status of this commission was as hard to define as the status of the "government" which sent it. The provisional Cuban government which was organized in 1895 had never been officially recognized by foreign governments, and in October of 1898 this shadow government was finally abandoned and replaced by a body known as the Cuban Assembly, which frankly represented the Cuban army. It consisted of the commanders of thirty-one so-called army corps, supposedly elected to membership by the troops under their command. The Cuban Assembly never exercised any real legislative power, but was supposed to be a kind of central board of the revolutionary movement. General Gómez had announced that he regarded the Assembly as the only body with authority to disband the Cuban army, and in that, perhaps, lay its greatest practical significance.[15] But the Assembly's direction of the revolutionary party was still shared with General Gómez, who commanded the army, and with the Cuban junta in New York, which had had charge of dealing with the United States government and public.

The Cuban commission which went to Washington in November came in the name of the Cuban Assembly, but included two representatives of the New York junta, Quesada and Rubens, and was headed by General García, the principal lieutenant of Gómez. Thus it represented all the major factions of the Cuban revolution, and was received, though not as representing a government, by the United States government. It was clearly expedient to come to some sort of terms with the group in order that the United States occupation of Cuba could begin on firm ground.

The Cubans, for their part, hoped to gain some idea of the intentions of the United States toward Cuba. Back in May, the Council of Government had urgently requested information on this subject from Estrada Palma in New York. The delegate was instructed to find out what parts of Cuba were to be occupied by the American army, and under what conditions. He was to continue to work for the official recognition of the Cuban insurgents by the United States, and to make the Americans understand that "there will be here no other order of things than that founded on our Constitution." Estrada Palma was to apply himself particularly to learning "who will have authority to keep order and tranquillity" during the American intervention, and to keep his superiors informed on the over-all policy of the United States with respect to future relations with Cuba.[16]

Since May, the Cubans had continued their inquiries. In addition, they had put an increasingly high priority on securing money from the United States government to pay their ragged and penniless army, and this was the second main object of the Cuban commission. The commission's instructions from the Cuban Assembly indicated that the Cuban army might well be disbanded entirely, unless the Americans wanted part of it to remain under arms to help keep order. But to disband the army, it was necessary to pay it, and the mission to Washington was to ask the United States to advance a "reasonable" sum for this purpose.[17]

The visit of the commission began auspiciously enough, with the usual receptions, dinners, and speeches. It was promptly accorded an interview with the President himself, in which the talk turned mainly about paying off the Cuban army. Since this body represented the only tangible threat to American rule in Cuba, the Americans wanted to get rid of it as quickly as possible. The Cubans seemed willing to cooperate, but they were divided over the policy to be pursued in paying the soldiers.

The Cuban army had never been paid regularly, but had lived largely by taking what it needed from the countryside. In theory, however, its soldiers were earning a liberal monthly wage, considerably higher than that given to members of the United States army, which was to be paid after victory was achieved. The majority of the Cuban commission wished to float a loan, to be secured by the future customs revenues of Cuba, big enough to pay the Cuban army a large part of the back pay due it at this somewhat inflated rate. Since the Cubans had neither money nor control of the island's revenues, any amount which the United States could be induced to advance would represent a windfall, and in the opinion of the majority, the larger the amount the better. But Generals Gómez and García took a somewhat longer view of the matter. They feared that a large loan to pay off the army would entangle Cuba so deeply in debt as to lessen her freedom of action, and might very possibly delay the day of her independence. They thus favored payment of a minimum amount, just large enough to enable the soldiers to return home and begin useful work.[18]

At the White House interview, McKinley asked the Cubans how much money they thought necessary to disband the army, and García promptly replied, "Three million dollars." The other Cubans, who had hoped for much more, protested immediately, but García had tipped their hand and thereafter McKinley held to the lesser figure.[19]

The President's attitude, however, was not entirely negative. According to the Cuban commission's report, he suggested that the Cuban army might be discharged gradually over a period of time, and that a portion of it, perhaps ten thousand men, might be incorporated into the United States army of occupation as a "colonial army," to be paid by the United States. He also promised that Cubans would occupy the civil offices, and would be consulted in public affairs.[20]

After this first interview, McKinley turned the negotiations over to Robert Porter. In the subsequent negotiations the Cubans fought hard to raise the amount of payment for their army, and quoted some fantastic figures in the process. If, as some of the Cubans asked, the soldiers were given their full back pay at the rate promised them, the total bill would amount to no less than $57,000,000. Even at the pay scale of the United States army, the total was calculated at around $30,000,000. It is doubtful if many of the Cubans really expected to secure such amounts as these, but most of them agreed that the $3,000,000 offered was too little to do any good. Porter, on the other hand, clung to the $3,000,000 figure because this amount could be supplied from the balance of the $50,000,000 appropriated for defense just before the outbreak of the War with Spain. The act appropriating this sum specified that it was to be spent at the discretion of the President, making possible the disposal of the ticklish Cuban army issue without a special Congressional appropriation.

The commission also asked for money to cover the accumulated debts of the Cuban Republic, which they estimated at between two and a quarter and two and a half million dollars. But the answer remained the same: the three million dollars were all that was available, and the Cubans must take it or leave it.[21]

At the same time that the Cubans were negotiating with the executive for financial aid, they were sounding out Congressional opinion. Among the first they approached was Senator John T. Morgan of Alabama, an influential Democrat and a member of the Senate Committee on Foreign Relations. Though he had long been an advocate of the extension of belligerent rights to the Cuban Republic, the Cubans soon found that Morgan was first and foremost an American expansionist.

Morgan met the Cubans with a prepared written statement of his views on Cuban-American relations. Before the meeting, which took place in a room in the Hotel Raleigh, he had sent a copy of this document to the Secretary of State. It consisted of sixteen propositions, the effect of which was to dash cold water in the face of Cuban hopes.

Morgan began by pointing out that Congress had refused to recognize any Cuban government except that of Spain, and that the failure of the Senate's resolutions recognizing Cuban belligerency left the Cubans in the status of mere insurrectionists. He explained that the purpose of the war with Spain was to avenge wrongs done to the United States, not to Cuba. He reminded his hearers, rather unkindly, that during the war all Spanish subjects were technically enemies of the United States, including Cubans. Perhaps most important of all, Morgan contended that the Teller Resolution itself, although morally binding on the United States, "is not an agreement with anybody, nor is it a decree or a law," and that it would be executed "in such manner and at such time as the competent authority in the United States shall provide."

Morgan further told the dismayed Cubans that military occupation by the United States was the necessary first step in Cuba, and that during this occupation sovereignty in Cuba must lie with the United States, with primary authority in the hands of the President. The peace between the United States and Spain, he said ominously, did not insure that there would be peace in Cuba if any group there offered resistance to United States military authority. Finally, when the time came to establish the permanent government which would replace American rule, the military authority must keep the initiative in framing it, though they should act "with reference to the wishes" of all the Cuban people.[22]

The Cubans disagreed violently with much of Morgan's analysis, and they attacked his conclusions in a written reply signed by Calixto García. Summarily rejecting the theory that the future of Cuba was "at the discretionary power of the American government," the commission insisted that the Teller Amendment was a law like any other law, and was legally as well as morally binding upon the actions of the United States.

Then the Cubans asked a number of questions about the American military government of which Morgan had spoken. Would it be "a government absolute and limitless, as if it were that of a Sultan, for example?" Could each American military chief establish whatever rules he pleased in his own district? Or would this interim sovereignty be limited to ordinary administration and the maintenance of public order, "touching our laws only at points where they are completely incompatible with the new order of things?"

The Cuban reply to Morgan ended in a warning. While disavowing any thought of violence against the United States occupation, the commission announced its intention to withhold its approval of any American government which violated accepted Cuban procedures or ideals. In such a case, "we will see the necessity of standing to one side, of not cooperating in the work of the government and policy of the American military authority, leaving to it the most absolute responsibility for the results. . . ."[23]

At this time the work of the Cuban commission was brought to a close by the sudden death of General García on December 11, 1898, after a brief illness. He was given an impressive funeral in

Washington, which was made the more impressive by the evident determination of President McKinley to show the old soldier all possible respect. The United States Army provided a large honor guard, Secretary of State John Hay represented the administration, and a crowd of American generals and officials escorted the body to its temporary resting place in Arlington National Cemetery.[24]

After the funeral the rest of the Cuban commission returned to Cuba to report the results of their activities to the Assembly. In its formal report, the commission neither favored nor rejected the American offer of $3,000,000 to pay off their army. They recommended instead that the Assembly accept the offer in principle, but continue to work to increase the amount. As for the over-all policy to be followed by the United States in Cuba,

> it was absolutely impossible [the report said] for the commissioners—in spite of their determination and their insistence—to obtain any explanation, but only vague manifestations, and even phrases more or less evasive, either from the President, or the Secretaries, or from the other persons whom they consulted . . . ; although everyone declared that they were resolved to comply faithfully with the resolutions of Congress of 19 April, 1898, they never let a word escape regarding the means they would adopt to obtain this result, nor the duration of the occupation of the island, as if they really had no definite political program. . . .[25]

In the same month, President McKinley sent his Annual Message to Congress. The section of the message which referred to Cuba was unexceptionable, even reassuring, to those who feared for Cuban independence. The President said that as soon as the military government was in possession of Cuba and had pacified the island, it would be necessary to give "aid and direction" to its people to form a government. This should be done "at the earliest moment consistent with safety and assured success." He called for friendship between the two peoples, and close and reciprocal commercial relations. It was the duty of the United States, McKinley said, first to rebuild Cuba and then to assist the Cubans to form "a government which shall be free and independent," "just," "benevolent," and capable of performing all its international obligations. It should encourage thrift, industry, and prosperity, and promote peace and good will. There was, however, one condition attached to this shining forecast: "Until there is complete tranquillity in the island and a stable government inaugurated military government will continue."[26]

All this seemed straightforward and reasonable. Yet over in England the daily press expressed doubts. Whether more sophisticated or merely more cynical, the editorial writers of London saw things in McKinley's message which escaped the vision of their colleagues across the Atlantic.

The *London Chronicle,* for example, politely questioned the timing of the schedule laid out for Cuba: "The President is naturally compelled to add that until complete tranquillity prevails in the island, and a system of government is inaugurated, the military occupation will be continued. We shall not be thought discourteous or cynical if we remark that this is precisely the language that successive British Governments have maintained about Egypt, with a result known to the world, and an omen which is certainly not inapplicable."[27]

The *London Daily Telegraph* took an almost exactly similar view, even to drawing the same parallel with "the words so frequently used by British Ministers in the not dissimilar case of Egypt."[28] The *London Standard* spoke even more plainly. The President, it said, seemed to aim at Cuban independence "on the surface," but made the achievement of this independence conditional on American assistance and participation. Furthermore, the attributes which the free and independent Cuba must possess were "defined on such an Utopian model, that the day of emancipation from military tutelage may be indefinitely postponed."[29]

Shortly after issuing his Annual Message, McKinley began the final preparations for the initiation of military government in Cuba. There was considerable speculation as to who he would select as military governor. One candidate frequently mentioned was General James Wade, who was head of the United States Evacuation Commission in Cuba and who came from Ohio, McKinley's home state. But the man actually chosen was Major-General John R. Brooke, a long-time career soldier and one of the three major generals in the regular army. Brooke was sixty years old, and had been in the service continuously since 1861. He had seen much fighting in the Civil War, and risen to the rank of brigadier general of volunteers. In the war just ended, he had led one of the invading columns in the virtually bloodless conquest of Puerto Rico, and since the end of hostilities had been serving as military governor of that island.[30]

At the same time another action was taken preparatory to beginning the job of civil government. On December 13, the War Department established a new agency to handle the paper work relating to the civil administration of the new dependencies of Cuba, Puerto Rico, and the Philippine Islands. Known at first as the Division of Customs and Insular Affairs, this body became the Division of Insular Affairs after its reorganization by Elihu Root in 1900, and was raised to bureau rank in 1902. It continued to be a central part of the government's machinery for administering its overseas possessions for the next two generations.[31]

The completion of these and other preparations occupied the remainder of December, and then at last the time was at hand when the United States should begin actually governing the island of Cuba.

5

The Occupation Begins

In spite of the ceremony and pageantry with which the United States assumed the rule of Cuba, the transfer of government from Spain to the United States on January 1, 1899, was marred by serious ill-feeling between Cubans and Americans. The Cuban leaders had planned a great victory celebration on the occasion of the termination of Spanish sovereignty, but they never held it.

The revolutionary patriotic committees of Havana had prepared the program, which was to last for five days. They had planned a public dinner for the insurgent soldiers, and a series of banquets, speeches, and balls. Most important of all, there was to be a great parade of Cuban troops through the city on the very day of the transfer, while the Spaniards would still be boarding their transports on the Havana water front. At the last minute, however, these plans were brought to an abrupt halt. General Brooke notified the Cubans through General William Ludlow, the designated military commander of Havana, that no insurgent troops would be allowed in Havana at the time of the transfer of government.[1]

The reason for Brooke's action was not political, but practical. The month of December had witnessed mounting violence between Spaniards and Cubans in Havana, particularly between officers of the respective armies. On December 11–13 there had been three days of riots and shooting affrays in which a number of people were killed and wounded, and since then the situation in Havana had been tense.[2] Brooke feared that if both Cuban and Spanish troops were allowed in Havana on January 1, a day which was sure to inspire deep emotion on both sides, there was danger that general fighting might break out.[3]

The Cubans received Brooke's decision with angry protests. A deputation of Havana leaders saw Ludlow and offered to make themselves personally responsible for good order during the celebration. General Máximo Gómez, the Cuban commander-in-chief, announced that he would not come to Havana unless he could be received there by his army. Perfecto Lacoste, chairman of the Havana committee, complained of the Americans' lack of understanding. "For years we have suffered," he said, "only to see, at this hour, our emotions changed from pleasure at the departure of the Spaniards to apprehension at the arrival of the Americans."[4]

There was dissatisfaction in the United States, too, when the news of Brooke's decision appeared in the press. Senator Teller wrote the President protesting the action on the grounds that it was ungenerous to our allies, and that it would create an unfortunate impression in Cuba. To deny them their victory celebration, Teller said, "will create a false idea of what our course is to be in dealing with them, and our difficulties are quite great enough now without any additions."[5]

But Brooke refused to take the risk, and McKinley refused to overrule him. By Brooke's special invitation a number of Cuban commanders were present at the transfer of government ceremony on January 1.[6] But the Cuban army was absent, as was Máximo Gómez, its chief, and there was no great victory celebration in Havana. Among the crowds of Cubans who witnessed the Spanish departure were many whose relief was mingled with bitterness and fear for the future. Even if Brooke's action was justified by the circumstances, it had transformed the celebration of a joint Cuban-American victory over Spain into an occasion for demonstrating the subordination of the Cubans to American authority.

On January 1, 1899, General John R. Brooke inaugurated the United States Military Government of Cuba by issuing a proclamation from Havana addressed "To the people of Cuba." He came among them, Brooke said, as the representative of the President of the United States, to further the humane purposes for which the United States had intervened in Cuba. These purposes he proceeded to define: "The object of the present Government is to give protection to the people, security to person and property, to restore confidence, to encourage the people to resume the pursuits of peace, to build up waste plantations, to resume commercial traffic, and to afford full protection in the exercise of all civil and religious rights." The new governor promised that the civil and criminal codes formerly used in Cuba would remain in force, except for such modification as might be found necessary in the interests of good government. He urged the Cubans to cooperate with the new government and to show "moderation, conciliation, and good will one toward another." Finally, Brooke promised to receive citizens who wanted to confer with him about public matters.[7]

The statements of Brooke's proclamation were drawn directly from President McKinley's letter of instructions to him, written a week earlier. In this letter, dated December 22, 1898, McKinley offered "a few unofficial suggestions" to Brooke about the policies he should pursue in Cuba.

United States authority in Cuba, McKinley wrote, was derived from "the law of belligerent right over conquered territory." Brooke would rule there as the direct representative of the President, who as commander-in-chief of the armed forces was at present the sole possessor of this authority. This must be the case until Congress provided otherwise, or until the Cubans had established a government of their own stable enough so that the President could "deem it safe" to withdraw American forces. Brooke's government, McKinley said, was "not in the interest or for the direct benefit of this country," but rather that of the Cubans, and of those who had "rights and property" in Cuba. Although a military government, it was established for non-military purposes.

McKinley then gave a series of directions to the new governor, many of them vague and platitudinous. Brooke should mingle with the leading men of Cuba and secure the peoples' confidence; he should try to unite all factions, but avoid offending any particular faction; he should be sympathetic, relieve destitution, and encourage municipal reforms; he should end aggression and extortion, and protect the ignorant. The President laid particular stress on preventing depredations by American troops, and warned: "let your government be a government of laws, not one of military force."[8]

To General Brooke, faced with the task of creating a new regime in Cuba, these instructions offered little practical help. Nevertheless, Brooke and his subordinates immediately began the organization of a government, and by the end of January the main outlines of the United States Military Government of Cuba were complete. Since Brooke and the others had been notified of their new positions barely two weeks before their duties began, their work had necessarily to be done in a hurried, and sometimes improvised fashion. The government they created was in reality a dual structure composed of two separate organizations, one civil and one military. The Military Governor, by virtue of his position as the head of both, held powers which were limited only by his own superiors, the President of the United States and the Secretary of War.

General Brooke created the structure of the civil administration by two civil orders of January 11 and 12. The civil government was divided into four departments, each headed by a Cuban secretary. These four secretaries, besides administering their respective departments, formed an advisory body which soon came to be known as the Cuban Cabinet. Of the four departments, two were "catch-all" agencies which combined two or more separate functions. José Antonio Gonzáles Lanuza was named Secretary of Justice and Public Instruction, while Adolfo Sáenz Yanez became Secretary of Agriculture, Commerce, Industries, and Public Works.[9]

Pablo Desvernine was Secretary of Finance (*Hacienda*) in the new administration, but his functions were carefully limited. The bulk of Cuban government revenue during the occupation came from customs duties, collected by a Customs Service which was entirely independent of the Department of Finance. This customs service was run by the United States army, and it turned over its receipts to the North American Trust Company, which acted as fiscal agent for the Cuban government. Finally, an auditing system was also set up independently of the new Secretary, making his department, as he later compained, a mere collecting agency and advisory group for the scanty internal revenues.[10]

The most important of the four departments was the Department of State and Government, whose Secretary was Domingo Méndez Capote. It had general supervision of the provincial governments and of municipal administration within the provinces. Cuba had a unitary government which integrated local, provincial, and insular administration into a single hierarchy. At the bottom was the municipality, consisting of a town or village and the country around it, governed by an *alcalde* (mayor) and municipal council. All of Cuba was divided into such municipalities. Above them were the six provincial governments, each headed by a governor. The provincial governors supervised municipal administration in their areas, kept public order, granted permits for meetings and parades, and titles to mining and timber rights, oversaw public works, and handled many other details of administration. The governors were responsible in turn to the Secretary of State and Government, who headed this entire civil hierarchy with the exception of the judicial system, which fell under the Secretary of Justice and Public Instruction. In addition, he carried on the housekeeping duties of the central government, including the administration of the civil service.[11]

At the beginning of the occupation, the framework of local government was taken over more or less intact from the previous regime, but was firmly subordinated to the new government by making all of its officers, from Secretary of State on down to municipal *alcaldes,* appointed by the Military Governor.[12]

Outside the structure of civil government, and superior to it, was the military command system. The Military Division of Cuba was created by the War Department on December 13, 1898. General Brooke was the commanding officer of this unit as well as Military Governor of Cuba. The Military Division included seven geographical departments corresponding to the six Cuban provinces and the city of Havana. Each of these departments was commanded by an American general, who exercised authority over the provincial and municipal administrations, and was in charge of all United States troops in the command area.[13]

Although in theory the department and local commanders were to work through the appropriate levels of civil government, at first they were forced to do relief and rehabilitation work directly, for want of adequate civil machinery. Thus the lines of jurisdiction between civil and military agencies were for a time blurred or nonexistent. As the situation cleared and the system of government crystallized, it was possible to let the civil authorities assume more of the work and to cut down the number of military commands. Reorganizations of April 19 and July 1, 1899, reduced the number of military departments to four: the six provincial departments were consolidated into three, of two provinces each, while the Department of the City of Havana was retained intact. At the same time it proved possible to reduce the number of American troops in Cuba. At the beginning of the occupation, United States forces numbered about 24,000 officers and men. These were rapidly increased in the first, uncertain months, reaching a peak in March of almost 45,000, and then declining steadily during the rest of the year. By the end of 1899 about 11,000 army personnel were left in Cuba.[14]

While the main machinery of the occupation government lay in the Civil Administration and the Military Division of Cuba, there remained a number of government agencies that did not fall within either organization. The Customs Service, headed throughout the occupation by Colonel Tasker H. Bliss of the regular army, was staffed with United States army officers, assisted by Cuban and American civilians. The postal service was under the supervision of the Postmaster General of the United States, and was unique in being almost wholly independent of the authority of the Military Governor. The Treasurer of the island was an American army officer, and its fiscal agency was the North American Trust Company of New York. The quarantine service was organized and run by the United States Marine Hospital Service, but employed many Cuban doctors. Telegraph and telephone lines were in charge of the United States Army Signal Corps.[15]

One of General Brooke's first problems was that of manning this complex and hastily assembled governmental structure, some of it improvised and much of it taken over bodily from the Spanish regime. The positions of the civil administration he staffed with Cubans; on the lower levels, some former civil servants simply remained in their jobs. On the higher levels, however, there was a wholesale redistribution of offices, much of it designed to placate the leaders of the Cuban revolutionary movement. An American departmental commander stated that, all other things being equal, "the officers of the successful revolution should have preference for civil employment over those who had supported the Spanish government or stood neutral between it and those who were contending for independence."[16] Brooke himself followed this rule in most of his appointments. Méndez Capote and Gonzáles Lanuza both resigned from the Cuban Assembly to accept cabinet posts from Brooke, and Méndez Capote was actually president of the Assembly at the time of his resignation. Of the six provincial governors appointed by Brooke, all but one were ex-generals in the Cuban army, and the lone exception had been a volunteer officer in the Medical Department of the United States army.[17]

Of the choice of army personnel for the Cuban occupation, Brooke had little to say. Yet next to Brooke himself, the most important men of the early occupation were a little group of senior officers who commanded the military departments and headed Brooke's staff. These men were a remarkably diverse lot, with wide and varied experience, and at least six of them were to play important roles at some time during the occupation. General Adna R. Chaffee and Colonel Tasker H. Bliss were successful career soldiers. Chaffee was Brooke's chief of staff, while Bliss headed the Customs Service; each ended his career as chief of staff of the United States Army.[18]

Of the four departmental commanders who survived the consolidations of the first months, General William Ludlow was the only old career soldier. Ludlow, who commanded the Department of the City of Havana, was first of all a military engineer. He had had wide engineering experience in the army, including a term (by special permission of Congress) as chief engineer of the Philadelphia Water Department. Like Chaffee, Ludlow had commanded a brigade in Shafter's army during the Santiago campaign.[19]

General Fitzhugh Lee, whose department finally included the provinces of Pinar del Río and Havana on the western end of the island, was perhaps the most colorful figure in the occupation. An old Confederate cavalry commander, Lee had been four years governor of Virginia, and later gained prominence as United States Consul in Havana in the years prior to the outbreak of the war with Spain. Round-faced, pop-eyed, and bewhiskered, the ebullient Lee was a well-known figure both in the United States and in Cuba.[20]

General James Harrison Wilson had also been a cavalry general in the Civil War, but on the Union side. Like General Lee, he had been out of the army between the wars, and had made a successful career as a railroad builder and executive. A prominent Republican and a National Committeeman from Delaware, Wilson knew many important men in Washington and New York, including President McKinley. It was no secret that Wilson had wanted Brooke's job as military governor of Cuba, but he had to settle for command of the Department of Matanzas, to which was soon added the province of Santa Clara, making Wilson's department comprise the middle third of Cuba.[21]

The youngest of the major commanders in Cuba was General Leonard Wood. Only thirty-nine years old in 1899, Wood began his military career as an army contract surgeon participating in the pursuit of the Apache chief Geronimo in 1886. He soon secured an appointment in the Medical Corps, and during a tour of duty in Washington, D. C., became the family physician to President McKinley and his chronically ailing wife. Wood's close acquaintance with the President led to other contacts; when war broke out with Spain he teamed up with Theodore Roosevelt to organize the famous "Rough Rider" regiment of volunteer cavalry. He made a good reputation by his handling of this unit during the Santiago campaign, and was promoted to command of a brigade. In a short time he was a general and was left in command of Santiago after its capture from the Spanish. In time his department included both Santiago and Puerto Principe Provinces, comprising the eastern end of the island.[22]

Beneath these principal commanders was the great mass of the army of occupation, whose blue-clad files, white tents, and recurrent bugle calls soon became familiar features in the life of every important Cuban city. In the opening months of the occupation the quality of this army left something to be desired. Since most of General Shafter's forces had returned to the United States after the Santiago campaign, the new army of occupation had to be built almost from the ground up, largely of volunteer units. Some of the best of the volunteer regiments so hurriedly raised after the declaration of war had campaigned with the regulars at Santiago, and had already left Cuba. Many others were sent to swell the growing army in the Philippines, where trouble with the natives threatened. The residue which was left for duty such as that in Cuba varied greatly. It included some excellent units, but also some which had been passed over as unfit for more demanding duties because of their lack of training and discipline.

Such troops had caused trouble even while Shafter still occupied Santiago. An early example was a volunteer regiment which arrived after the end of the fighting, and was used to relieve regular troops in policing the city. Instead of keeping order, the new arrivals drank, fought, fired off their rifles indiscriminately, and were charged with a number of robberies by the irate citizenry. Shafter withdrew them in disgust, and replaced them with another regiment.[23]

When the new occupation began, a stiffening of regulars was provided to do some of the most demanding work, and to keep the volunteers in line. By this time, however, the regulars had their own troubles. The rapid expansion of the army had overloaded many regiments with green recruits, at the same time that a disproportionate number of regimental officers were being detached for the many special duties of the occupation. The result was a slow assimilation of the newcomers, and, for a time, a low degree of efficiency. In May, 1899, General Brooke forwarded to Washington a report on the troops stationed nearest his own headquarters in Havana. An inspecting officer had found that most of them "do not know the names of their equipments [*sic*]; do not know the number of their squad or who is in charge of it; . . . do not know how properly to care for their own equipments," and were ignorant of drill and weapons alike.[24]

As a final complication, some American newspapers accused the army of introducing southern race prejudice into Cuba, where racial relations had previously been smooth.[25]

Most of these conditions disappeared with time. The bulk of the volunteer troops eventually made good soldiers, and at any rate all of them were withdrawn and discharged after the first year. The regulars regained their normal state of excellence, and Cubans and Americans learned to live together reasonably well. But the stresses of the early days came at the time when the American military government of Cuba faced some of its most difficult times, and added a special irritant to the many worries of the commanding general.

Such was the organization with which General Brooke began the formidable task of bringing order to Cuba. The condition of the island in January, 1899, was appalling. The devastation of the past three years had crippled Cuba's economy and reduced thousands of people to misery and starvation. An emergency existed which required vigorous government action, but the universal neglect and destruction made it difficult for the new government to perform even routine functions. Estes G. Rathbone, the new Director-General of Posts, complained of the condition of the Havana post office when he took it over: "The Spanish government on retiring left no records for my guidance, and not one stamp of any denomination, nor a cent in money. In fact, about all that was found was a great quantity of undelivered mail matter, some of it dating back as far as the year 1891; a disreputable old post-office building in very bad sanitary condition, and a miserable post-office outfit."[26]

Colonel Tasker Bliss of the Customs Service found things even worse at the Havana customs house. The building had been stripped of equipment and furniture, and the records removed or destroyed. "Had it not been for a personal appeal to my retiring predecessor I doubt if there would have been left on January 1 a table at which to write or a chair in which to sit," Bliss reported. The floors and courtyards were covered with trash and dirt, while six cesspools were found beneath them. Bliss estimated later that his clean-up crews had removed over 1200 cubic yards of rubbish and filth from the building alone. Other customs houses reported similar conditions.[27]

The condition of the rest of Havana was no better. Arriving Americans were at first struck by the city's attractive appearance from the harbor, where the sea wall was backed by a wide promenade and lined with parks and fine buildings. The old stone houses were picturesque in pastel tints softened by time, and topped with the universal red tile roofs. It was a pleasing panorama, but on closer approach every traveller noted a new fact—Havana smelled bad! To a good deal of old dirt had been added masses of newer refuse resulting from the breakdown of municipal services. The city was full of sick and starving people, the streets littered with dead horses and dogs.[28] General Ludlow, the departmental commander, reported that "the commonest and most imperative requirements of a city government were abandoned; to clean the streets, rescue the dying, even to bury the dead."[29]

In Santiago Province, at the far end of the island, General Wood had had several months to make headway against similar conditions, but still had to deal with a devastated society. In a letter to President McKinley written in November, 1898, Wood said that "It is almost impossible to appreciate the entire destruction of the interior estates in this Province," and declared that it had become "almost a wilderness."[30] Wood wrote elsewhere that during this period, "in many of the interior villages women were compelled to keep out of sight when strangers appeared, as they had only skirts and waists made of bagging and other coarse material."[31]

The same story came from almost every part of Cuba. In the central part of the island General Wilson estimated that the fighting and its disastrous aftermath had cost the lives of one-third of the population of Matanzas Province and one-seventh of the population of Santa Clara Province. According to Wilson's figures, over nine-tenths of the horned cattle of the two provinces had disappeared, and of well over 1,000,000 animals less than 100,000 remained.[32] And from Cienfuegos on the south coast, a sugar plantation manager reported that business had come to a standstill and that the merchants of Cienfuegos refused even to bring in goods until American troops had arrived to insure order.[33]

Faced with these conditions, Brooke quickly organized an emergency relief program designed to alleviate the effects of hunger and disease. He ordered food supplies shipped to all major towns, and to many interior points, for free distribution by the army. Bliss's efficient Customs Service began almost at once to return revenue to the government, and these funds were used to pay for rations for the poor. Army medical officers and Cuban doctors took over appropriate buildings and began treatment of the diseased, while local commanders began vigorous sanitation measures in their areas.

In Havana, whose quarter of a million inhabitants made it Cuba's only large city, Ludlow's energetic action was typical of the whole relief program. He divided Havana into districts for the distribution of rations and medicines, and organized a house-by-house inspection system for reporting the cases of need in each district. A citizens' committee helped the army to administer relief and to channel it where it was needed. During January and February, twenty thousand people in Havana and its environs were fed from five army-run food distribution centers.[34] At the same time the city water supply was overhauled, street cleaning begun, a system of disposing of refuse instituted, and hospitals and asylums established, while a large crew of men was put to disinfecting houses at the rate of 125 per day.

Similar measures had been taken by Wood in Santiago before the occupation began, and were quickly copied in the other provinces. From the first of January to the end of November, 1899, a total of 5,493,000 free rations (a ration was enough food to feed one adult for one day) were distributed in Cuba by the United States army, most of it paid for out of insular revenues. But while rehabilitation was a continuing long-term problem, emergency relief needs dwindled quickly after the restoration of order and the renewal of economic activity, Once allowed back on the land, their fertile soil and tropical climate allowed the Cubans to feed themselves again in a startlingly short time. Few free rations were distributed after the first of July except to hospitals and asylums.[35]

All this work had brought results by the middle of 1899. In six months, the new regime had ended the emergency phase of postwar recovery. A great deal remained to be done, but most of the people had returned to their normal pursuits, wholesale sickness and starvation had been brought under control, and order was restored to the island. Accomplishing this, and bringing into being the organization with which to do it, filled the time of the American authorities for many weeks after the occupation began. Even while they labored, however, new problems had emerged to command their attention.

6

The Military Government
Establishes Its Authority

At the same time that the new government was straining
all its energies to relieve distress in Cuba, General Brooke had to
cope with threats to his authority from both within and without.
Within the military government trouble came almost immediately
from a rebellious subordinate. Outside of it a far graver problem
was posed by the continued existence of the Cuban army.

The dissatisfied subordinate was General Leonard Wood, who
commanded the Department of Santiago. Of the departmental
commanders, Wood was in a unique position. Santiago Province
had been occupied by American forces ever since the surrender
of the Spanish General Toral to Shafter's army in July of 1898,
while General Wood had been in charge of the province since August. A young and ambitious general, Wood had had over four
months to work out his own policies in Santiago, and it was with-
but pleasure that he saw his administration subordinated to the
direction of the central government which Brooke was now creating.

The occupation was barely a week old when Wood rebelled
against this new subordination. The issue he chose for his challenge was the disposition of the customs receipts from his department. In the preceding months, Wood had collected these revenues himself and spent them locally on projects of his own choosing. Now Bliss's Customs Service collected the money, and its

disbursal was controlled by the central government at Havana. Wood's administration was reduced to fiscal dependence on the central treasury, and his projects now needed the approval of General Brooke's headquarters.

In a long memorandum to the War Department, Wood protested against the whole policy of central control. Rather than re-centralizing the Cuban government in Havana, he urged a decentralized military administration in which each department commander would have a large measure of autonomy. Specifically, Wood urged that the revenue collected in each province should be held there to be spent by the local commander as he thought best.[1] Coincident with this appeal to Washington, the Santiago merchants and press began violent protests against the diversion of Santiago revenues to Havana. Rumors soon spread that Wood controlled the Santiago press and had inspired the protests.[2]

General Brooke took action in two directions against this threat to his authority. He fired off a letter to the War Department protesting Wood's insubordination in going over his commander's head with complaints. And Chaffee, Brooke's gruff, outspoken Chief of Staff, sent Wood some directions. "Customs revenues belong to the Island of Cuba as a whole, not as of right to the particular province in which collected," Chaffee wrote Wood. Either the Santiago newspapers did not understand the President's purpose of working for the general good, or they were trying to dictate to the President on the matter. In either case, Wood should make it clear to the offending newspapers that further agitation on the subject would result in their suspension. As for Wood himself, Chaffee declared, he would "be expected to conduct the affairs of [his] Department along the lines *prescribed for guidance*" [emphasis Chaffee's].[3] In an accompanying order Chaffee announced that Wood's past appointments to civil offices would be reviewed in Havana, and further that such appointments would be made from there.[4]

The War Department's failure to support his one-man rebellion, and Chaffee's blast from headquarters, forced Wood to back down. Brooke's authority survived the episode unimpaired, but it marked the beginning of a permanent hostility between the military governor and his well-connected subordinate.

A much more serious threat to the military government was the external one posed by the Cuban army. This organization had not only continued to exist, but had actually performed the duties of an interim government in large parts of Cuba. As the Spanish army withdrew from the interior in the closing months of 1898, Cuban army units moved in and took charge of evacuated regions. General Brooke reported that in most such areas, the Cuban army had performed police duties well and effectively maintained order. Even during the opening weeks of the occupation this situation continued in many areas. It took time to extend American control to all parts of the island, and the Cuban forces did valuable work in the interval.[5]

In spite of the genuine contributions of the Cuban army, however, it was a serious embarrassment to the new government. The existence of a large armed force of uncertain attitude and independent leadership was certain to be a threat to the effectiveness of Brooke's control. To make matters worse, there was recurrent friction between the American and Cuban armies, which might some day blaze into open conflict. And finally there was the question that underlay all the others: would the Cuban revolutionary leaders, who had fought for three years to throw off the control of Spain, now submit peacefully to alien control from another source?

Brooke had gotten off on the wrong foot at the very start, with his refusal to allow the Cubans their victory parade. Adding to the atmosphere of uncertainty in which the occupation began was a proclamation issued to the Cuban army by General Gómez. Writing from his camp at Narciso, two hundred miles from Havana, Gómez issued his statement on December 29. In part it was conciliatory. His absence, Gómez said, would help to smooth the transfer of government at Havana. The period of transition was ended and the sovereignty of the United States was beginning in Cuba. Cuba was not yet free and independent; "For that reason we must dedicate ourselves to bringing about the disappearance of the causes for American intervention." This should be done by peaceful cooperation to restore order and prosperity to Cuba. To all this, however, Gómez added significantly that the Cuban army could not be disbanded until it had been paid. Until this had been done Gómez would remain in command and the army would continue its organized existence.[6]

A week later, Gómez expressed his concern for the future in a letter to the Executive Committee of the Cuban Assembly, which had adjourned in December to await the report of the Cuban commission on the results of its activities in Washington. Describing the moment as one of "transcendent gravity," the old warrior urged the committee to convoke a constitutional convention as soon as possible, and establish the framework of a government to which the United States could relinquish its authority. The letter contained an implied rebuke to the Assembly leaders for their past inaction, and warned that the United States occupation "constitutes a danger to the absolute independence of Cuba" which must be cut as short as possible.[7]

The Assembly's Executive Committee replied to this clarion call with a soothing answer. They could decide nothing, they said, until they had received the report of the commission. This would be ready in a few more days, at which time the entire Assembly could meet and decide what to do. In the meantime, there was little to worry about; relations with the American authorities were good, and growing better. The committee expressed itself as "a little surprised" at Gómez's impatience, and assured him that it knew what it was doing. The best way to cut short the American intervention, its letter concluded, "is in avoiding words or acts which give our enemies a chance to accuse us of impatience or bad feeling, and our allies of jealousy or perfidy."[8]

As January wore on, and the whole issue of the Cuban army hung in the air, impatience mounted in Washington. The harassed Brooke, busy creating a government and coping with a national emergency, attempted to win over the Cuban leaders by the shrewd use of patronage. But he made no attempt to contact the distant Gómez, while Gómez himself seemed content to wait in his camp in the interior. To break the seeming impasse, McKinley determined to send the ubiquitous Robert P. Porter back to Cuba once more as his special representative.

Porter arrived in Havana on January 30, accompanied by Gonzalo de Quesada of the Cuban junta. Upon his arrival he delivered a letter to Brooke signed by the Secretary of War, which said that "Mr. Porter has the entire confidence of the President, who directs that any subject he may bring to your attention shall receive your careful and immediate attention and cooperation." On the authority of this sweeping declaration, Porter got Brooke to write a letter to Gómez, inviting him to come to Havana and confer with Brooke about paying the Cuban army.

Armed with Brooke's letter, and accompanied by Quesada and by Captain J. A. Campbell of Brooke's staff, Porter left Havana immediately for Remedios, where Gómez now had his camp. On February 1 there was a general conference at Gómez's headquarters. Speaking at first through Quesada, Porter presented to the Cuban commander the same offer of $3,000,000 that he had held out to the Cuban commission in Washington. He explained the President's strong desire to accomplish the disbandment of the Cuban army, and stressed the benefits that would result to Cuba through returning the soldiers to useful occupations. Porter insisted that the American money must not be considered a part payment of the back wages owed the Cuban soldiers, but only a relief fund to facilitate their demobilization. The United States government, in other words, was not accepting responsibility for any Cuban revolutionary debts. At the same time, however, Porter held out the possibility of converting a large cadre of the Cuban army into a national police force at some time in the future.[9]

This last idea may have been a variation on the Cuban "colonial army" of which McKinley had spoken to the Cuban commission, back in December. It also struck a responsive note in Máximo Gómez, who had a pet scheme for adding several Cuban regiments, manned by his own soldiers, to the American occupation forces.[10] In suggesting a civil rather than a military force, however, Porter indicated the adoption of a new model for such plans. General Wood had recruited a mounted police unit called the Rural Guard from Cuban army veterans in the autumn of 1898. Its purpose was the suppression of banditry in Santiago Province.[11] Porter's projected national police force was simply an extension of this Rural Guard to all the rest of Cuba, a program which was carried forward steadily in the months following Porter's conference with Gómez.

To Porter's relief, Gómez was courteous and receptive. He

agreed that it would be desirable to return the Cuban soldiers to peaceful occupations. The Cuban general had always favored a moderate level of payment for the army, rather than the grandiose schemes of the Cuban Assembly which were based on securing large foreign loans. Nevertheless, even to Gómez $3,000,000 seemed too little money to pay off his army; he compared it to "the miracle of the loaves and the fishes." But Gómez concluded that, since the amount was not his fault, he would do the best he could with it. He refused, however, to be personally responsible for the money, and emphasized that it must be in charge of General Brooke rather than himself. He readily gave his promise to confer with Brooke, and, at Porter's suggestion, sent off a cable to President McKinley in Washington: "It has afforded me great pleasure to have conferences with your commissioner, Porter, introduced by my friend Quesada, and I am informed and satisfied with your wishes. In a short time I will go to Havana to have conferences with General Brooke, that all may run smoothly, following your advice and gladly contributing to the reconstruction of Cuba."[12]

In another cable to Havana, Gómez assured Brooke of his regard and announced his intention of coming "soon" to the capital. This ended the conference.

That evening all of the participants attended a reception and ball at the local theater, where both Porter and Quesada spoke. In his speech Quesada assured the audience that the United States would never annex Cuba against the will of her people. After the speeches came the dancing, which Gómez led personally and which lasted until early morning. The surprising success of this single day's work convinced Porter that his mission had been accomplished, and he immediately returned to the United States, leaving Brooke to handle the actual negotiations when they should begin.[13]

Although the Americans were greatly encouraged by General Gómez's surprisingly cooperative attitude, relations with the other Cubans again became clouded within a few days of Porter's departure from the country. The occasion for this new friction was a misunderstanding connected with the final burial of Calixto García. On February 9, the body of General García arrived in

Havana aboard the United States gunboat *Nashville,* where it was received in state by a multitude of Cubans and a United States military escort headed by General Ludlow.[14]

Recognizing the desire of the Cubans to honor a national hero, the military government authorized a great procession for February 11, to escort the corpse to its final resting place in Havana. A number of patriotic orations were to be given by Cuban leaders, and prominent places in the procession had been allotted to the Cuban army and the Cuban Assembly. When the line formed, however, an American cavalry unit mistakenly crowded into the place intended for the Cubans. The latter sought out Brooke and Ludlow, who were further forward in the line, and protested their exclusion from their places. But Brooke apparently misunderstood the Cubans' complaints. Thinking that they were demanding a position preceding his own, he angrily refused to do anything, and the march began.[15]

Rather than trail along behind it, the Cubans withdrew from the procession entirely, troops, generals, Assembly, and all. When the cortege arrived at the cemetery, the Cuban speakers and guard of honor were missing, and an embarrassing situation resulted. The Americans were left to conduct the ceremony themselves, and the proceedings ended in confusion and bitterness.[16] In the minds of many Cubans, this blunder confirmed the impression, first created by the cancellation of the victory celebration of January 1, that the Americans were following a deliberate policy of humiliating Cuban leaders and monopolizing public events.

At this time the problem of the Cuban army gained new urgency from events which occurred on the other side of the world. In the Philippines, as in Cuba, American forces had allied themselves with a native insurrectionary movement in the fight against Spain. After the Spanish surrender the question arose there, as it had in Cuba, whether the rebel leaders would choose to submit to United States authority, or to fight for freedom from all foreign control. The Filipinos had chosen to fight. Large-scale hostilities broke out near Manila on February 5, 1899, and it soon became clear that the American forces faced a national uprising which could be subdued only at the cost of a full-dress war.

The parallel with the still uncertain Cuban situation was too obvious to be overlooked, and from this time forth the administration in Washington faced the specter of a Cuban uprising similar to the one already in progress in the Philippines. From his point of vantage in the capital, Henry Adams noted the impact of the Philippine Insurrection on the attitude toward Cuba. He reported, probably with some exaggeration, that "the President and everybody else are almost as eager now to get out of Cuba as they were a year ago to get into it. They are as docile as lambs. The thought of another Manila at Havana sobers even an army-contractor." "If the Democrats were united," Adams concluded, "I think Bryan might be President after all. . . ."[17]

To add to the President's anxieties, General Gómez continued to delay his promised visit to Havana. Instead of going to confer with Brooke, he made a triumphal tour of the island, reviewing parades, occasioning speeches, and arousing patriotic enthusiasm everywhere he went. The Americans began to have horrid doubts about the intentions of the Cuban commander, and regiments of reinforcements continued to swell the strength of the occupation army, but Gómez finally arrived at the capital on February 24.

This time there were no awkward blunders. The American commanders received Gómez with full military honors. What was more important, they at last allowed Cuban troops to parade in Havana for their leader, who reviewed 2,500 of them from the balcony of the governor's palace.[18] When Brooke and Gómez got down to business, it was in an atmosphere of cordiality which had been sadly lacking before. During the following days, the two commanders worked out the details of the plan to pay off the Cuban army. As a result of the Porter mission, Gómez had already agreed in principle to the demobilization of his army in return for the distribution to it of $3,000,000 by the United States government. He and Brooke now decided that each Cuban soldier should receive $100. They would make the official rolls of the Cuban army the basis of payment, and the actual disbursal would be done by a mixed Cuban-American commission named by Gómez and Brooke.[19]

The formulation of these plans, however, reopened the old disagreement between Gómez and the Cuban Assembly over the payment of the army. The Cuban Assembly had not given up its hopes of procuring vast sums of money for the army by means of borrowing abroad. Now in session again, the Assembly grew increasingly critical of Gómez for agreeing to disband his forces in return for a paltry $3,000,000. It was an open secret that the Assembly leaders were seeking a loan from private sources in the United States, and wished to delay proceedings until they could locate a lender.

Nevertheless, when the Assembly openly broke with Gómez and challenged his authority, Brooke seems to have been taken by surprise. On March 9, the Assembly sent a committee to Gómez with the demand that he adhere to the decision to hold out for more money. The old general replied on the following day that he had already made an agreement with the American authorities, and that rather than go back on his word he would pay off the army himself. On March 11, the Cuban Assembly deposed Gómez by the simple expedient of abolishing the army grade that he occupied. They charged that Gómez had been insubordinate in accepting Porter's offer and in dealing with Brooke without consulting the Assembly, and that his actions threatened to ruin negotiations for a loan in which the Assembly was involved. They also attacked Gonzalo de Quesada for the part he had played in the Porter mission. The Assembly declared that the $3,000,000 was insufficient and that they had never agreed to accept it.[20]

There was a reason for the Assembly's agitation. As they had suggested, the Cubans were deep in negotiations for a private loan. The prospective lender, a mysterious American named C. M. Coen, had come to Cuba to meet a committee of the Assembly early in March. Challenged to present his proposals in writing, Coen submitted them to the Assembly in a letter signed "C. M. Coen of self and Associates."

What Coen proposed was to give the Cubans $12,400,000 in return for Cuban bonds to the amount of $20,000,000, which were to pay 5 per cent interest and to be redeemed at face value within thirty years. The money which the Cubans received must be used solely to pay off the army, and for no other purpose. The contract must meet the approval of the President of the United States, or it would be entirely voided. Coen undertook to secure this approval through his "associates," but the Assembly must

DICKENS UP TO DATE

OLIVER TWIST OF CUBA: "Please, sir,
I want some more."

—*The Dispatch*, Pittsburg
Reprinted in *Literary Digest*, April 1, 1899.

also send a commission to Washington to ask the President's permission for the loan. In the meantime, the contract must remain
secret.[21]

This offer left the Cubans with mixed emotions. If McKinley
approved it, it promised them a large sum of money in a short
time, but the terms of the loan gave them pause. They were to receive only 62 cents on the dollar for their $20,000,000 in bonds,
but had to pay back the full face value, plus 5 per cent interest on
it dating from the time they received Coen's money. Furthermore,

no one knew anything about Coen, and Coen himself refused to tell who was behind him, although the provisions for Presidential approval suggested someone in the group with White House connections.

After three days of hot debate, the Assembly voted to approve the Coen contract, though by no means unanimously. In the dark days of the revolution, Estrada Palma had been forced to dispose of Cuban bonds in New York at discounts of 75, and even 90, per cent in his desperate search for funds, so the Assembly was not unaccustomed to such transactions.[22] The vote of approval came on March 9, and led directly and immediately to the break with Gómez and his deposition from command of the army.[23]

This action of the Assembly raised an obstacle in Brooke's way just when he thought the Cuban army problem well on the way to solution. The military governor at once announced that he would continue to recognize Gómez as the true representative of the Cuban army. He also sent a wire to Washington requesting permission to abolish the Assembly by decree, but received an answer counseling delay and advising against such action.[24] It soon appeared that, with the Cuban army and the public in general, Gómez's prestige far outweighed that of the Assembly, and on March 14 Brooke wired the Secretary of War that action "of the kind suggested" would probably not be needed.[25]

On the same date, Brooke informed the War Department that "a man named Cohen" was in communication with the Cuban Assembly, and had promised to get the approval of President McKinley for a private loan to the Assembly of $20,000,000. Brooke asked to be informed of his government's position in the matter.[26]

The War Department referred this message to the President. On the following day, McKinley's secretary wired the Secretary of War that he was "directed to say that no one has any authority from the President to communicate with the Cuban Assembly, that he does not recognize the Assembly, and that whatever communication he may have to make to the Cuban people will be made through official channels."[27]

On March 17 Brooke wired that the Assembly wished to send another committee to Washington to confer about a loan. Brooke believed that no such committee would be sent, however, if he were authorized to state that it would not be received in Washington. He even thought it possible that such an announcement might lead to the dissolution of the Assembly.[28] The War Department's reply, sent the same day, said that the "so-called Assembly or any part of it will not receive recognition by this Government under any conditions whatever."[29]

But the Assembly still held one card. It had possession of the rolls of the Cuban army, without which payment could not be made, and it refused to relinquish them either to the American authorities or to General Gómez. A virtual stalemate ensued which lasted throughout the month of March.

At this time Brooke attempted to find out for himself the remaining strength of the Cuban army. Most of it had been allowed to go home on indefinite leave, and few elements were still actually in the field. On March 18 Brooke's headquarters wired all departmental commanders, requesting the number of Cuban troops in each department who still retained their organization.[30] But the results of this poll were indecisive. The commanders in Puerto Principe Province and Havana City each reported only three or four hundred Cubans still in the field in their areas. The commanders in Havana Province and Santa Clara, however, wired the total numbers still enrolled in Cuban units, getting the information from the Cuban provincial commanders. In this case the totals were about 2,000 for Havana Province and almost 5,000 for Santa Clara. The commander in Pinar del Río found it impossible to get the information quickly, while General Wood at Santiago insisted that the Cuban army no longer existed in his province. General Wilson in Matanzas gave double figures: he found about 450 men still in the field, while the local commander assured him that about 2,200 men in the province had preserved their organizations.[31]

Since it was impossible to tell how many Cubans were still subject to recall, or how many of these would actually respond, the real strength of the Cuban army remained a matter of conjecture. However, Brooke's problem soon began to work itself out, as the Cuban Assembly showed signs of final collapse.

In spite of the uncompromising attitude of the American government, the Cubans had persisted, after long discussion, in sending their agents to Washington on behalf of the Coen loan. A committee of two men managed to get an interview on March 31 with John Hay, the Secretary of State. Speaking for McKinley, Hay told them that it was out of the question either to authorize any loan to the Assembly or to augment the sum already offered to pay off the Cuban Army.[32]

When the two emissaries wired their news to the Assembly, it was clear that further efforts were pointless. As the agents reported, "the Assembly can hope for nothing from the American Government."[33] The $3,000,000 offered by McKinley was the only money in prospect, and no action of the Assembly had been able to change this. On April 4, the Cuban Assembly gave up the fight. It voted, almost unanimously, to disband the army, to dissolve itself, and to turn over the army rolls to Brooke so that he could proceed with his plans.[34]

While this finally opened the way for Brooke and Gómez to go ahead with their arrangements, it also raised new problems. They had already suspected that the poll of department commanders instituted on March 18 showed too few Cuban soldiers. General Wood, for example, reported none at all in Santiago Province, but subsequent investigation indicated that several thousand armed men met there every fortnight for drill and review, and then dispersed again until the next muster. Now that the rolls were at hand, however, they showed the startling total of 48,000 Cuban army veterans to be paid. Although this figure was undoubtedly padded, there was no way to go behind the rolls, which were the only official records available.

Since the amount of money available was fixed, the only thing to do was to change the details of the payment plan. Brooke and Gómez agreed to reduce the amount per man from $100 to $75, and to eliminate payment of the several thousand Cuban veterans who held paying jobs in the military government as clerks, officials, or rural police. They agreed further that any remaining money was to go to a list of disabled officers to be made up by Gómez, but this list was never prepared, and the surplus funds were finally returned to the United States Treasury.[35]

Brooke also stipulated that at the time of payment the Cubans must surrender their arms to the commission which distributed the money. Though Gómez agreed to this, many of the Cubans objected strenuously. Feeling ran so high that none of the Cuban officers named by Gómez to the mixed payment commission would accept the duty. The Americans, it appeared, would have to do the job unaided. To soothe Cuban feelings, Brooke ordered that the arms should be deposited with the mayors of the municipalities in which payment took place, rather than given up directly to the payment commission.[36]

These new problems and delays created fresh uneasiness in Washington, where everyone was preoccupied with the Philippine Insurrection. Russell A. Alger, the Secretary of War, wrote McKinley in mid-May: "I do not like the Cuban situation. While there is nothing serious yet the delay in paying off the insurgent forces seems to be breeding discontent."[37] A letter from General Brooke to the War Department late in May added to these apprehensions. Brooke found "a deep-seated suspicion in the minds of the Cubans" toward the United States government. Brooke added, however, "I think it would be the same with any government."[38]

The actual payment of the Cuban army began in Havana on May 27. Accompanied by a guard of infantry, Major Francis S. Dodge of the Paymaster's Department drove up to the selected open-air site in a wagon containing $30,000 in gold and $9,000 in silver. General Juan Rius Rivera, the civil governor of Havana, was there to receive the arms turned in, and a group of Cuban officers and American reporters came to watch the proceedings. Major Dodge set out a bag of gold on the rough wooden table, clerks arranged their muster rolls, and the infantrymen stationed themselves to direct the expected crowds.

To the dismay of the Americans, almost no one came to be paid. While some of the Cuban officers jeered, the unit paid exactly seven men in the course of the day. Word soon leaked out that a group of die-hard Cuban officers in Havana had organized a boycott of the payment, seeking by patriotic appeals and personal threats to dissuade the veterans from collecting their money. Most effective of all, they simply neglected to announce the payment to their men. The fiasco of the first day was a victory for this group, and for a moment they seemed to constitute one more obstacle to the dissolution of the Cuban army.

On the next day, however, the Cubans began to appear in small but increasing numbers. Many had just learned that the payment was taking place; others had finally decided to brave the threats of their officers. By the third day, May 29, hundreds of Cubans thronged about the pay-table. The lure of $75 in cash had broken down all opposition, and the boycott was a complete failure.[39]

Assured of success, the occupation government organized special army pay units to travel from place to place about the island until every Cuban veteran had been paid and disarmed. The work took all summer, but on the whole things ran smoothly. In some towns entire Cuban army corps assembled to receive their pay, while in others only a few hundred, sometimes less, could be reached at once. The clerical work was formidable. One pay unit, headed by Colonel Edward Moale and active from June 16 to August 27, alone paid out $1,728,000 to over 23,000 men.

This was not accomplished without incident, however. At Manzanillo in Santiago Province, Moale found two Cuban regiments, totalling 2,300 men, awaiting him on July 4. When he produced the pay rolls, the Cuban commander announced that he would not allow any of his men to be paid unless all were paid, regardless of whether they were listed on the official rolls or not. He would not even allow the rolls to be called, and for a time trouble threatened. Moale wired Havana for instructions, and was told to pay the Cubans upon the certification of their officers that they were bona fide members of their units. This proved satisfactory to everyone, and the day's difficulties soon ended.[40]

Probably more typical was the experience of Major Frank H. Edwards, who paid troops in Pinar del Río Province. Edwards reported: "At all points at which payments were made the people present were invariably good natured, well behaved and gave no trouble whatever."[41]

When the payment was under way, Máximo Gómez issued a farewell manifesto to his army. He was going away, he said, to visit his old home in Santo Domingo, but before leaving he had "a parting word to the people for whom I have sacrificed thirty years of my life." The old chieftain's tone was blunt but pacific. "Now we no longer want soldiers but men for the maintenance of peace and order, which are the basis of Cuba's future welfare." Nevertheless, he expressed no satisfaction with American rule. While granting that "We wanted and depended upon foreign intervention to terminate the war," Gómez declared that "none of us thought that this . . . would be followed by a military occupation of the country by our allies, who treat us as a people incapable of acting for ourselves, and who have reduced us to obedience, to submission, and to a tutelage imposed by force of circumstances." Bitter a dose as this was, Gómez urged peaceful cooperation with the Americans in a task "which is as disagreeable for them as for ourselves." Cubans should draw together in unity, organize politically, and "make useless the presence of a strange power in the island." They should help the Americans to complete the "honorable mission" which had been forced on them by circumstances. "This work was not sought by those rich northerners, owners of a continent. I think doubts and suspicions are unjust." Finally, Cubans must form "a committee or club, to be the nucleus of a government."[42]

This dignified and realistic message seemed to guarantee that to Gómez the Cuban Revolution was over, at least for as long as the Cubans could believe in the good faith of the Americans and in their own ultimate independence.

By late summer of 1899 the payment project was completed. Following the lead of Máximo Gómez, the Cuban army had peacefully accepted the authority of the United States, and the possibility of armed rebellion in Cuba had been immeasurably reduced. Although, as General Brooke complained, "The amount of labor given to this matter and the time consumed was out of all proportion to the work in hand,"[43] nevertheless the military government had scored a major victory and established its authority on firm ground.

Growing Divergence over Cuban Policy

While General Brooke's government was successfully establishing United States authority in Cuba, back in Washington Congress had come forward to define one important aspect of American occupation policy. This was the question of the granting of public franchises, which must play an important part in any American economic penetration of the island.

Many in America assumed that such penetration would result from United States rule as a matter of course. In July of 1898, an editorial in the *New York World* pictured "our next invasion of Cuba" as one of merchants and investors, and declared that "whatever may be decided as to the political future of Cuba, its industrial and commercial future will be directed by American enterprise and stimulated with American capital."[1]

The expected influx of American businessmen and promoters began as soon as peace was restored in the island. One observer of the occupation's early days described the first wave of these as the skirmishers of a new army—"that of commercial occupation." Within a few months their numbers had swelled to thousands. Their activities ranged from the struggle of rival financial syndicates for control of the Havana street-car line to the unsuccessful efforts of a Grand Rapids furniture agent to penetrate the Cuban market with his product. One goal, however, they held in common: most of them hoped to see, with the beginning of the American military administration, an open door to grants and concessions of all kinds.[2]

Among General Brooke's earliest instructions was an order from the War Department expressing the President's wishes on this subject. The substance of this order was that no local governmental body in Cuba should grant concessions or franchises for public works, railways, telephone or telegraph lines, water or gas works, and the like, without Brooke's approval. Also, before giving such approval Brooke himself must get specific authorization from the Secretary of War.[3] Thus the control of such grants was largely removed from the military government in Cuba, and centralized in the hands of Russell Alger, the business-minded Secretary of War.

On February 10, 1899, the *Washington Evening Star* carried an article announcing the creation by the War Department of a new board. Its function was to review applications for franchises, railway grants, street car line concessions, electric light monopolies, and similar privileges, in Cuba and Puerto Rico, and to make recommendations to the Secretary of War regarding them. The board's president, General Robert P. Kennedy of Ohio, stated that the board would leave for Havana within a week or ten days, as soon as a clerical force could be assembled. It was their intention to visit "every port, large city, and province on the island," taking a month or six weeks to do so.

"Very many applications have been referred to us by Secretary Alger and Assistant Secretary Meiklejohn," Kennedy was quoted as saying, "and not a few calls have been made by applicants in person." According to Kennedy, some requests for grants or concessions were from American syndicates, but most were from corporations already established in Cuba. None of them would be approved, he said, "until we have gone over the ground and carefully looked into the advantages or disadvantages of each."[4]

Senator Joseph Benson Foraker of Ohio read this article with care. According to Foraker, this one newspaper article was all the information that he ever received concerning the government's franchise policy in Cuba, but it served to arouse his interest in the subject.[5] On February 28, the Ohio Senator introduced an amendment to the current army appropriation bill. The first section of the amendment forbade the granting of franchises or concessions of any kind in Cuba, by United States authorities, for the duration of the American occupation. The second part declared that, the pacification of Cuba having been accomplished, the President was authorized to withdraw the army and leave the Cubans to govern themselves.[6]

This measure was referred to the Senate Committee on Appropriations, where it disappeared briefly from sight. When it reappeared on the Senate floor, the second part, relating to the termination of the occupation, had been removed, but the section on franchises remained unchanged.

The general debate on the Foraker Amendment occurred on March 3, 1899, the last day of the final session of the Fifty-fifth Congress. Foraker led off with a vigorous defense of his measure. If a program of granting franchises began, he said, and American economic penetration was given an open field, "it means that the United States will not get out of Cuba in a hundred years." The Senator was equally blunt in urging a quick end to American occupation and early self-government for the Cubans.[7]

Foraker received support from oddly disparate sources. The anti-imperialist Senator George F. Hoar of Massachusetts approved of the amendment.[8] On the other hand, no less an imperialist than Senator Henry Cabot Lodge declared that he also favored the measure. Lodge thought it "of the last importance that Congress should say by statute, and say to all the world, that while we are holding these islands by military authority, we are not going to have them exploited for commercial purposes."[9]

Senator Orville H. Platt of Connecticut and Senator John C. Spooner of Wisconsin, both leading administration spokesmen, led the opposition. Platt argued that the amendment was unnecessary, as no one had any notion of giving away franchises in Cuba. Besides, he said, such a measure would be a reflection on the honor of the administration. In reply, Foraker demanded what the purpose of the Kennedy Board could be, if not to grant franchises, and Lodge indignantly denied any reflection on the administration's honor. If the President really did not want to give away Cuban franchises, Lodge said ingenuously, then the Senate was only endorsing his policy by barring them.[10]

Senator Spooner was made of sterner stuff than his colleague.

He declared flatly that the President's authority in Cuba came, not from Congress, but from his constitutional position as commander-in-chief of the armed forces. This being the case, Spooner concluded, then Congress had no right to legislate on Cuba at all.[11] But this argument failed to convince the Senate, which promptly passed the Foraker Amendment with only eleven dissenting votes. As finally passed by Congress, the Amendment said that: "No property franchises, or concessions of any kind whatever, shall be granted by the United States, or by any other military or other authority whatever in the Island of Cuba during the occupation thereof by the United States."[12]

A curious feature of the debate on this act was that no one ever openly defended the granting of franchises, though many congressmen would do so later when the full effects of Foraker's action became visible. Like the Teller Resolution, the Foraker Amendment probably passed at least in part because politicians were afraid to take a public stand against it. And, also like the Teller Resolution, it represented another important change imposed by Congress on the President's Cuban policy.

While both the Executive and the Legislative branches of the government were busily shaping American occupation policy in Cuba, they failed conspicuously to define the ultimate purposes of the United States intervention there. This question had presumably been decided in April of 1898, with the passage of the Teller Resolution. Whatever the disagreements about the proper duration of the American occupation, Senator Teller's "self-denying ordinance" seemed to assure that Cuba would be left free and independent whenever conditions there had been properly tidied up. But in the winter of 1898–99, senators and congressmen displayed a widening range of opinions about the "Cuban problem." It began to appear that the matter was not so simple as had been supposed.

A good deal of the debate over expansionism at this time centered about the Vest Resolution, introduced in the Senate on December 6, 1898, by Senator George Vest of Missouri. In his resolution, Senator Vest declared that "under the Constitution of the United States no power is given to the Federal Government to acquire territory to be held and governed permanently as colonies."

He went on to insist that the only legitimate purpose for acquiring new territory (aside from small naval bases and the like) was that of "ultimately organizing such territory into States suitable for admission into the Union."[13]

It was no coincidence that the Vest Resolution made its appearance in the Senate just prior to the opening of debate on the peace treaty with Spain. The treaty would be debated in executive session, behind closed doors. The Vest Resolution, like several others introduced in this period, was a device of the anti-expansionists to get the expansion movement out in the open where they could attack it publicly.

Most of the ensuing debate concerned the disposal of the Philippine Islands, but some statements about Cuba appeared as well. Perhaps the most significant of these was that of Senator Teller, whose position on Cuban independence had been evolving rapidly since the spring of 1898. On September 8, Teller had made a speech at Colorado Springs which already departed considerably from the language of his resolution. The Cubans, he said then, should have a territorial government "something on the order that we had in Colorado for fifteen years," in which their individual rights would be safeguarded, but the United States government would be in control. The main thing was to "put a strong hand on them and give them a good government."[14]

Senator Teller clarified his new position in a Senate speech of December 20, 1898, in which he attacked the Vest Resolution. He began by vigorously justifying the position of the United States in Cuba. "It is not necessary," Teller said, "that we should have a concession from Spain to say that Cuba is ours . . . if we choose to assert our right" to hold it. And he asked, "Who else can govern Cuba today but the United States?"

Teller agreed, however, that the United States had a moral obligation to give its new acquisitions self-government when they were ready for it. Some day they must all be either self-governing or a part of the United States. The question was, which should it be? "Nobody wants to make Cuba or Porto Rico or the Philippines States of the Union," the Colorado Senator said flatly. But at present the Cubans were not ready to govern themselves. He did not want to see the people of Cuba "turned out to take care of themselves so far as international affairs are concerned," Teller announced. The great danger was of interference with the new government by some foreign power. To this danger there was only one answer: "In all their international relations I believe, for many years to come at least, the Government of the United States must speak to the world for Cuba."

The next question was that of the internal government of Cuba. Teller thought that it was "not necessary . . . that we invite every man in Cuba to participate in the government that we there establish." The "unstable and unsafe" elements of the population must be excluded from political participation, if not by the Cubans, then by the United States authorities. But if the Cubans were able to maintain by themselves a government "of the character I have mentioned . . . then we should let them do so in all their local affairs."[15]

All this was far removed from the Teller Resolution. Instead of renouncing "sovereignty," and even "control," over Cuba, the United States was to establish a protectorate there, take complete control of foreign affairs, and refuse even local self-government to the Cubans until they complied with the specific requirements of the United States.

If this call for the continuation of United States authority in Cuba came from a seemingly unlikely quarter, so did one of the clearest demands that such authority soon be ended. Senator John C. Spooner of Wisconsin was one of the most prominent and dependable administration spokesmen in the Senate, but in his speech on the Vest Resolution he took an unexpectedly independent line. Speaking to the Senate on February 2, 1899, Spooner voiced his distrust of the whole movement for territorial expansion. He believed, he said, in commercial expansion, including an increased navy and merchant marine, and the acquisition of necessary naval bases. But he had grave suspicions of any attempt to annex permanently areas far away, inhabited by alien peoples, and located in tropical climates where white men could not work. "Every argument," Spooner said, "which has been made in support of the doctrine of territorial expansion . . . seems to me to be superficial, some of them sentimental, and some of them fantastic."

These sentiments Spooner applied specifically to Cuba. "Of course we can not take Cuba," he said: "I hope, for the honor of America, no man would think of such a thing. We promised the world to make Cuba free and to enforce law and order in that island until the people there could form a government. When that is done our pledge will have been splendidly redeemed. . . . The jingle of words which we read every day about 'hauling down the flag' does not in the least either thrill me or impress me. Our flag has been hauled down before. . . . It will be hauled down again." And the Wisconsin Senator pointedly expressed the hope that it would not be long before the flag was taken down in Cuba and the island left to govern itself.[16]

Other senators, it appeared, were justifiably confused by all this. Senator W. J. Sewell of New Jersey wrote to President McKinley in April, plaintively requesting enlightenment. The Cuban situation, he said, "is such that men in my position are loaded down with inquiries, as to what its future is going to be." As for himself, "I have always been in favor of the permanent occupation of Cuba, and deprecated the passage of the Teller Resolution." But not even the meaning of the famous resolution was clear, for "I was answered by a number of senators, that it did not mean any more than the oft made statements of British Diplomatists that they would give up Egypt whenever a stable government could be formed, which nobody believes now."

Sewell complained that the uncertainty as to Cuba's future was holding up United States investment there, and its consequent economic development. So was the Foraker Resolution, which blocked the construction of badly needed railroads. Finally, Sewell told the President, there were domestic political considerations. "We are rapidly approaching another Presidential Convention, and my views are very much sought after," but "I am utterly ignorant of what you expect to achieve."[17]

This lack of direction in Cuban affairs was apparent almost from the start to Washington insiders like Henry Adams. Adams, long interested in the Cuban question, wrote as early as January, 1899, that "the government lets everything drift. It professes earnestly its intention to give Cuba its independence, but refuses to take a step towards it, and allows everyone to act for annexation. It supports Wood at one end and Brooke at the other, pulling different ways."[18]

A similar confusion was evident in Cuba, where the chief officers of the occupation debated as to the part they should play there. General Brooke was as much in the dark as anyone else about the ultimate purposes of his government. Brooke had little to guide him but the Teller Resolution, which assigned no role to the United States authorities in the island except "the pacification thereof." But soon the island seemed as pacific as could be desired. What else was Brooke's government supposed to do? What was to succeed it? In short, what did the administration expect of him?

These same questions occurred to General Wilson, commanding the Department of Matanzas. They seemed so important to Wilson that he went to Havana in the opening days of the occupation to ask Brooke about them in person. But according to Wilson, Brooke could give him no answers. Instead, he complained that he had no more information on the subject than had Wilson. "We were left," Wilson wrote later, "absolutely to our own conception of the situation and what it required of us."[19]

At first, General Brooke had no great need for long-term goals. The day-to-day work of setting up a regime, getting a relief program under way, straightening out the tangled insular finances, negotiating the disbanding of the Cuban army, and a hundred lesser details, were ample to occupy his attention. Aside from such pressing matters, Brooke's policy was to take the "pacifying" instructions literally and otherwise to meddle as little as possible. He encouraged the Cuban department heads to use their own initiative, and when they spoke collectively as the Cuban Cabinet he usually listened to their advice. The immediate work of the occupation was done well. The Cubans were given real responsibility and experience in government. Beyond this, Brooke moved cautiously. "I wish to say that rapidity of action is not possible here," he wrote the War Department late in May, for in making changes "we are working against the habits of thoughts and action of this people."

The military governor also complained of the independence of his subordinates. Some of the department commanders had a disturbing tendency to strike out on their own, modifying the laws on their own authority. One solution to this growing problem, Brooke hinted, was more effective central direction: "the expression of the views of the President is very necessary to guide me in these matters."[20]

By far the most troublesome of the department commanders was General Leonard Wood, who carried things with a high hand in his part of the island. Robert P. Porter, an early admirer of Wood, wrote approvingly of the vigor and sternness with which Wood enforced his sanitation program in Santiago. The struggle against dirt and disease in the face of local resistance, he declared, "has been as sharp and hot as the charge on San Juan Hill." In the course of this fight, "The doors of houses had to be smashed in; people making sewers of the thoroughfares were publicly horsewhipped in the streets of Santiago; eminently respectable citizens were forcibly brought before the commanding general and sentenced to aid in cleaning the streets they were in the habit of defiling." The result of these somewhat heroic measures was, understandably enough, "complete surrender to the sanitary authorities." The Santiagans, wrote Porter, had "had their first object-lesson in the new order of things inaugurated by the war."[21]

Balked in his frontal attack on Brooke's authority in January, Wood kept up thereafter a constant sniping from under cover. This was the more effective because of his many contacts with highly placed politicians, including President McKinley himself. Wood had maintained a personal correspondence with McKinley ever since he left Washington to organize the Rough Riders, and Theodore Roosevelt, his partner in that enterprise, was his enthusiastic partisan.

For a few months in the autumn of 1898 Wood also had a paid agent, A. E. Mestro, promoting his interests in the United States. Mestro had orders to see a number of prominent men, including the President, on Wood's behalf; he also acted as a public-relations man with the newspapers. In October, 1898, Mestro wrote Wood that he had spoken to the editor of the *New York Evening Sun* about getting Wood appointed Governor of Havana. The editor agreed to help, and the result was an editorial, printed October 15, 1898, which supported the appointment. Shortly after this Mestro quit Wood's service to accept a private job in Havana.[22]

Wood had opened his campaign against Brooke's control with his January "memorandum" to the War Department, which advised against putting any single person at the head of the military government. Instead, he recommended autonomous rule by the departmental commanders, who could coordinate their separate policies by holding frequent joint conferences. He had also advised going slow in the establishment of any general government for Cuba. "It is absolute folly, in my mind," he wrote, "to begin the details of government among a people who are in arms and starving." The development of a civil government should follow, rather than precede, social and economic rehabilitation.[23]

Although Brooke swiftly rebuffed this early move for independent action, Wood continued to advocate it. In mid-February he wrote Theodore Roosevelt that "the people" in Cuba wanted provincial and municipal autonomy, "and they are bound to have it. . . . They abhor the idea of re-centralizing everything in Havana."[24]

To this theme Wood soon added another, the desirability of continuing the United States rule in Cuba indefinitely. As usual, he ascribed his new policy to the desires of "the people." Writing McKinley in April, Wood said that "The sentiment for our remaining here forever is becoming very strong in this part of Cuba, and I think we shall have hard work to get away." He added significantly that "they are a quiet people, without enough force of character to be seriously troublesome if we can only keep them moderately busy."[25]

At first, however, Wood was cautious in his annexationism. In an article written for the May issue of the *North American Review,* he again urged a plan for provincial autonomy in Cuba, "as in our federal system." But he soft-pedalled annexation talk, declaring that the military government should last only until a civil government could be set up to take its place. Wood even suggested that the Cubans might be better fitted for self-government than had been thought. Nevertheless, he advised a period of education and adjustment for the Cubans, and recommended a slow, step-by-step approach to the problem of building a civil government.[26]

Soon Wood was speaking somewhat more boldly. He visited the United States in June, and conferred with McKinley on Cuban policy. Interviewed at this time by a newspaper reporter, the General gave a summary of his current views which included a thrust at the Brooke regime.

"The Cuban problem can easily be solved," he said. "With the right sort of an administration everything could be straightened out in six months. Just now there is too much 'tommy-rot.'" What was needed, according to Wood, was "a firm and stable military government in the hands of men who would not hesitate to use severe measures should the occasion arise."

The propertied classes in Cuba, Wood declared, and all the foreigners there, including the Spaniards, favored the annexation of Cuba by the United States, "because they realize that we can give them a stable government." At the same time, Wood's confidence in the ability of the Cubans to govern themselves had suffered a decline. He would not discuss the point, he said, because "If I said they were [able to do so], a lot of cranks would at once shout for the immediate American evacuation of the island; if I said they were not, I would have all the Cubans down on me." He believed that "the establishment of another Haitian Republic in the West Indies would be a serious mistake." If Cuba were left to herself, international complications were sure to result. But fortunately the Cubans were gaining in understanding. "They are rapidly realizing that annexation is the best thing for them, and the awarding of the officers to them has satisfied them that the United States does not wish to do any grasping."[27]

While Wood became a leading annexationist and a rallying point for opposition to General Brooke, another of the occupation generals was working out his own theories about the future of Cuba. General James Harrison Wilson was well connected too, and like Wood he had a boundless confidence in his own judgment. He also had a long-standing political friendship with Wood's own friends, Theodore Roosevelt and Senator Henry Cabot Lodge of Massachusetts. When the Spanish War broke out, Roosevelt thought at one time of joining Wilson's staff, though his martial ambitions soon outgrew such modest bounds.[28] Senator Lodge, however, actually did request a place on Wilson's staff for his son-in-law, Augustus P. Gardner, which Wilson promptly arranged.[29]

In the autumn of 1898 both Lodge and Roosevelt had pleaded with President McKinley to appoint Wilson military governor of Cuba. The idea seems originally to have been Lodge's, but Wilson was soon actively seeking the command on his own behalf.[30] Like Leonard Wood, Wilson got press support for his claims. He was a lifelong friend of Charles A. Dana, editor of the *New York Sun,* and of Dana's son Paul, who ran the paper after his father's death in 1897. Wilson also had the benefit of the political contacts resulting from his years as a Republican national committeeman, and his many acquaintances in the Senate.

In the event, Wilson got command only of a department, not command of the division of Cuba. McKinley appointed Brooke to the coveted post in mid-December; a week later Wilson seriously annoyed the President by placing him in an embarrassing position. While on a Southern tour, McKinley came to Macon, Georgia, to review troops, some of them under Wilson's command. After the review the President and a number of generals gave speeches. Wilson, a long-time expansionist, gave a spread-eagle speech foreseeing the day when "the flag will fly over every foot of the continent from the northern extremity of the Dominion of Canada to the Gulf of Mexico." He hoped to see this day "before the next administration of the President closes," for "we are too big and powerful and progressive to have neighbors on this continent."[31] This somewhat startling demand, made from a platform shared with the President of the United States, brought forth a scathing attack from the *New York Times,* considerable unfavorable newspaper comment elsewhere, and a conviction on the part of McKinley that Wilson talked too much.[32]

While often indiscreet, however, Wilson had great energy and considerable ability. In the spring and summer of 1899 he visited all the towns and villages in Matanzas and Santa Clara Provinces, talking to almost everyone of even local importance. He delegated to his staff the task of making studies of the economic, political, sanitary, and military conditions in his command. Then, in the absence of an announced administration policy, Wilson formulated his own.

The first step, Wilson thought, was to get the land of Cuba back into production as soon as possible. Cuba was primarily an agricultural country, but the revolution had left the work cattle decimated and the land laid waste. The basic means of production were often lacking. One observer saw farmers plowing with an old piece of barrel hoop in one place, and in another, three men dragging a plow guided by a fourth. With almost everything else lacking, agricultural credit was lacking too. Cuba had few banks, farm loans were almost impossible to get, and interest rates were prohibitively high.[33]

On May 9, Wilson wrote to Havana recommending a general scheme of agricultural rehabilitation. He requested that the central government send each province $20,000 per month, to be used for loans to small farmers. These loans, which would make possible the purchase of tools, seed, and work animals, need not in any case be larger than $400 to any one individual. The money could come from Cuba's own revenues, which were already accumulating a surplus due to the combination of an economical government and an honest administration of the customs.[34]

Others besides Wilson had considered this problem, and devised similar plans. In January Fitzhugh Lee had made a speech to the Cubans in which he advocated the establishment of agricultural banks, and loans of cattle and seed to deserving farmers to put them back into production. Later on, General Wood endorsed a plan similar to Wilson's.[35]

General Brooke was also thinking about the problem, but in slightly different terms. While Brooke agreed that some sort of rehabilitation scheme was absolutely necessary, he was opposed to the kind of scheme suggested by Wilson. He recognized the need for putting animals and implements in the hands of the Cubans, but feared the principle of government loans to individuals, and had little faith that they would ever be repaid. Rather than embroil the government in such paternalistic schemes, Brooke advised giving the needed materials to the farmers outright and avoiding the pernicious loans.[36] But in practice, nothing was done. Brooke refused to approve the loan policy, while the authorities in Washington took a dim view of making outright gifts to Cuban farmers.

General Wilson also considered the problem of Cuba's future government. His ideas on this subject began to take shape in a letter he wrote in May to Senator Foraker, another old acquaintance with whom he was in regular correspondence during 1899. To begin with, Wilson expressed his regret at the passage of the Teller Resolution. It would have been better, he thought, if Congress had openly announced an intention to annex Cuba. But instead it had promised not to do so, and the promise must be kept, once made. Now the question was what to do next. If he had supreme command in Cuba, Wilson said, he would call together Máximo Gómez, the Cuban Assembly, and other leading Cubans, and would get them to cooperate in drafting a Cuban constitution. The President should send down a committee of United States senators and judges to "advise" this constitutional convention. When it had produced a suitable constitution, the new government should be inaugurated, and the President should withdraw all United States troops.

At the time the Cubans assumed their own government, however, it was of the utmost importance that a treaty be negotiated which would regulate the future relations between Cuba and the United States. As Wilson envisaged the treaty at this time, it would embody a sweeping United States protectorate over Cuba. The United States would furnish Cuba with military protection, and maintain common diplomatic, customs, and postal services with the Cubans, but "leave them free to manage their internal affairs in their own way." The treaty should also provide for mutual free entry of natural and manufactured goods and establish an identical tariff against outsiders; in short, "an American zollverein with Cuba."[37]

Wilson regarded this "zollverein," or customs union, as basic to his program. Only by giving Cuban sugar free entry into the United States, he believed, or at least a greatly reduced tariff rate, could the island be assured of any permanent prosperity. Falling sugar prices, ruinous competition from foreign, state-subsidized beet sugar, and restrictive tariff barriers had combined to ruin the Cuban economy in the first place. The last straw was the repeal of the reciprocity arrangement with the United States during Cleveland's second term. It was the subsequent economic breakdown that was responsible for all of Cuba's troubles, even the revolution, Wilson thought, for political conditions could only reflect the economic chaos. If Cuban sugar were denied a favorable market in the United States, then all other efforts to rehabilitate Cuba, and even the war itself, would be wasted.

There was another and broader dimension to the plan for a customs union. Wilson favored the future annexation of Cuba as much as Wood, but he privately believed that any attempt to maintain the occupation indefinitely or to annex Cuba outright would lead to resentment, resistance, and trouble. The Philippine Insurrection gave a fair forecast of what could be expected from such tactics. On the other hand, if the United States ran the occupation honestly and efficiently and then ended it as had been promised, it would leave the island amid general good feeling. The subsequent treaty and tariff arrangements would tie the Cuban government and economy closely to the United States, while self-rule would give the Cubans experience in democracy. In a few years, Wilson thought, these factors, working together with their own economic self-interest, would draw the Cubans steadily toward their powerful neighbor until annexation could be easily and peacefully achieved. This was the real purpose of the plan Wilson described to Foraker.[38]

Ten days later Foraker replied to Wilson's letter, expressing complete agreement with his basic premises. Like Wilson, he said, he did not like the Teller Resolution, which barred the annexation of Cuba at the present time. Foraker hoped that the Cubans would soon want annexation, but Cuba "can be annexed only as Hawaii was, on her own voluntary application." Since this was the case, the sooner the United States could end the occupation, the better.

The great danger, Foraker thought, was an armed clash between Cubans and Americans, similar to what had happened in the Philippines. If this should take place: "well, the mischief will be to pay generally, and the Administration at Washington will have to pay it, and I predict there won't be funds enough on hand for the purpose." He had urged McKinley three months ago, he said, to withdraw from Cuba as soon as possible, but "instead of determining upon a policy, and indicating to them what it is, the President carefully abstains from allowing any Cuban, or any American for that matter, so far as I can learn, to know what his policy is, or whether he has any policy whatever, except only to hold on by military force to the control of the Island, including the Customs Houses and all other sources of revenue."[39]

General Wilson's first official expression of his plans for Cuba was contained in a report dated June 20, 1899, in which he included his scheme for a Cuban constitutional convention, withdrawal of American troops, and a special treaty between the two countries. In this version he toned down his original sweeping protectorate slightly by eliminating the "common diplomatic service" mentioned earlier, but in other essentials it was simply a more specific statement of the same plan. The treaty, Wilson said, should contain four general points:

1. The United States should "guarantee" Cuba a peaceable and stable government, republican in form.

2. The two nations should enter into a customs union, with free trade between them and a common tariff against all others.

3. The Cuban Customs and sanitary services should be supervised by commissioners appointed by the government of the United States.

4. There should be a postal union between the two countries; Cuba should cede a naval station to the United States (preferably at Matanzas, the site of Wilson's own headquarters); and any other matters of mutual concern should be agreeably adjusted.[40]

By July, Wilson was seeking support for his program from Theodore Roosevelt. His Cuban plan, he wrote Roosevelt, was the best one now possible, and he declared that "if my views are carried into effect Cuba will be in the Union within ten years."[41] In his reply, Roosevelt declared himself in substantial agreement with Wilson's plan. He asked Wilson to write him another letter explaining it, which he could send to McKinley with his own endorsement. As to McKinley's present position, Roosevelt admitted, "I do not know what policy he intends to follow out as regards Cuba."[42]

Thus by mid-summer of 1899 the position of General Brooke had become distinctly difficult. Generals Wood and Wilson, both possessing influential connections, were insistently proposing definite lines of policy regarding Cuba's future, not through the regular army channels, but by seeking political support for their ideas in the United States. The goal of both men was the eventual annexation of Cuba to the United States, yet Brooke still had no notion of whether his superiors favored annexation or not. Besides their schemes regarding Cuba's external relations, Wood and Wilson, as well as most of the other departmental generals, had favorite internal policies which they wanted the occupation government to adopt. If General Brooke, like a good soldier, refused to advance without orders, his subordinates were less restrained. As the year progressed, the occupation generals became ever freer in criticizing Brooke, expressing their own views, and appealing for political support in Washington. In default of a declared official policy for Cuba, everyone felt free to work out policies of his own.

Back in February, Henry Adams had written with characteristic pessimism that "a dozen Major Generals are all pulling different ways, in Cuba, Brooke and Ludlow and Lee, Jim Wilson, Wood, and I don't know how many more, are pulling different ways, on totally different lines, and only by the greatest effort has a grand dissolution of ties been avoided thus far. . . ."[43] If this was an overstatement of the situation in February, by June it came close to being the truth.

8

Efforts to Displace Brooke

In an effort to reduce the squabbling and disagreement among his subordinates, and especially to achieve some kind of agreement about the pressing problem of agricultural rehabilitation, General Brooke called a meeting of all his departmental commanders on June 1, 1899.[1] As an attempt to secure any sort of unity, the meeting was a dismal failure. General Wilson began by urging on the group his program of loans to small farmers, but Brooke was still solidly opposed to it, and the others were rapidly losing interest. Their attention was swinging now toward Wood's scheme for departmental autonomy.[2]

Tempted by the alluring prospect of freedom from central control, Brooke's generals, led by Wood and Ludlow, threatened a new revolt against his authority which posed a more serious challenge than mere disagreement about specific policies. Before the meeting had ended, Wood, Ludlow, and some of the others had demanded a fixed revenue from customs, amounting to substantial financial independence of Brooke's headquarters.[3]

General Ludlow in particular was now wholly converted to the Wood approach. It was really in complete harmony with Wilson's plans, he wrote Wilson shortly after the meeting. If each department received a specific portion of the insular revenues, Ludlow argued, then every department commander could give his own area whatever he thought it needed—municipal engineering works

in Ludlow's Havana, agricultural rehabilitation in Wilson's farm-
ing provinces. "It has seemed to me and still does that the autonomy of the Provinces was the first point to secure," Ludlow concluded, and charged that Brooke's control "cramps and dwarfs the
exercise of discretion by the Departmental Commanders."[4]

When the subject of Cuba's political future was introduced, the
generals found new grounds for disagreement. Ludlow was now in
agreement with Wood about the desirability of staying in Cuba.
According to Wilson's account, Ludlow and Wood talked as
though the occupation were to go on indefinitely. Wilson challenged
this idea, and precipitated an argument with Ludlow. When he
asked Ludlow where he had acquired his views, the latter replied
that he had got them directly from President McKinley.[5]

If this conference of June 1 indicated the growth of dissension
among the occupation's leaders, an even stronger proof of it lay
in the mounting efforts of Brooke's subordinates to replace him in
command. The maneuvers to this end long centered about the person of Theodore Roosevelt. Roosevelt was at this time in a highly
nervous state about the whole colonial program of the McKinley
administration, and advocated a wholesale change in top personnel. "I do wish that President McKinley would get rid of Alger!"
he wrote Lodge. "Bryan is I believe a good deal stronger than he
was three years ago, and it looks now as though it was going to be
a serious struggle in 1900. . . . While Alger is in the Cabinet I
always have a feeling of uneasiness about Cuba and the Philippines."[6]

Roosevelt expressed the same fears to Secretary of State John
Hay: "I am uneasy at the way things seem to be going both in the
Philippines and in Cuba, and also at the mutterings of discontent
with what we have done in those islands, which can be heard here
and there throughout the country even now. A series of disasters
at the very beginning of our colonial policy would shake this administration, and therefore our party."[7] One of the precautions
which Roosevelt had been urging was the replacement of General
Brooke with Leonard Wood in Cuba. Late in February, Roosevelt
and Lodge had gone to the President to ask for Wood's promotion
to Brooke's place.[8] Roosevelt recommended the same thing to
Hay, and declared that this action had the support of Senators
Platt and Lodge.

In July Roosevelt sent Wood an account of his latest approach to McKinley, whom he had visited overnight in the White House. The President thought that conditions were satisfactory in Cuba, Roosevelt reported glumly. "I told him plainly that I did not think so, and that I did not think they were growing better; but he takes the opposite view, and that is all there is to it." However, McKinley finally did promise that he would "ultimately" put Wood in charge of the whole island, and, said Roosevelt, "I suppose we have got to be content with this."[9]

The noncommittal President was being besieged, not only by the partisans of Wood, but by those of Wilson as well. Senator Foraker saw McKinley early in March to press Wilson's promotion to Brooke's command, and Foraker was moderately hopeful of the result.[10] Wilson was still getting favorable notice from the Roosevelt-Lodge group, too. Although they now wanted Wood to command in Cuba, Roosevelt for a time pushed Wilson as the best man to straighten things up in the Philippines.[11] But their shift to Wood left Wilson's influence perceptibly weaker, as Senator William P. Frye of Maine found when he saw McKinley on Wilson's behalf. He had repeatedly urged McKinley to put Wilson in charge in Cuba, Frye wrote Wilson, but "somehow or other I do not seem to have met with the profoundest kind of success. Somebody has a stronger pull than I and I thought mine was reasonably strong."[12]

The movement against Brooke was not limited to his rivals and their friends. Even Russell Alger, himself the target of a barrage of criticism ever since the Spanish War, advised Brooke's replacement by "a younger and more vigorous officer." Although Brooke was "faithful, honest, conscientious and true," Alger warned McKinley, "I doubt if he has quite the tact which is necessary to inspire the confidence and affection of the Cuban people so as to enable them to govern themselves, as they must do in the near future."[13]

Brooke did not bear all these attacks without fighting back. He saw from the first that his most dangerous enemy was Leonard Wood, the man most capable of undermining his position with the administration and the public. In April, Brooke sent Chaffee, his chief of staff, and Pablo Desvernine, the Cuban Secretary of Finance, to Washington to state to McKinley the case against Wood.

In an accompanying letter Brooke urged the President to question his emissaries about conditions in Santiago Province. "I am not at all satisfied with the conditions existing there," Brooke wrote guardedly. If McKinley would talk to Chaffee and Desvernine, he "would be put in possession of information which I do not wish to write. I am satisfied that the situation is grave and the remedy should be applied at once."[14]

As time passed, the Wood-Brooke feud grew even fiercer. In July Wood poured out his wrath in a long and angry letter to Roosevelt. Wood had had "a great deal of trouble with General Brooke," he said, and he found it "discouraging and disgusting." He had recently received a telegram from Brooke's headquarters, sent without cipher, charging him with "great folly in building roads, haphazard methods of doing business, and submitting reports for six months which were a disgrace to the Army." This message went through routine channels and became common knowledge in Cuba. Wood had sent a copy of it to the Secretary of War with a demand for a court of enquiry, whereupon Brooke sent a "half-hearted retraction." Wood described the incident as "a peevish outbreak from an old man."

Then Wood launched into a sweeping arraignment of Brooke's rule in Cuba. The condition of the island, he said, was disheartening. No important reforms had been instituted. What was needed was "good courts, good schools, and all the public work we can pay for," reform of municipal administration, and "a business-like way of doing things."

Instead of reforming the legal codes, Wood said, Brooke had restored the old Spanish laws and customs. "Nothing more idiotic can be imagined than the attempt to establish a liberal government under Spanish laws," and the Cuban people were disgusted. This was bad enough, but even worse was the sinister purpose behind it all. Brooke was a mere tool of the Cuban Cabinet, Wood declared, and this body was really working to produce friction between the Americans and the Cuban people. The Cabinet wanted to block the establishment of stable, successful government by the Americans, and to prevent needed reforms. "Their hope is that Cuban discontent will be of such character that there will be a general expression of disapproval and that the 'Mugwumps' at home will side with the discontented people in asking for the withdrawal of our occupation." Then "these little rascals who have made all the trouble" would be in a position to assume power in their own right. It was "maddening" to see the military government "in the hands of transparent little rascals being led into pitfalls which a child ought to see." Six months or a year of "decent, candid, courageous government" would turn Cuban sentiment "all our way," while "six months of this sort of thing and no one will know what will turn up." Under the circumstances, "the system of civil government which is being developed here has got to be uprooted and suppressed entirely in the end and every day makes it more difficult to do so without more or less trouble."

Wood airily described this blast as "only a growl of mine to you personally and confidentially." He ended the letter, however, with the hope that Roosevelt could find a way to convey its contents to the newly appointed Secretary of War, Elihu Root, "not for any purpose of furthering my advancement or anything else, but simply as a statement of conditions which actually exist."[15]

Less than a week after receiving Wood's angry indictment of Brooke, Roosevelt summed up the current state of Cuban policy in a letter to Henry Cabot Lodge:

Wood and Wilson, who are in that order the two best men in Cuba, advocate utterly different policies. Wood believes that we should not promise or give the Cubans independence; that we should govern them justly and equitably, giving them all possible opportunities for civic and military advancement, and that in two or three years they will insist upon being part of us. Wilson believes that we should now leave the island, establishing a republican form of government and keeping a coaling station, etc., together with tariff arrangements which would include them with us as against all outsiders, and he thinks that in a very few years they would drop into our hands of their own accord. I told the President (who is inclined to Wood's policy) that probably either policy would do, but that whichever is adopted must be followed out vigorously, intelligently and with tact.[16]

In the weeks that followed, the bitter, undercover struggle for influence continued. Roosevelt gave Root, the new Secretary of War, a copy of Wood's letter attacking the Brooke regime, and offered to tell him "everything that Wood has told me, and show you all his letters. . . ."[17] Wood continued to insist on the impossibility of ending the occupation. "To abandon the Island of Cuba today would be a crime," he wrote. "To govern it firmly and wisely is an absolute obligation."[18]

James H. Wilson also continued to scheme for power, but in the face of growing obstacles. At the end of June, Robert P. Porter declared himself against Wilson's proposals for a Cuban constitutional convention and a special treaty with the United States. In a newspaper interview, Porter stated that the future of Cuba "can only lay [sic] in annexation," which should be delayed as little as possible. Anyway, he considered Wilson's scheme impractical: "We cannot, in my opinion, make a special treaty with Cuba as an independent State, any more than a man can ask his own consent to marry his own ward in chancery." "The United States is responsible for Cuba," Porter concluded firmly, "and that responsibility is recognized throughout the world."[19]

Porter, however, sailed off the scene to Europe on a new commercial mission for President McKinley. More important than Porter's opposition was the evaporation of Theodore Roosevelt's support. Wilson tactlessly insisted to Roosevelt that he, rather than Wood, should succeed Brooke in Cuba, "not only on account of superior rank, but also on account of a very much wider experience and knowledge."[20] But Roosevelt was losing interest in Wilson's demands. When Russell Alger was finally to be replaced as Secretary of War, Roosevelt supported another man for the post rather than Wilson, who wanted it. In August, Roosevelt openly abandoned the Wilson camp. His letter to Wilson on this occasion showed more than a trace of irritation: "I have on different occasions applied on your behalf for the Administration to give you the Secretaryship of War, the Governor Generalship of the Philippines, the Governor Generalship of Cuba and supreme command in Porto Rico. But, my dear General, you know that when one's original recommendations are not taken, or when one is informed that certain arrangements are impossible, it is not possible to make the same suggestions over again."[21]

Senator Frye continued to assure Wilson of his support, and so did Foraker, but the latter was in a poor position to ask favors of the President. Not only had Foraker been a political rival of McKinley back in Ohio, but he was now a leading critic of the administration's Cuban policy. He had not seen the President lately, Foraker wrote Wilson late in July: "He does not care for my opinion anyhow, and I do not intend therefore to obtrude it upon him."[22]

In Cuba itself Wilson saw one of his favorite schemes, that of loans to small farmers, doomed to failure. He had continued to push hard for his program. For a time he worked through another of his political acquaintances, Postmaster General Charles Emory Smith, who gave copies of the Wilson plan to McKinley and Root.[23] General J. P. Sanger, writing from the War Department, told Wilson in November that his loan scheme would certainly have been adopted but for the strenuous opposition of General Brooke. Sanger later told Wilson that even Root had tentatively favored the loan program.[24] But Brooke soon brought the matter to an abrupt halt.

In his Civil Report of October 1, 1899, Brooke blasted the loan plan once and for all. Such schemes, Brooke said, would induce pauperism and destroy the self-respect of the people. Those who did not receive aid would be jealous, and ill-feeling would certainly result. The whole idea was "paternalistic" and "a most dangerous implanting of a spirit alien to a free people." Besides these drawbacks, the thing was impractical. The entire insular revenues would not meet "all demands of this kind." Cumbersome government machinery would be required, and years of time, to carry the plan into effect. The real solution, Brooke said firmly, was the formation of banking firms by private enterprise which could tap the capital lying idle in Cuba. And this would occur spontaneously, "were the capitalists assured as to the future."[25]

Another long-continued argument also came to a head at the end of the summer. This concerned the advisability of recruiting Cuban regiments, officered by Americans, for duty with the American occupation forces in Cuba. McKinley had shown interest in such a plan since before the occupation began, and Porter had mentioned its possibility in his conversation with General Gómez. This idea had also attracted the attention of Leonard Wood. As Wood saw it, such a course would have multiple advantages. The Cubans would have less objection to occupation by troops of their own nationality; the bolder spirits of the Cuban army could be attracted to enlist, and could thus be safely supervised; most of the American troops could eventually be relieved from occupation duty. Even more important, the army service would help to Americanize numbers of young Cubans, who would "become intensely loyal to us," and aid in spreading annexationist sentiment. If the Americans followed such a policy, and in addition carried out needed reforms, Wood concluded characteristically, "I do not believe you could shake Cuba loose if you wanted to."[26]

Wood had advanced this plan periodically, and McKinley had favored trying it; it had never been implemented due to the determined opposition of General Brooke.[27] But when Root came to the War Department, the subject was reopened. Root was attracted by the idea, and he recommended it to McKinley in August. As Root outlined it, the United States should recruit three Cuban regiments. The officers of the rank of captain and above should be Americans, as well as the sergeants, while the lieutenants and enlisted men would be Cubans. Like Wood, Root felt that this kind of service by Cubans would "educate them into Americans."[28]

McKinley took up the matter once more, but again found Brooke strongly opposed. Brooke wired in September that he had polled his departmental commanders, and found only Wood in favor of the project. His own feeling was that such action would make a very bad impression on the Cubans, for two reasons. First, it would lead them to think that the army could not cope with the Philippine Insurrection without cutting its commitments elsewhere, and second, it would "add to the distrust" about the intentions of the United States in Cuba. This last point, Brooke declared, had occurred to some of the other generals as well as himself.[29] Brooke's message must have carried weight with McKinley, for no program to recruit Cuban army units was ever carried into effect.

On the surface, Brooke appeared to have scored victories over both of his major rivals. Wilson's scheme for agricultural loans was not put into effect, nor did Wood have any success with his plan for enlisting Cuban regiments. Yet Brooke's own position was no stronger than before, and nothing positive had really been decided.

Amid confusion and disagreement in Cuba, the summer of 1899

merged into autumn. The work of the first phase of the occupation had clearly ended; it was time to move on to the next steps, whatever they were to be. Yet the continuing silence from Washington made further steps impossible, for no one knew in what direction they should go. The one thing that seemed certain was that the days of Brooke's command in Cuba were numbered. Brooke had failed to master his unruly officers, and he was not the man to strike out on his own initiative. Lacking either political influence or a favorable press, he had waited patiently for guidance from Washington while his subordinates hopelessly undermined his position. Who was to succeed him, no one knew. As a declaration of United States policy became increasingly imperative, all eyes began to turn toward Elihu Root, the vigorous new Secretary of War, who had thus far kept his own counsel.

The Advent of Elihu Root

The United States military government of Cuba carried out its functions under the direct supervision of the War Department and the ultimate authority of the President of the United States. It would be expected, therefore, that the commander in Cuba would look for guidance chiefly to the Secretary of War, and that this official would be a key figure in the working out of policy decisions. But during the first six months of the occupation, this was not the case. The War Department was in near-chaos, and the Secretary of War, Russell A. Alger, was one of the most thoroughly discredited men in Washington.

At one time Alger had been a leader of the Republican party. A general in the Civil War, he had settled in Detroit after peace was restored, and soon made a large fortune in the lumber industry. In 1889 he became national commander-in-chief of the politically potent Grand Army of the Republic, and he was a contender for the Republican nomination for President in 1892. When McKinley formed his cabinet in 1897, it was natural that Alger should become a member of it.

A year later came the Spanish War, and with it the ruin of Alger's reputation. The position of Secretary of War had become largely an honorific one by 1898. The army had changed little for a generation, and was fettered by the outworn belief that its chief function was the prosecution of the Indian wars that had long since died away. The conversion of this sleepy and impoverished establishment into a national war machine was a task to challenge an administrative genius, which Alger most decidedly was not. As a result, the luckless Secretary bore the blame, not only for his own very real shortcomings, but for all the blundering and confusion inevitable at the beginning of any war. By the time the fighting ended, he had become a kind of national scapegoat, with large portions of the press clamoring for his removal.

McKinley, however, refused to abandon Alger under fire. Instead, he appointed a special presidential commission to investigate the War Department's conduct of the war. This group began its hearings in September of 1898, and the unhappy War Department experienced new woes as everyone from Alger down tried to shift the responsibility for their sins. Before the investigation ended, the nation was treated to the spectacle of the Commissary General of the Army giving the lie to its Commanding General, and being cashiered for it. While the investigating commission was cautious in its conclusions, it left no room for doubt that there had been grave maladministration in the War Department.[1]

McKinley still refused to ask for Alger's resignation, but the hapless Secretary was totally discredited and left without influence. The results in Cuba were serious, for the consequent headlessness and lack of direction was one of the heaviest handicaps of Brooke's new government. Early in the occupation, Henry Adams offered the opinion that "Alger is very much broken, and his mind so weakened as to be incapable of consecutive thought. As a matter of fact, the President long ago set Alger aside, and this is one reason why he cannot remove him, because Alger is really not responsible, but McKinley is." The War Department, Adams concluded, "is not run at all."[2]

In spite of the clamor for his removal, Alger himself clung to his office with an iron grip. In April he authorized the Associated Press to deny the widely circulated rumors of his resignation. He intended, he said, to stay in office until the end of the current administration, barring unforeseen circumstances in his private life.[3]

Nevertheless, Alger finally lost his job, not because of his incompetence, but for political disloyalty to McKinley. In the spring

of 1899 he was approached by the reform-minded Governor of
Michigan, Hazen Pingree, who proposed that Alger should run for
the United States Senate with the support of the Pingree group,
and on an anti-trust platform. The incumbent was a staunch Mc-
Kinley supporter, while Pingree was a bitter enemy of the administration. The offer was really an invitation to Alger to desert to
the opposition, bringing his remaining influence in Michigan state
politics to Pingree's aid. Without much hesitation, Alger agreed to
do so. Word of it soon reached McKinley, and his patience came
to an end. After a chilly interview in the White House, Alger submitted his resignation in July of 1899.[4]

When the nature of Alger's new political alliance became public, it was clear to everyone that his days were numbered as a member of McKinley's cabinet. Theodore Roosevelt immediately began pushing the candidacy of Francis V. Greene, a New York
general and politician, for Secretary of War, while other candidates, among them General Wilson, fished for the appointment in
the troubled waters of the capitol.[5] But McKinley chose none of
these. Instead, he selected as Alger's successor a prominent corporation lawyer named Elihu Root, who had long been active in
New York state and city politics but who was little known to the
country at large.

Many years later, Root told the story of how he came to the
War Department:

I was called to the telephone and told by one speaking for President
McKinley, "The President directs me to say to you that he wishes you to
take the position of Secretary of War." I answered, "Thank the President for me, but say that it is quite absurd, I know nothing about war.
I know nothing about the army." I was told to hold the wire, and in
a moment there came back the reply, "President McKinley directs me
to say that he is not looking for any one who knows anything about the
army; he has got to have a lawyer to direct the government of these
Spanish islands, and you are the lawyer he wants."[6]

Thus Root's appointment represented, at least in part, a conscious
attempt of the President to provide the Cuban occupation with the
direct supervision it had so far lacked.

Elihu Root formally took office on August 1, 1899. The new
Secretary of War spent his first weeks in Washington largely in

listening attentively to the opinions of others, and gathering information about his new responsibilities. His reticence to express his
own views and his eagerness to hear those of others encouraged
partisans on all sides to hope that in him they might find an ally.
Theodore Roosevelt, who had known Root well in New York,
wrote Wood that "Root is a thoroughly good fellow and I believe
he is going to steadily come around to your way of looking at
things."[7] A week later Senator Foraker wrote Wilson that he, too,
had conferred with the new Secretary, and believed that "in the
main" Root agreed with the Wilson-Foraker view. He thought
that "action will be taken in the near future, looking to the establishment by the Cubans of a Government of their own." The Senator warned Wilson that he suspected a disposition on Root's part
to " 'string out' the program a little," but he was confident that
things could be hurried up afterwards, if only a proper start were
made.[8]

Though he kept his intentions to himself, Root lost no time in
attacking the Cuban problem. He initiated two significant actions
during his first month in office, one of which was a holdover from
Alger's administration. Back in July Alger had instructed J. P.
Sanger, the Inspector General of the Army, to prepare a memorandum on the subject of organizing a national census for Cuba.
Sanger consulted with the United States census officials and gave
his plans to Root when the latter took office.[9] Less than three
weeks later a proclamation "To the people of Cuba" appeared
over the signature of President McKinley. The President announced his intention to conduct a census of Cuba, and described
the project as one of "the successive steps by which you will proceed to the establishment of an effective system of self-government."[10]

At the same time Root implemented another program for securing information about Cuba. On August 18 General Brooke's
headquarters sent identical messages to all departmental commanders. The generals learned that "in order to comply with the instructions of the War Department" they were each to submit a
special report on civil affairs. The purpose of these reports was
"to form the basis for the deduction of the results of the American
Occupation."[11]

The reports which came in during the following weeks revealed a cross section of military opinion on the question of a Cuban policy. Since these were official statements, however, the Wood-Ludlow wing spoke cautiously. General Wood's report was specific only in its short-term recommendations. Wood urged judicial reform, including "a radical modification" of the Cuban criminal code, a more equitable tax system, and an immediate effort to build up public education. He also recommended holding municipal elections after the census had been completed. Wood's references to annexation were oblique. He said only that "many of the class possessing property are annexationists," including the Spaniards, and that: "Manifestations of hostility to our occupation are limited almost solely to the press in certain large towns, which find it necessary to serve up exciting and incendiary articles in order to maintain a large circulation."[12]

General Ludlow's language was similarly veiled. Ludlow spoke up for agricultural rehabilitation and an effective public school system. Beyond this, he merely suggested that a large part of Cuba's population was either illiterate or politically self-seeking, and that "it is the interests of the civilized world at large that must determine the future adjustment" of the Cuban problem, "not the views or opinions of theorists or sentimentalists."[13]

General Wilson, who preached at least a technical compliance with the Teller Resolution, had no need for such evasions, and was therefore able to give a detailed outline of his favorite plans. He asked again for agricultural rehabilitation, urging that "if the plan which I have submitted be not regarded as feasible some other plan with the same end in view be substituted for it." As for Cuba's future, Wilson gave a rosy picture of the capacity of the Cubans for self-government. He repeated the program contained in his report of June 20, calling for a constitutional convention, withdrawal of American troops, and the negotiation of a special treaty between the United States and Cuba. This program, Wilson said, would not only give "almost instantaneous relief" to Cuba, but also "it would put matters on the best possible footing for the ultimate absorption of the latter into the Union by natural, voluntary, and progressive steps."[14]

The last of Brooke's chief lieutenants, Fitzhugh Lee, had earlier placed himself in the Wilson camp. In August Lee had echoed, with some changes, Wilson's proposal for a constitutional convention and an election of national officers as soon as possible. The United States, Lee thought, should keep troops in Cuba until the success of the new government had been established, at which time the Cubans themselves should be allowed to choose between an American protectorate, or annexation to the United States.[15]

In September, Lee submitted his special report in response to the call from headquarters. He stressed the desirability of ending the uncertainty about Cuba's future, which was holding off foreign investments. The Cubans "are as capable of organizing a form of government today as they ever will be," and should be allowed a fair trial. If they could achieve stable self-government, they deserved to have it. If not, "the strong hand of the United States must be placed again on the helm. . . ."[16] Writing to General Wilson a few weeks later, Lee admitted that if he were asked whether Cuban self-government could suceed, "I would be obliged to reply that 'I am not answering conundrums.' "[17]

The last voice heard from was that of General Brooke, who confined his recommendations to more sanitation, sewerage, and new dwellings. He pointedly declined to comment on political questions, saying: "The kind of government to be established, and when, is not a subject which the military governor believes to be a matter which can be discussed in this report, if at all. Obviously, this must be determined by higher authority, to whom such matters properly pertain."[18] A few days before, however, Brooke had ventured a cautious statement on the subject in a personal letter to President McKinley. Feeling that at last "I should express to you my opinion as to the ability of this people to govern themselves," the General concluded: "I do not think the time has yet arrived when this people can establish a stable government."[19] But he made no attempt, then or later, to spell out the implications of his conclusion in terms of policy.

Thus Root's survey showed opinion within the occupation to be neatly divided. Wood and Ludlow talked only of internal reforms and hinted at staying on indefinitely in Cuba, Wilson and Lee proposed taking immediate steps toward the establishment of internal self-government there, and Brooke, as always, refused to speculate about policy at all. It appeared to be up to Root alone to guide matters to a solution.

As a result, much of the pressure and propaganda hitherto aimed at McKinley now centered about the Secretary of War. The indefatigable Theodore Roosevelt redoubled his efforts to get some sort of commitment from Root, but never succeeded in extracting anything very definite. In September Root finally acknowledged the letter from Wood which Roosevelt had given him, and which contained Wood's July outburst against Brooke. "I have Wood's letter safely stowed away [Root wrote Roosevelt], and will return it to you very soon. The matter to which it relates has depressed me very much. I sincerely hope for the good of the service it will not go any further, for there was certainly enough to try any man's patience severely."[20] This was encouraging, if vague, and Roosevelt promptly saw both McKinley and Root again on behalf of Wood's appointment to the Cuban command. But although convinced of Root's sympathy, Roosevelt could only report to Wood that Root "did not think it prudent to answer."[21]

Wood himself, however, carefully continued to aim his campaign at McKinley as well as Root. He wrote the President late in September that "the people are all very much interested in the taking of the census and are looking forward to municipal and town elections with great interest." But, he said, "I do not think they are fitted to go beyond town and municipal elections for some time." "The great bulk" of Cubans, according to Wood, looked on the presence of American troops as their only safeguard. "The people who are talking 'Cuba Libre' and the total withdrawal of the American Army in the daily press represent at most not over five per cent of the Cuban people." When the voice of the people was really heard, Wood concluded, "there will be many more voices for annexation than there is at present any idea of."[22]

There was similar activity in the Wilson camp. General Wilson wrote lengthy letters to both Roosevelt and Lodge, explaining his plans for Cuba all over again.[23] In early November he wrote to Root himself, in a last desperate effort to secure the adoption of his policy. In his appeal to Root, Wilson unmasked his intentions more completely than ever before, and revealed the potentialities which he saw hidden in the terms of his draft treaty for Cuba.

In his proposed treaty, Wilson said, the United States would guarantee the Cuban people a government which was stable, peaceable, and republican in form. If this article were properly phrased, the United States would be left "as free to interpose for the prevention of rebellion and anarchy in the Island of Cuba, as it is under the laws to intervene in the affairs of any state of the Union." By establishing a customs union between Cuba and the United States, Wilson hoped to oppose Cuban nationalism with the force of economic self-interest. While Wilson believed that "the great majority of the Cuban people are earnestly in favor of independence," he thought that Spaniards, planters, merchants, and other influential classes would come to favor annexation in order to insure the permanence of free trade with America, once they had had a taste of it.

His proposals for the administration of the sanitary and customs services by the United States "would put the control of the revenue of the island largely in our hands." The cession of one or more naval stations would give the United States "a lodgement for our troops . . . in case the necessity should arise for the use of troops in the maintenance of a peaceable and stable government."

"I have not felt it necessary," Wilson wrote, "to explain to you or anybody else that such a treaty as I have proposed would practically bind Cuba, hand and foot, and put her destinies absolutely within our control." Yet this course would also "save the pride and feeling" of the Cubans. It would secure for the United States almost the entire foreign trade of Cuba, while leaving open the option of annexing the island or merely controlling it. Best of all, it would even comply legally with the provisions of the Teller Resolution, for "we have made no promises either to the Cubans or to the world at large" about what terms could be demanded in a treaty with a sovereign and independent Cuba!

Thus Wilson laid out for Root's appraisal a glittering array of tools for the indirect control of Cuba. On the copy of his letter which he kept for his own files, he added a mournful handwritten postscript: "It is worthy of note that although I have known Root from boyhood he made no reply whatever to this letter. But he and the President having chosen another for the chief command in this island, it may be fairly assumed that it is to carry out some other policy than the one herein outlined."[24] It was one of the few times that General Wilson ever sold himself short. The techniques which he had described in his letter were to dominate American diplomacy in the Caribbean for many years to come.

Meanwhile the clamor of opinion swelled, as General Ludlow now came out with an outspoken attack on the idea of Cuban self-government. Visiting the United States in November, he spoke on the Cuban question before the New York Chamber of Commerce. In Ludlow's view, the "present generation will have to pass away before the Cubans can form a stable government." Any attempt to give universal suffrage to such people would make of Cuba a second Haiti. The Cubans, he said, "are not as we. They are Latin, and belong to a dying race" which could not be made into a stable people like the Anglo-Saxon.[25]

At this point Senator Foraker made another attempt to assess the political picture. "I have had several conversations with Mr. Root," he wrote Wilson. "His own judgment and personal inclinations run along the same line with yours and mine." But the Senator was haunted by a conviction that "the President through somebody's influence is not in exact accord." He had noticed that "General Ludlow and others who have recently talked with the President are saying in interviews that the Cubans will not be ready for self-government for many years." What the result would be, Foraker ended gloomily, no one could tell.[26]

Wood Replaces Brooke

In November, 1899, the discussion of Cuban policy took on an unexpected new dimension. Rumors began to appear with increasing frequency, to the effect that the administration intended to replace the existing, and avowedly temporary, military government of Cuba with a United States Civil Government. This would be in the charge of United States officials appointed by the President, a sort of colonial administration for Cuba. The rumors had begun in October, and Fitzhugh Lee had promptly attributed them to the influence of Leonard Wood, who had, Lee told Wilson, "a number of his newspaper friends and others in Washington . . . engaged in working the matter up."[1]

However, others beside Wood probably agitated for the proposed change. According to Horatio Rubens, it was the Director General of Cuban Posts, Estes G. Rathbone, who hoped to become civil governor under the new dispensation. George D. Meiklejohn, the Under Secretary of War, also figured in some of the rumors as a potential governor.[2]

After weeks of hints and predictions, the whole affair came out into the open on November 9. A front-page story in the New York *Evening Post* stated that a civil administration was to be established in Cuba, and that Wood was to be in charge of it. The *Post*'s correspondent declared that "a source above question" had told him that McKinley regarded Brooke's government as a failure, and had decided to replace it. Wood would relieve Brooke on January 1, 1900, the story said, at which time the new form of government would replace the old.[3]

The press in Cuba was already alert to the new development. The Havana daily, *La Discusión,* commented editorially on November 4 about the rumors from the north. Admitting at the beginning that the stories of the establishment of a civil government were as yet unconfirmed, the editorial warned that every Cuban who wanted to see his country independent would have to oppose such a step. To replace the military government, which had always been understood to be only temporary, with a regular colonial administration could mean only that the United States intended to stay in Cuba. The plan, *La Discusión* said, sounded like a "snare prepared by the annexationists of both here and there."[4]

The rumors continued, and ten days later the same newspaper reacted with a vigorous statement of Cuban rights: "Cuba is not American territory, it is not a state, nor a conquered country like Puerto Rico or the Philippines, which were ceded to the United States without reserve, condition or restrictions."[5] Other Havana dailies struck a similar note; protesting articles appeared in *La Patria* and *La Tarde* during November, as well as in the magazine *Cuba y América.*[6]

In the meantime General Wilson endeavored to find out whether the rumors were true, but reports from Washington varied. Senator Foraker wrote to Wilson: "As to a Civil Governor, I think as you that the President has decided to appoint one, and that he will select General Wood. Everyone here is of this impression."[7] Wilson's son-in-law, Henry B. Thompson, who held Wilson's position by proxy on the Republican National Committee, went to Washington to learn what he could. He reported that the administration wanted to appoint Wood governor of Cuba, "whether it is to be Civil or Military." There was "a strong press bureau behind Wood." As for the rumored change in the form of government, "the scheme of appointing him Civil Governor seems to have been held up, and apparently the Cabinet decided last week to hold this matter over until Congress meets."[8]

On November 22 Leonard Wood was called to Washington, and the suspense grew more intense. "It is not to be doubted," the *New York Tribune* reported confidently, "that the name of the General has been under consideration" for the chief post in Cuba, "when the change is made from a military to a civil form of government." However, said the *Tribune,* Generals Wilson and Ludlow were also being considered.[9]

In Cuba, General Brooke warned of the mounting tension. "I believe a reduction of our force inadvisable," he wrote, "until it shall be determined that military occupation shall cease at some fixed time in the near future. . . . A material reduction of our force now would foster an existing sentiment, *known to me,* that I deem it prudent to keep down [emphasis Brooke's]."[10]

Suddenly, at the end of November, the unrest and excitement which had been growing in Cuba produced an overt protest movement of sobering proportions. Telegrams denouncing the change to a civil government began to pour into the headquarters of the military government from dozens of mayors, municipal councils, Cuban army veterans' organizations, civic clubs, and even civil governors of provinces. The Veterans of the Independence of Cuba held a mass meeting in Havana. City councils passed formal resolutions of protest in provincial capitols like Santa Clara and Matanzas, while on November 29, the mayor of Cienfuegos wired Havana that "an imposing popular demonstration has just taken place." P. E. Betancourt, the Civil Governor of Matanzas Province, described the protest movement in his province as a "spontaneous and unanimous demonstration." From November 29 through the first week in December, there was hardly a pause in the series of rallies, resolutions, and demonstrations that swept over Cuba.[11]

Although all observers agreed that the Cubans' activities had so far taken only legal forms and that disorder was at a minimum, the excitement in Cuba produced alarm in Washington. This was heightened by excited letters from Americans in Cuba, warning of imminent revolt. One such letter, which found its way to the White House, stated that bands of guerrillas had "taken to the woods" all over the island, but the writer doubted that open rebellion would break out until after Congress had met and declared its intentions.[12]

On November 28, when the mass protests had just begun, Elihu Root wrote to Estes G. Rathbone, requesting information: "I perceive that there seems to be a good deal of excitement now in Cuba

over the subject of the supposed intention to establish a civil government there. Can you give me any idea of the cause or origin of
this sudden excitement?"[13]

Rathbone, who had favored the change of government, replied
with some embarrassment that only "60 days ago" the Cubans
would have welcomed the civil government plan. But "someone"
had mysteriously induced an agitation which had changed Cuban
sentiment, at least on the surface. The main reasons for the popular opposition to an American civil government, Rathbone said,
were twofold. First, there was a general conviction that it meant
the postponement of Cuban independence and the continuation of
United States rule. Second, some people feared that the change
would be a move to allow the granting of concessions and franchises to the great corporations. (Such grants were blocked by the
Foraker Law, which apparently was erroneously believed by some
Cubans to apply only during the duration of the military government.)

The present excitement, Rathbone thought, would fade away in
time, and at any rate the administration should not let its decisions
be swayed by public opinion. But the postal head warned against
raising any native regiments at this time, or placing arms in Cuban hands in any other way, and admitted his distrust of the loy-
alty of the Rural Guard.[14]

On the same day that Root wrote to Rathbone, the Cabinet met
in Washington to consider the Cuban crisis. According to the
Washington correspondent of the *New York Tribune,* Root stated
after the meeting that the government had "no immediate intention" of establishing a civil government in Cuba. The *Tribune* reporter took this to mean simply that a decision on the matter had
not yet been reached. He had it, however, "on high authority,"
that the agitation in Cuba "may result in allowing the present military government to continue longer than it otherwise would." In
the view of this "high authority," the administration would not
force a civil government on Cuba if the Cubans objected to it
strongly.[15]

On the following day a soothing statement came from General
Wood, who had been conferring with McKinley on Cuban affairs.
The rumors of an impending revolt in Cuba were groundless, he

said. He knew nothing about a plan to appoint a civil governor, and had not been offered such a post. At any rate, the Cuban excitement about such a plan "grows, I think, from their misunderstanding of the meaning of the term civil governor," which did not necessarily "mean permanent American government for the island."[16]

In private, administration leaders were gravely worried. Several years later, Elihu Root thought that "we were on the verge daily of the same sort of thing that happened to us in the Philippines," and he recalled that "I had an uneasy life for a long time with the apprehension that the morning paper when I looked at it any morning might contain the news of American troops firing on Cubans."[17]

At the same time that independence sentiment was mounting in Cuba, a surge of annexationism swept a large part of the American press. From October through December of 1899, dozens of newspapers in all parts of the country reacted to the uncertainty over Cuba's status with demands for the continuation of United States rule there. The *Chicago Inter-Ocean* declared editorially that "To abandon Cuba in the near future would be to deliver the island up to the fate of Hayti and San Domingo. . . . The American people cannot be hoodwinked into a policy of scuttle in Cuba."[18] The *Chicago Times-Herald* agreed that the Cubans were unready for self-government: "Surely they must see that annexation would be a blessing to them."[19] "We suppose it is pretty generally agreed among the great majority of the American people," declared the *St. Paul Pioneer Press,* "that by far the best thing which could happen to Cuba and the Cubans would be the annexation of the island to the United States."[20] The *Kansas City Star* used similar language: "When the question is raised, 'What is the best thing for Cuba and the Cubans?' the answer is 'Annexation.' "[21] The *Boston Herald* judged: "That it is the ultimate destiny of the Cuban people to be incorporated with our republic we think no intelligent observer of the events of the world doubts."[22]

Similar editorial sentiments appeared in the press of St. Louis, New Haven, Cleveland, Memphis, Dallas, Boise, Portland,[23] and many other cities. While this was by no means the tone of all American newspapers, it indicated that any expansionist policy pursued by the administration in regard to Cuba could count on a widespread and vociferous support in the United States. It was equally evident that any such policy might encounter a dangerous degree of opposition among the people of Cuba.

At this point, when interest was at its peak in both countries, the long-awaited announcement of the intentions of the United States in Cuba came at last. On December 1 the War Department made public the text of the Annual Report of the Secretary of War, dated November 29, 1899.[24] In this document, Elihu Root laid out clearly and specifically the steps which were to be taken in Cuba. He began with a statement of general principles:

Our temporary occupation of the island of Cuba involves a very simple plan of operation, with some difficulties in its application which are apt to be overlooked by those who are impatient for immediate results. The control which we are exercising in trust for the people of Cuba should not be, and of course will not be, continued any longer than is necessary to enable that people to establish a suitable government to which control shall be transferred, which shall really represent the people of Cuba, and be able to maintain order and discharge its international obligations. . . . Our present duty is limited to giving every assistance in our power to the establishment of such a government and to maintaining order and promoting the welfare of the people of Cuba during the period necessarily required for that process.

The details of Root's program followed. First, the Cuban census which had just been taken must be tabulated and totaled, in order to give correct information upon which to base suffrage and representation in coming elections. This would be the work of some months. In addition, no elections could properly be held until after April 11, 1900, for on that date the year of grace expired within which the residents of Cuba could elect either Cuban or Spanish citizenship, according to the terms of the peace treaty. Only after that date would it be possible to know definitely who were citizens of Cuba and who were not.

When these necessary delays had passed, municipal elections could be held, resulting in the establishment of local governments. The next step would be to call a constitutional convention, which would frame a central government to which the United States could surrender power in Cuba. "When that government is established," Root promised, "the relations which exist between it and the United States will be a matter for free and uncontrolled agreement between the two parties."

Having outlined his political plan for Cuba, the Secretary of War turned to economic matters. In words reminiscent of General Wilson, he declared that the prosperity of Cuba really depended on the condition of the American sugar market. The first consideration, therefore, of any Cuban government would be to secure some tariff arrangement with the United States. Root declared his confidence that the United States would "deal generously" with Cuba on this point, when the time came. For the duration of the occupation, he recommended the reduction of United States duties on Cuban sugar to a point no higher than the rates proposed for Jamaican sugar under the pending reciprocity treaty with the British West Indies.[25]

The effect of Root's statement was immediate in Cuba. The press response there was mixed, but largely favorable. Many Cubans agreed with the Havana daily, La Patria, that Cuban independence now appeared to be safe,[26] and tensions relaxed visibly.

Nevertheless, the public uneasiness was not entirely quieted. Some newspaper editors complained that there was still no date set for Cuban independence, and the more suspicious-minded found loopholes in Root's wording. Indeed, the situation still appeared sufficiently strained so that the Havana Commercial Company, which owned large plantations in Pinar del Río Province, renewed its request to General Brooke for a contingent of soldiers to guard its properties. The company's manager declared that "the spirit of disaffection is spreading, and is liable soon or late to burst into flame."[27]

Back in Washington, Leonard Wood wrote Roosevelt that "I do not believe in any civil government for Cuba at present."[28] But it was William McKinley who would make the final decision. The President's annual message to Congress was due in a few days, and his words then would be the acid test of whether Root spoke only for himself, or for the administration as a whole.

The President's annual message for 1899 went to Congress on December 5, and like Root's report, it contained a section dealing with the political future of Cuba. In contrast to the clarity and precision of Root's program, however, the President's intentions were but dimly visible behind a cloud of words. Some of McKinley's statements seemed to be clear enough. In reference to the vital Teller Resolution, he said: "The pledge contained in this resolution is of the highest honorable obligation and must be sacredly kept." But this was followed by a declaration that the new Cuba "must needs be bound to us by ties of singular intimacy and strength." The President could not yet say even "whether those ties shall be organic or conventional," which was really the central issue involved. He was certain only that "the destinies of Cuba are in some rightful form and manner irrevocably linked with our own, but how and how far is for the future to determine in the ripeness of events."

The one thing that emerged clearly from McKinley's words was that, on his part at least, the Cuban problem would be worked out with a comfortable lack of haste. The creation of the new Cuba, the President said, must not be "a hasty experiment bearing within itself the elements of failure. Our mission . . . is not to be fulfilled by turning adrift any loosely framed commonwealth. . . ." Cuba's "chief and immediate need," he concluded, was the restoration of prosperity, a reassuring but safely nonpolitical objective.[29]

It was the editors of the anti-imperialist New York *Evening Post* who drew most acidly the inevitable comparison between this statement and that of Root. "If anyone expected Mr. McKinley to express clearcut convictions about our duty or policy [in Cuba]," said a *Post* editorial, "he will be disappointed." After stressing the evasions and contradictions of the message, the editorial concluded: "We fear that despondent Cubans and exultant annexationists alike will read those words and say, with the Irishman, that they are 'so ambiguous that only one construction can be put upon them.' "[30]

By the middle of December, however, the choice of Brooke's successor and the definite continuation of the military government had ended some of the uncertainty in Cuba. The contest for the chief command had reached its peak in November, when Wood's principal rival, General Ludlow, had attempted to reach a compromise solution. In a remarkable letter to Elihu Root, Ludlow insisted on his great seniority to Wood, but suggested three alternative courses which would be acceptable to him. The first possibility, he said, would be to divide the Cuban command into two parts having coordinate commanders. Wood could command in the East and Ludlow in the West, both reporting directly to the Secretary of War. A second solution would be to give Wood a command in the Philippines and put Ludlow in sole charge in Cuba. Finally, Ludlow would be willing to see Wood commanding in Cuba, provided he himself was given the present command of the retiring General Merritt in the United States.[31] These proposals, however, merely underlined the fact that Wood had the political power to get what he wanted.

Senator Lodge's son-in-law, Augustus P. Gardner, and Senator Foraker both made a last try to secure the appointment of General Wilson. They found that the choice was limited to Ludlow or Wood, Foraker receiving this information directly from McKinley and Root.[32] Given this choice, there could be but one result. On December 13 the War Department published the order which assigned Leonard Wood to the command of the Division of Cuba in place of Brooke.[33]

"I know you were pleased by the appointment of Wood in Cuba," Root wrote Roosevelt a few days later. "The situation there is exceedingly delicate and difficult. Anything which the thoughtless and uninstructed would consider absolute success is practically impossible, but I think Wood is competent to secure a greater degree of success there than any one else."[34]

On December 20, General Brooke issued a brief final report. It had been difficult, he said, to work "in a foreign country, under a different form of government than the one to which we were accustomed, among strangers, a strange people, speaking a foreign language." Nevertheless, Brooke concluded: "Progress may have seemed slow to others, but the foundations of a future government were being laid, and upon its being well and securely done rested the safety of the whole structure."[35]

Thus the year 1899 drew to a close with the promise of a new order of things in Cuba. Yet no one was sure exactly what had taken place during November and December. One view was that stated by the New York *Evening Post*. President McKinley, a *Post* editorial charged, had intended to make Wood civil governor of Cuba, "but this plan caused such commotion among the Cubans themselves that it was dropped even more hastily than it was taken up." Instead, Wood became the second military governor of Cuba. The change was important, the *Post* said, because, "while the name will make no difference as regards the kind of rule exercised by General Wood, there is a material difference as to its duration."[36]

Even if this version of the story were the true one, however, it still left many questions unanswered. The program contained in Root's annual report had the appearance of a carefully thought out plan rather than a hasty surrender to unexpected pressure. This would indicate that Root, at least, had not intended that the United States should stay on indefinitely in Cuba. Senator Foraker had written Wilson that Root and McKinley were not in accord on Cuban policy. Had McKinley reverted to his old habit of making colonial decisions without reference to the War Department, only to be stopped short by Cuban protests? Or had both Root and McKinley been thinking of establishing a purely temporary American civil government, which would have had no serious effect on the duration of United States rule? And finally, why, if McKinley was still as undecided about the future of Cuba as his annual message indicated, had he allowed Root to issue an official report which committed the government to a definite course of action? No one knew, and the outcome still lay with the future.

11

Short-Term Steps and Long-Term Prospects

General Leonard Wood took over the command of the Cuban occupation from General Brooke at noon on December 20, 1899. Brooke boarded a ship and left the country, while the Cuban Cabinet he had entrusted with civil administration promptly tendered its collective resignation. These latter Wood asked to remain until the following day, when he and Chaffee conferred with them. Wood asked the four secretaries point blank if their resignations were merely a matter of form, or if they really wished them to be accepted. All four declared their determination not to stay in office, and Wood accepted their resignations without further parley. He had neither liked nor trusted them, he reported to Root, and was pleased to see them gone.[1]

Freed of the old cabinet, the new Governor was able to reorganize the civil administration during his first two weeks in office. The Department of State and Government, and that of Finance, retained their old organization, but the other two departments were each divided in half. Justice and Public Instruction, formerly lumped in one department, were entrusted to two separate agencies, and the same thing was done with Public Works, and Agriculture and Commerce. Thus there were now six administrative departments instead of four, all with new heads appointed by Wood. The revolutionary leaders were still represented, however, in the persons of two prominent veterans of the Cuban army:

126

José Ramón Villalón became Secretary of Public Works, and Juan Rius Rivera, Secretary of Agriculture, Industry, and Commerce. In Wood's view, all six of the new department heads "represent the Cuban party but are strong, thoroughly able and competent."[2] The rest of Brooke's government was left largely as it had been. Of the seven provincial governors appointed by Brooke, six remained in office until the end of the occupation, while most of the lesser officials stayed at their posts.[3]

Wood's first great task in his new post was to quiet the popular unrest which had flared to such a dangerous level in the preceding weeks. To do this, it was necessary to placate the old revolutionary leaders. Wood and Root had persuaded Horatio Rubens, formerly the lawyer for the Cuban junta, to precede Wood to Cuba "to reassure the troubled minds" of his old associates, and Rubens spent ten days in preparing them for the advent of the new governor.[4]

As soon as he arrived, Wood took further conciliatory steps. In addition to appointing two spokesmen of the Cuban army element to his cabinet, he attempted to secure the good will of Máximo Gómez by offering him a government sinecure. The old revolutionary chieftain was to become head of a committee to look after aged and crippled Cuban veterans, at a salary of $5,000 per year. Other Cuban generals could be added to this committee, at somewhat lower salaries, if it seemed expedient. "These men have great influence with the army and great influence among the people," Wood wrote Root. Gómez and some of the others were currently living on the charity of friends. Wood's plan would take care of them and "put them in a position where they will apparently be working for the benefit of their late comrades."[5] This attempt at polite bribery failed, however, when Máximo Gómez returned a dignified refusal to Wood's offer. His only remaining mission, Gómez said, was to help secure the liberty of Cuba.[6] The committee on veteran's welfare was never established.

But Wood was already going ahead with other plans designed to reassure the Cubans about the future. The day after assuming office, he had invitations sent to a number of prominent leaders, calling them to a meeting to be held in Havana on January 1, 1900. Aside from high officials like the civil governors of provinces, the notices went mainly to the old leaders of the Cuban army and revolutionary movement, including General Bartolomé Masó, ex-president of the Cuban Republic. "I intend to keep them here only a day or so," Wood wrote, "and simply desire to explain to them our policy."[7]

When the meeting was held, Wood found the Cubans alert and distrustful. They knew perfectly well that he favored permanent United States control in Cuba, and they feared the results of his appointment to supreme command. These fears were voiced openly by one of the Cuban generals, José Miró, who charged Wood with working for annexation instead of Cuban independence. The military governor calmed the Cubans by affirming, on his honor, that "by the instructions of my government, we are marching toward independence."[8]

In addition to the existing popular distrust in Cuba, Wood and Root faced the potential hostility of the influential Wilson-Foraker alliance. Senator Foraker's suspicions of the administration were aroused anew when he was excluded from membership on the permanent Senate Committee on Relations with Cuba which was organized in December of 1899. "When it came to making up the committee in the Senate," Foraker wrote Wilson, "it was made apparent that my known views . . . were not acceptable." In Foraker's opinion, the committee actually chosen would be in no hurry to set up an independent government in Cuba: "I do not think they intend to do it either this year, or next year . . . the program is to so direct matters that as a result of it all this government will probably not withdraw from Cuba at all until conditions arise to compel such action."[9]

General Wilson had as little faith as Foraker in the intentions of his government. He believed that although both the President and Congress had come to see the necessity of abiding by the Teller Resolution, there was still a wide divergence of opinion as to what constituted a proper fulfillment of the pledge, and as to when this should be done. He agreed that "the President and his close friends who constitute all that is worst in 'Imperialism' " would try to prolong the occupation. Senator Foraker, on the other hand, "backed by a powerful element in the Republican Party," would work to end the occupation as soon as possible. Thus Wilson foresaw, in the near future, a "struggle between these two lines of policy." He had advised the Cubans with whom he came in contact to be quiet and well behaved in order to avoid giving any excuse to prolong the occupation.

As for his own position, Wilson by now considered it hopeless. Since the administration evidently disagreed with his policy, he thought it likely that it would soon retire him from the army in order to get him out of the way.[10]

While Foraker and Wilson thoroughly distrusted the administration, this feeling was reciprocated in full. Both Root and Wood soon regarded Wilson as a dangerous man to have in a responsible position within the occupation. They feared that his insistence on quick action could jeopardize the success of their program, and their correspondence at this time was full of references to "Wheeling," the code name which they gave to Wilson.[11]

"I should prefer to have 'Wheeling' moved from the Island as soon as convenient," Wood wrote Root immediately after taking command. "He is sore, discontented, and appears to be a man with a grievance." Wood had conferred with Wilson, and explained his intention to hold municipal elections and gradually to build up a Cuban civil government, but Wilson expressed "lack of sympathy" for the Wood program. "He can do no serious harm," Wood wrote hopefully, "but better be transferred."[12] This belief in Wilson's harmlessness, however, soon disappeared.

The most immediate danger from Wilson sprang from the coming municipal elections. These were important in themselves, but even more so in that they furnished the occasion to set up the ground rules for Cuban elections in general. Since the election law for them would set a precedent for subsequent voting regulations in Cuba, the terms of suffrage which it contained were considered of great future significance. Both Root and Wood regarded it as vitally necessary to establish from the first the principle of limited suffrage. For one thing, they sincerely distrusted the ability of the illiterate masses to use their franchise wisely. But there was another consideration. Both Wood and Wilson had agreed that pro-United States sentiment was strongest among planters, merchants, and the upper classes generally, while they attributed Cuban nationalism chiefly to the revolutionary party and to the propertyless working class.[13] Whatever the future held in Cuba, the advantage of securing as friendly and moderate an electorate as possible was clear to everyone. The question was, how would the Cubans react to such a restriction of their suffrage?

This was where General Wilson came in. He had gained influence among the Cubans through his supposed faith in their capacity for self-government, his urging of a quick end to military control, and his efforts toward agricultural rehabilitation. Public criticism of the election law from him might help set off another wave of distrust among the people, and by the end of December, Wood was highly suspicious of Wilson's intentions. Wood had recently sent Horatio Rubens to the United States carrying confidential information for Root. On January 1, 1900, he cabled Rubens in cipher: "there is sure to be trouble unless Wilson leaves—action cannot be deferred." Rubens forwarded this message to the Secretary of War, who promptly took the problem into his own hands.[14]

Choosing to employ the personal approach, Root called Wilson to Washington, where the General arrived on January 8. Root and Wilson had daily conferences all week at the War Department, but Wilson afterward claimed to have been little impressed. "Root asked me 'to support the policy of the Administration,' " he declared, "without getting further than telling me it had been decided 'to qualify the suffrage' and 'to hold the municipal elections.' "[15] Nevertheless, Root felt that he had accomplished a good deal. He wrote Wood that when Wilson arrived he was "wholly irreconcileable," but that before he left "he seemed to feel much better, and gave me the absolute and unconditional promise to do everything in his power towards carrying out the policy of the Administration in Cuba." In particular, Root got Wilson's promise that he would support the limited suffrage which was to be provided for in the municipal election law.[16]

At this time Root was seeking general support for the policy he intended to embody in the election law. In a letter to Paul Dana, editor of the *New York Sun,* he argued for a suffrage in Cuba based on literacy, property ownership, or past service in the Cuban army. He advanced three reasons for such limitations on the franchise: it would "secure a conservative and thoughtful control of Cuba" during the formative period, make the suffrage respected, and stimulate the people to thrift and education. Wood, Fitzhugh

Lee, and Ludlow all agreed with this view, he wrote, "and Wilson, with whom I have discussed it at length, is going back to Matanzas, agreeing to secure the adherence of the people of his Department to this basis."[17]

By the end of February, Wood was optimistic about the outlook in Cuba. "The limitations of suffrage as proposed met with the approval of practically all the best people here and are acceptable to the people generally," he wrote Root. "Giving the vote to the ex-soldiers has removed the only element which would be in any way dangerous." The educated classes had been relieved of their fear that the illiterate masses would dominate the political scene. Altogether, Wood concluded, "there is infinitely less opposition to the limitation of suffrage than I expected."[18]

Wood wanted to publish the suffrage regulations immediately in order to quiet speculation, but Root called for delay until the census report was finished. They could expect attacks on their policy, he told Wood, and might need the census data to aid in its defense. Also, since the census had been officially described as a first and necessary step in building a Cuban government, "it would seem rather absurd if we take this most important step . . . just before the census is concluded, and in ignorance of what it shows."[19]

The results of the census were available in Washington early in April, and were published in English and Spanish editions in May.[20] The figures showed that two-thirds of all adult Cubans were illiterate; roughly a third of the total population of a million and a half was non-white. Root used these figures to good advantage, arguing that the suffrage limitations were adopted principally because of the high rate of illiteracy which the census revealed.[21]

On February 16 Wood appointed a commission to draw up an election law. Headed by Diego Tamayo, the Secretary of State and Government, the commission contained thirteen Cubans and two Americans. The Americans, James E. Runcie and Horatio Rubens, were both men whom Wood trusted, and were included in the group to safeguard his policies. After some weeks of wrangling, the commission brought in two plans. It had split, not over the basis of suffrage, but upon the details of the nature and operation of the electoral machinery. Runcie and Rubens favored the minority report, while most of the Cubans backed the majority plan. It was the minority report that Wood accepted.[22]

The completed electoral law of April 18, 1900, embodied Root's franchise qualifications substantially unchanged. Potential voters must be male, over twenty-one years of age, and citizens of Cuba according to the terms of the treaty of peace. In addition, they must fulfill at least one of three alternative requirements: possession of the ability to read and write, ownership of property worth $250 in United States gold, or service in the Cuban army prior to July 18, 1898, which had been terminated by an honorable discharge.[23]

While Root and Wood worked out the details of the election law, discussion about the long-range planning for Cuba continued. General Wood, as always, favored continuing the occupation as long as possible. In Wood's opinion, the emergency of November and December was entirely ended. "There is nothing in the present situation which need give you any anxiety or concern," he wrote McKinley in February: "The announcement that it was the intention of our government to carry out the resolutions of Congress, provided the people wished them carried out, produced a general good effect and has resulted in a good many people here advising us not to go too rapidly. The Cuban people, as a whole, realize very fully that they are not ready for self-government and the only people who are howling for it are those whose antecedents and actions demonstrate the impossibility of self-government just at present."[24]

However, Wood recognized the need to take some action toward Cuban self-government. In February he reported that the time had come for the gradual transfer of all civil affairs to the civil authorities, retaining in the military government only the necessary degree of supervision. "We have got to trust them with the handling of affairs under our supervision and in this way teach them," he wrote.[25] But there was no question of trusting the Cubans with *unsupervised* self-government, at least for some time to come. As he told Root, there was "not a sensible man" in Cuba who thought that the American authorities could leave for a long time, "not measured by months, but by years; several of them at least." To go at present "would be to betray the cause of civilization."[26]

The Governor had revealed one aspect of "civilization" back in January: "The people ask me what we mean by a stable government in Cuba? I tell them that when money can be borrowed at a reasonable rate of interest and when capital is willing to invest in the Island, a condition of stability will have been reached."[27]

As General Wilson had predicted, some elements in Congress proved restive about the uncertain duration of the occupation and kept up a steady harassment. On January 17 the Senate passed a resolution of inquiry demanding a detailed accounting from the War Department of all expenditures of Cuban revenues since the occupation began.[28] Later in January Democratic Congressman Henry D. Clayton of Alabama introduced a joint resolution in the House aimed at withdrawing all United States forces from Cuba, and in April a similar resolution was introduced in the Senate by Senator William E. Mason of Illinois, a Republican. Both were referred to committee, where they were safely buried.[28]

Outside of Congress, too, there was some hard thinking about Cuba. Richard Olney, Cleveland's Secretary of State, analyzed the Cuban situation in an article in the *Atlantic Monthly* of March, 1900. In general, Olney favored overseas commercial expansion but opposed the actual acquisition of large territories, such as the Philippines. Cuba, however, was a different case, being a "natural appendage" of the United States. As Olney saw it, the Spanish War had ended in the acquisition of Cuba by the United States, an event fated to occur sooner or later in any event. While it might be argued that Cuba was technically not an "acquisition," Olney said, "the expression conveys the substantial truth, notwithstanding a resolution of Congress which, ill-advised and futile at the time of its passage, if now influential at all, is simply prejudicing the interests of Cuba and the United States alike." No such resolution "should be allowed to impede the natural march of events."

Having thus disposed of the Teller Resolution, Olney called for a permanent political settlement in Cuba. He assailed the current uncertainty, which would end only "when Congress ceases to ignore its functions and makes Cuba in point of law what she already is in point of fact, namely, United States territory."[30]

General Wilson privately charged Senator Orville Platt, chairman of the Committee on Relations with Cuba, with a similar disregard of the Teller Resolution and of Elihu Root's report. A Senate sub-committee led by Platt visited Cuba in March to gather information. According to Wilson, "Platt came down to Cuba—told my officers—more than one of them, that the troops would not be withdrawn and that we should 'never relinquish Cuba.' "[31]

Whitelaw Reid, expansionist editor of the *New York Tribune,* friend of McKinley, and one of the peace commissioners of 1898, expressed the sober second thoughts of many expansionists in his letters to Wilson at this time. Reid looked upon the Teller Resolution as "singularly unfortunate," since he regarded Cuba as clearly not ready for independence. He was also "strenuously opposed" to the admission of Cuba into the union, then or later. The people of Cuba were "not adapted to the working of our Republican institutions," and it was not likely that, "in our lifetime at least," enough Americans would go there to comprise a majority. Under the circumstances, the best that could be done for Cuba would be to "give it such a measure of self-government as experience may show that its people can sustain in an orderly manner," while maintaining a United States protectorate which would conduct foreign affairs and insure internal stability.[32]

Besides these political considerations, Reid discussed the possibility that Cuba and the other Spanish islands would demand admission within the United States tariff and immigration barriers. Such a result would not only "destroy the present revenue system of the United States" by costing many millions of dollars a year in lost customs revenues, but it would arouse the opposition of American capital and labor. The free immigration of cheap tropical labor would be such a danger to workingmen that "it would absolutely consolidate them against the party that proposed it," while any major tariff concession "breaks down the protective tariff to which the Republican party is devoted."[33]

Given Reid's conclusions, and those of many other prominent Americans, it appeared that Cuba must be strictly controlled by the United States, while being rigidly excluded from sharing the benefits of the American economic system. The problem was to get the Cubans to be satisfied with such a position.

The Administration
Is Driven to Speed Its Pace

Elihu Root and Leonard Wood found their problems complicated at this time by a series of troubles within the occupation which were to put in jeopardy the administration's entire Cuban program, and which would end by crystallizing the vacillations of the government into a definite line of action.

The internal affairs of the military government had suffered from chronic discord during the Brooke regime, and they failed to run more smoothly in the first months of Wood's rule. The new Governor found it almost as difficult to control his subordinates as had Brooke before him. To add to his difficulties, he had previously been involved in disagreements of some kind with everyone except Fitzhugh Lee.

The other American generals all presented problems for Wood. General Chaffee, who had been closely identified with General Brooke in his fight against Wood, soon requested a transfer from his uncomfortable position. Here the new Governor showed a generous spirit, writing Root that Chaffee should be promoted for his hard work in Cuba: "He is a fine old soldier and an honest straightforward man, and whatever he thinks of me, I wish him good luck and good fortune everywhere."[1]

General Wilson was still a thorn in Wood's side. He had taken advantage of his summons to Washington in January to appear before the Senate Committee on Relations with Cuba and attack the Wood administration. He told the committee then that the powers of the military governor should be confined to maintaining order and to collecting the revenues, which ought to be conserved.[2] Wilson continued to hammer away at Wood's program of internal reforms after his return to Cuba. "I do not consider that the immediate future of Cuba depends chiefly upon schools, road-making, improved sanitation or judiciary reform," he said in a newspaper interview in March. The best internal program, Wilson insisted, was one of agricultural rehabilitation such as he had long urged.[3]

Until Chaffee left, Wood had hoped to put him in command of Wilson's department and get rid of the troublesome Wilson. He wrote Root in March that Cuba would be "much benefitted by disposing of General Wilson," of whom he had "exactly the same opinion as I had when I came here in December."[4]

Wood also had trouble with one of his Cuban subordinates. General Juan Rius Rivera, the Secretary of Agriculture, Industry, and Commerce, had been chosen for his post partly because of his reputation as a leading spokesman of the views of the Cuban army. In April, however, he performed this function rather too well for Wood's taste, publishing a letter which called for the immediate recognition of Cuban independence. Wood reprimanded him for releasing an unauthorized public statement, which he privately described as "a very silly letter," and Rius Rivera resigned.[5]

A slightly different kind of problem was presented by General Ludlow. Though Ludlow had resented his subordination to Wood, he had accepted it quietly. But unfortunately, he had also become deeply involved in a complex legal-political squabble in Havana concerning the paving and sewering of the city's streets.

Back in 1895, the Havana authorities had accepted plans for this work which had been prepared by an American construction firm, Michael J. Dady and Company. By Spanish law, the fact that they had prepared the plans gave Dady and Company certain special rights and claims on the project when bids were placed for its construction. The Dady bid was also approved by the Havana authorities, just prior to the beginning of American military government in Cuba. Because of the imminent change of authority, the Spanish governor general had refused to sign any new contracts, and the matter was held over for the Americans to settle.

Ludlow, who assumed command in Havana, was himself an engineer of wide experience. He prepared his own plans for the city engineering work, and refused to approve the old Dady contract on the ground that it was unduly expensive and legally incomplete. The Havana *ayuntamiento,* or city council, continued to favor its original arrangement, and the Dady people demanded compensation for their special rights in the case.[6] The upshot was an unseemly row in which all sides joined in abusing Ludlow, as did the Havana press. Ludlow lost his temper and began fining the publishers of offending newspapers, a course which Wood disavowed.[7] Ludlow became highly unpopular in Havana, and by February feeling had grown so intense that Wood packed the embattled general off to Washington on leave.

"Do give the General some good advice," Wood wrote Root, "and keep him in the States for a couple of weeks until things cool off." Wood unfeelingly blamed the situation on Ludlow's "natural inability to keep quiet,"[8] though before long he himself was drawn into just such a squabble as Ludlow's over exactly the same issue. Root was more sympathetic to Ludlow, reminding Wood that "your appointment to be Governor, over his head, was undoubtedly a jar to his feelings and he may be a little sensitive."[9] But the result was that on May 1, 1900, the Department of the City of Havana was discontinued. The city became a part of Lee's Department of Havana and Pinar del Río, while Ludlow left Cuba for duties elsewhere.[10]

These embarrassments were augmented in February, when there appeared in the *North American Review* a startling article by Major James E. Runcie, entitled "American Misgovernment in Cuba." Runcie, a retired army officer, was a close friend of Wood. Late in 1898 he had come to Santiago at Wood's request to act as an unpaid legal adviser, and had been one of Wood's aides ever since.[11]

Runcie's article had been written just before Wood's appointment to the Cuban command, though it did not appear in print until three months later. In substance it was a violent attack on the government of General Brooke, reminiscent of Wood's criticisms of the previous summer. Runcie contrasted a glowing picture of Wood's policies in Santiago with the dreary failure which he ascribed to all of Brooke's efforts. The chief charges against Brooke were that he failed to institute necessary reforms, and that he delegated too much authority to Cubans. An informal junta of Cuban revolutionary leaders had gained control of the government, Runcie charged, and had built an anti-American political machine which covered the whole island. Wherever Cubans had been trusted to govern, "the result has been worse than failure." On the other hand, those agencies completely under American control, such as the customs service and the treasury, were models of efficiency.

Wood himself had said all this in his private correspondence, although it was another thing to write it for publication. But Runcie went on to place a share of the blame on the McKinley administration. He charged, with some justice, that no one had bothered to plan for the occupation and government of Cuba in the six months before January 1, 1899. Instead, everything had to be done "as if the island had been captured the previous day." Worse, no general policy or specific instructions had been given the Military Governor, who was already handicapped, according to Runcie, by his lack of qualifications for his job.[12]

Coming from a source known to be close to Wood, this article created a minor sensation in the United States. Some people recognized the opinions as those held by Wood, and many charged that he had inspired the publication of the article in an attempt to discredit his predecessor. Wood denied any share of responsibility, writing Root that he had never seen the article until it was published.[13] Root, angry and embarrassed at this public washing of dirty linen, called the article "grossly improper." "I am trying to check the tendency to turn the Army into a newspaper debating society," he wrote in irritation, but he accepted Wood's disavowal.[14] General Brooke protested to the War Department against the personal attack upon him, while McKinley declared that Wood's "own sense of propriety will indicate the course which ought to be followed."[15] Wood understood, and Runcie was immediately cut off from all contact with the military government. Feeling that he had been betrayed, Wood's former friend brooded about in Havana, and soon became one of the Governor's bitterest enemies.[16]

Even the Runcie affair was trivial compared to the really serious scandal which burst upon the public in May. The trouble centered in the Cuban postal system, which had from the first occupied an anomalous position in the military government. By order of the President, the Director General of Posts in Cuba was subject to the direct authority of the Postmaster General of the United States, rather than that of the Military Governor. In January of 1900, however, Root grew dissatisfied with the financial irresponsibility of the Cuban postal system, and in the following months he negotiated with the Postmaster General for a better arrangement, while Wood began a routine army audit of the postal accounts.[17]

Root's worst fears were realized when, on May 4, Wood cabled him news of the discovery of large-scale embezzlements in the Havana post office. One postal official, Charles F. Neely, had absconded a few days before, but suspicion soon spread to others, including Estes G. Rathbone, Director General of Posts and a political protege of Senator Marcus A. Hanna of Ohio. Originally estimated at $100,000, the shortages, Wood feared, might prove even greater.[18]

Both Wood and Root at once saw the dangers of the situation. Wood wrote that "the only chance to free ourselves of blame is to smash the offenders without regard to who they are."[19] "I want you to scrape to the bone, no matter whose nerves are hurt by it," Root replied. "The first essential of administration in this Island is that we shall be perfectly honest with ourselves."[20]

Joseph L. Bristow, the Fourth Assistant Postmaster General of the United States, came to Cuba to take charge of a sweeping investigation, with orders from McKinley himself to "shield nobody who has committed a wrong."[21] But the damage was done. The American public, already a little wearied of the problems of imperialism, was shocked and disillusioned by the suggestion of robbery and corruption in Cuba, supposedly the show place of American rule. The general dismay was skillfully exploited by the Democratic press, which charged that the scandals were rooted in Washington as well as Havana, and that they were symptomatic of a general maladministration in Cuba.[22]

CAPTAIN KIDD: "We lived too soon!"

—*The St. Louis Republic*
Reprinted in *Literary Digest,* June 2, 1900.

It was in Congress that the reaction was most dangerous. The postal scandals gave the congressional anti-imperialists a formidable club with which to belabor the administration, and they lost no time in launching an assault on the entire Cuban occupation.

Senator Augustus O. Bacon of Georgia began the attack in the Senate on May 16. A leading anti-imperialist Democrat, Bacon had led the opposition to keeping the Philippines, and now he delivered a full-dress speech on the Cuban question. He alluded at length to the postal scandals, but charged that they merely exemplified a prevailing wastefulness, extravagance, and slackness in the military government of Cuba. After this prelude, Bacon raised the broader issue of whether the United States had any right to be governing Cuba at all. He demanded to know by what warrant the army stayed in Cuba, and why it should continue to collect money from the Cuban people by taxation.

The only just reason for the United States to exercise authority in Cuba, the Senator thundered, was to carry out the terms of the War Resolutions. Yet there had been peace in Cuba for nearly two years, and still a Cuban government had not been erected. The Teller Resolution, he pointed out, denied the United States, not only sovereignty in Cuba, but "jurisdiction and control" as well, and thus had already been violated. The immediate and only duty of the United States in Cuba was to erect a local government and get out. Congress should refuse to adjourn until it had fixed a specific and early date for complete American withdrawal from Cuba. In the meantime, Bacon called for a resolution of inquiry into the collection and expenditure of public money in Cuba.[23]

The administration's answer to Bacon's speech came a week later from Senator Orville Platt, chairman of the Committee on Relations with Cuba. Platt began with a vigorous defense of the occupation government. The Cuban administration, he said, had been neither careless nor extravagant, and although every one deplored the postal scandals, they were the single and unique blot on an otherwise excellent record. The scandals had been discovered and made public by the military authorities, and further investigation should have been left entirely to the executive branch of the government. However, since mudslinging had begun, Platt said, he favored a full Senate investigation to bring out the truth.

Next the Senator took up the real issue which Bacon had raised: why the United States governed Cuba at all. Bacon had missed the point, Platt said, by misunderstanding the word "pacification." When it evicted Spain, the United States became responsible for Spain's international obligations in Cuba and for the future of the island. It was not enough merely to stop the shooting; a stable and responsible government must be established. The establishment of such a government was proceeding as fast as possible, Platt insisted. He mentioned the unavoidable delays cited in Root's report: the free choice of citizenship did not end until April 11, 1900, and it had been necessary to complete the Cuban census. Now, he promised, the work would advance steadily. While the establishment of a stable government was not the work of a moment, much had already been done, and further progress would be pushed as fast as possible.[24]

Behind the scenes, Platt was fighting desperately to hold the Republican majority in the Senate solidly behind the administration. The difficulties and scandals in Cuba, when added to the revolt which had raged for a year in the Philippines, threatened to discredit the administration's entire colonial policy, and there would be a presidential election in only a few months. "The whole Congress is nervous [Platt wrote Wood], liable to take the bit in its teeth and say we ought to get out of Cuba, and it requires a sort of steady hand to keep things straight now in the last days of the session. We hope to adjourn on the 6th of June, and if we can accomplish it matters will be comparatively safe." The combination of the postal scandals and the coming presidential election made Cuba a very touchy subject indeed, Platt confessed. He had intended to propose a modification of the Foraker Amendment, but "to tell the truth I do not dare to do it now," for it would arouse the Democrats to reopen the entire Cuban debate. It would simply have to wait until after the election, by which time Platt hoped that full investigation would have restored confidence in Wood's government, and in its intention to work toward Cuban independence. "If we had made no promises there would be, I think, a strong annexation sentiment among the business people of the United States," Platt said regretfully, but as things stood, a Cuban Republic would have to be established. It would be necessary to secure such relations with the new government "as will safeguard and protect not only the interests of Cuba, but our own interests with relation thereto."[25]

By the first of June, the worst danger appeared to be over. Root wrote Wood: "I have not troubled you with letters during the recent excitement, but I want you to feel how entirely satisfactory your course has been. . . . We are flooded with resolutions of inquiry from both Houses of Congress, relating to pretty nearly everything the army has done for the past two years in the islands or elsewhere, involving an enormous labor, so that we can appreciate the position you are placed in Cuba when we forward such resolutions to you."[26]

On June 16, hard on the heels of the crisis in Congress, came the Cuban municipal elections. These went off quietly, though Wood was disappointed in the voters' choice of candidates. The old revolutionary element, represented by the Cuban National party, was generally successful, while the more conservative Union-Democratic party boycotted the elections in many areas where their defeat was assured. The result was a victory for Cuban nationalism and independence sentiment, or as Wood wrote, for "the extreme and revolutionary element."[27] General Alejandro Rodrígues, one of the leaders of the nationalists, rubbed salt in the wound by sending a victory telegram to McKinley: "The Cuban National Party, victorious in the election, salutes the worthy representative of the North American Nation, and confidently awaits an early execution of the Joint Resolution."[28]

Root was inclined to take the situation philosophically. "It was a great thing to secure the peaceful adoption of the basis of suffrage . . . and to carry the Cubans through their first real election so quietly and satisfactorily," he wrote Wood. While most people would take this achievement for granted, "we know better here." It was especially important, Root thought, to have excluded from the voting "so great a proportion of the elements which have brought ruin to Hayti and San Domingo."

As always, however, Root looked forward rather than back. Perhaps it was time to reduce Cuba to a single military department, he suggested, and thus get rid of Wilson and Lee as well as of some of the American troops.

Also, he wrote, "Admiral Bradford asked me the other day to say something . . . to you about the purchase of land for a naval station at Guantánamo."[29] The Navy hungered for advanced bases in the Caribbean, and it was inevitable that its leaders should try to seize the present opportunity to get something in Cuba. As early as the 1860's, Secretary of State William H. Seward had desired the acquisition of Caribbean bases, while President Ulysses Grant in the 1870's had embroiled his administration in an attempt to secure the Dominican port of Samaná Bay. By the 1890's, interest had focussed on Cuba, the unique strategic value of which was expounded by no less an authority than Captain A. T. Mahan, the famous theoretician of the United States Navy. Mahan noted that Cuba dominated both entrances to the Gulf of Mexico, and would equally dominate the routes from the Atlantic coast of the United States to the proposed isthmian canal. Compared with its rivals in the area, he wrote in 1897, "the advantages of situation, strength, and resources are greatly and decisively in favor of Cuba" as a base for naval power.[30] These considerations had been driven home during the war with Spain, which left the American admirals with a fixed determination to retain a Cuban port.

Root himself regarded the issue as important for other reasons. He wanted to see the United States secure early title to naval bases at Guantánamo and Havana, and if possible at some other points in the island. Root did not contemplate an indefinite continuation of the military government. When the Cubans became self-governing, he argued, the United States would have to guarantee the fulfillment of their international obligation to protect life and property. For this military footholds were required, and the Cubans would make much less objection to the possession of such footholds by the United States if this were an accomplished fact which predated the establishment of their government. The occupation of such bases, Root said, would involve "political as well as property rights."

Finally, Root asked Wood to get things into shape in Cuba so that he would be free to come to Washington and confer about preparing for a constitutional convention.[31] This was an action which Wood had previously suggested. On June 3, when Congress was acting most threatening, Wood suggested that a convention be called for some time in the autumn, provided that the elections went off quietly. "I am going to work on a Constitution for the Island similar to our own," he wrote. Embodied in this organic act would be "certain definite relations and agreements between the United States and Cuba." The finished product would be "presented to the Assembly as a model for adoption," and in order to prepare it Wood asked Root for a statement of the conditions "which our government is going to insist upon." Even after this "model" had been adopted by the Cubans, Wood thought, the occupation should continue; American troops should remain in the island, and the military governor should retain an absolute veto power over the Cuban government. Wood admitted that "such a form of government would not differ materially from the present," but the people *would* make their own laws, while the governor's veto would remove the risks this entailed.[32]

This scheme of government was designed to give the Cubans a sense of self-government without relinquishing American control. Wood continued to suggest ways of fostering such a feeling, and of soft-pedalling the role of the United States. A few days later he said: "I think on the first of July it will be a good idea to quietly authorize the floating of the Cuban flag from all municipal and civil buildings occupied by local authorities," including his own palace at Havana.[33] And at the end of June he wrote Root: "I want to go ahead with the Constitutional Convention as fast as possible, and follow it by the legislative assembly; the Military Governor to hold absolute veto. . . . I believe the adoption of a constitution here and the legislative assembly to be a fine thing for the Cubans and for the administration at home."[34]

Early in July, Wood's attitude toward Cuba's future changed as a result of news of the Boxer outbreak in China and the siege of the legations in Peking. Wood believed that there would be major fighting in China, and he was determined to take part in it. So eager was he to go that all other factors became secondary, even the Cuban situation. "I apply for service in China in case troops are sent," he wired Root. "This Island profoundly peaceful. Older men can do this work."[35] Not only was Mrs. Wood's sister feared trapped in the Peking legations,[36] but Wood thought that his very career was at stake. As things stood, he told Roosevelt, a Republican defeat in the November election, or even the failure of the new Army Bill to pass in Congress, would leave him without hope of early promotion.[37] And he complained to Lodge that "the people going to China will have the opportunity for the only thing which gives the man of the Army reputation."[38]

In his eagerness to leave Cuba, Wood now moved far toward adopting the program of General James H. Wilson. He even began cultivating Wilson personally, and their relations suddenly bloomed into an unprecedented cordiality. Under the influence of his new attitude, Wood wrote Root a long letter of persuasion.

"Let us rush the establishment of civil government," he began. "Everything is quiet and there is no use of prolonging the misery."

All was now well in Cuba, and a nominal garrison would suffice to keep order. Wood urged calling the constitutional convention "right away." A month would suffice to get ready, while the convention's work could quickly be finished. Simultaneously with the adoption of a constitution, the convention should sign a treaty which would define the relations between Cuba and the United States so as to "definitely bind the two countries." The United States might keep control of the Customs, and "if deemed advisable," the military governor could continue in office, holding an absolute veto power. To succeed him in this post, Wood recommended none other than General Wilson, his old foe. But he suddenly could see no merit in further delay. "We only give a cudgel to the Democrats and are allowing them to play on the suspicions of the Cubans."

"I am satisfied that the Island will run quietly," Wood declared, apparently forgetting that only three months before he had branded anyone who urged a quick withdrawal from Cuba a "coward" who would be "guilty of the greatest crime of recent years."[39] In words borrowed from General Wilson, Wood declared that "this rapid and positive action" would "do more to draw Cuba to the United States than anything else" and would "produce such a feeling of confidence and friendship that the future will not long remain in doubt." At the end of the letter, Wood returned to the point closest to his heart: "If there is going to be war in China I want to go. . . . I do not want to be left here to fossilize."[40]

Within a few days, Wood was on his way north to confer with Root and McKinley about the coming constitutional convention. The circumstances of the past months—the postal scandals and the near-rebellion of Congress, the imminence of the elections of 1900, the embarrassments in the Philippines, Wood's ambition to play a role in the Chinese expedition—had succeeded at last in bringing the administration, the Congress, and the occupation generals into a temporary agreement in favor of early action in Cuba.

On July 25 the American Military Government of Cuba published the civil order providing for the election of delegates to a Cuban constitutional convention. The election was to be held on September 3, under the terms of the Cuban election law of April 18; the time had come when Root's careful limitation of the suffrage was expected to pay its dividends. The convention was to

begin its sessions at Havana, at noon on the first Monday in November. Its duties were "to frame and adopt a constitution for the
people of Cuba, and, as a part thereof, to provide for and agree
with the Government of the United States upon the relations to
exist between that Government and the Government of Cuba, and
to provide for the election by the people of the officers under such
constitution and the transfer of government to the officers so
elected."[41]

"You will see," Senator Allison wrote Wilson, "that General
Wood's visit to Washington culminated in orders to carry out
what you have so often outlined as the true thing to do."[42]

In one respect Wood's trip to Washington was a failure: he was
not to go to China. That, the President said, was out of the question.[43] Instead, he stayed on in Cuba while the other remaining
generals left the island one by one. Chaffee and Ludlow had already gone; the next to leave was General Wilson. Wilson himself
was by now eager to go, and had recommended earlier that his department be discontinued.[44] Wood seconded this recommendation,
although, in the warmth of his new alliance with Wilson, he reported the surprising fact that "I shall regret to lose General Wilson's administrative ability."[45] The Department of Matanzas and
Santa Clara was incorporated with Lee's department on July 23,
and the whole was renamed the Department of Western Cuba.[46]
Wilson, ironically, was to join the American relief force in China
as second in command to Chaffee, who had been given the command there which Wood so coveted.

At the end of July, then, there were only two military departments left in Cuba. In October these two were combined into one,
and Lee left in his turn.[47] For the rest of the occupation Wood ran
the island without the aid of the departmental commanders, that
turbulent and unruly group which he himself had led in harassing
Brooke the previous year. Once the great advocate of departmental
autonomy, Wood was beginning to appreciate the advantages of
"re-centralizing everything in Havana." "It is pretty hard to handle a Latin population [he wrote Root] and those who have had
experience with them realize that it is necessary that they look to
some one as having ultimate authority and that decisions given by
this authority should stand."[48]

After his return from Washington, Wood's greatest preoccupation was with the coming constitutional convention. He reported to Root early in August that the Cubans seemed generally dissatisfied with the wording of the civil order announcing the convention. The order had specified that the convention should frame a constitution, and that it should provide for future Cuban-American relations "as a part thereof." The Cubans, Wood wrote, wanted the two matters to be considered separately, and to be embodied in two distinct documents. Wood was inclined to grant them the concession. "Every apparent string which we attach to Independence," he wrote, "only intensifies the desire for it." Nevertheless, he added, "if things go wrong in this convention, we can, of course, slow up on the subsequent procedure to any extent necessary."[49]

A week later, the Governor began a tour of the island designed to encourage the election of the "best men" as delegates to the convention. He told local political leaders that "they must not trifle with this Constitutional Convention" and that "if they send a lot of political jumping-jacks as delegates they must not expect that their work will be received very seriously."[50]

As he became resigned to staying on in Cuba, Wood began to sound more like his old self. He wrote McKinley that "conservative men" in Cuba were "for slow progress in the evacuation of the Island by American forces and Authority." Such men knew, he said, that "a control more or less strong must be maintained for some time, and they desired "a Constitutional Government under our supervision. According to Wood, the Cuban leaders really wanted the United States to move slowly, but did not dare say so.[51]

The Governor was even more cautious after seeing the results of the election of delegates. The Union-Democratic party, which represented the most conservative and pro-annexation Cubans, had shown little strength in the elections. The Nationalists, who stressed independence most strongly, had dominated the voting and would send the most men to the constitutional convention. Wood expressed disappointment in the voters' choices; he had hoped that they would elect only "their very best men." Instead, "I should say that we have about ten absolutely first class men and about fifteen men of doubtful qualifications and character and about six of the worst rascals and fakirs [sic] in Cuba." Not over 30 per cent of the qualified voters had voted, Wood declared. This indicated to him that the Cubans "lack confidence in their own people."[52]

The opening of the constitutional convention was set for almost the same time as the presidential election in the United States. The Republican convention had met in June and renominated McKinley, as expected. Interest had centered on the choice of a vice-presidential candidate. During the previous winter Elihu Root was the man most often mentioned for the nomination, and Roosevelt and Lodge had made tentative plans to secure Roosevelt's appointment as Secretary of War in Root's place.[53] But in time McKinley decided that he needed Root where he was, while a burgeoning movement for the nomination of Roosevelt resulted in his virtual draft by the convention.

During the convention, the Platform Committee delivered itself of a Cuban plank: "To Cuba independence and self-government were assured in the same voice by which war was declared and to the letter this pledge shall be performed."[54] There the Grand Old Party left the Cuban problem, with the less said about it the better. To Leonard Wood, however, this was an unsatisfactory course. He soon wrote Root that "the Republican Party should have some one here writing up the immense amount of work which has been done in Cuba." It would be useful campaign material, and also "the Democratic Party have a swarm of people here working against us and sending out all sorts of absolutely false reports."[55] He wrote in a similar vein to Roosevelt, who contacted Mark Hanna. Hanna saw the force of this, and replied that he would act on Root's suggestion.[56]

The main thing, however, was to avoid any more unpleasantness in Cuba, at least until after the election. Many years later, Horatio Rubens recalled that he made a suggestion to Wood at this time concerning land taxation, aimed at penalizing absentee landowners who kept their land idle. According to Rubens, Wood objected to the plan because it would arouse controversy, "and McKinley, who was facing a campaign for re-election, had asked him to keep things as quiet as possible in Cuba." This request from the President, Rubens concluded, "probably was the reason that so little friction arose between Wood and the Cubans—until after McKinley's re-election."[57]

Genesis of
the Platt Amendment

The Cuban Constitutional Convention began its sessions in Havana on November 5, 1900. It consisted of thirty-one delegates, apportioned among Cuba's six provinces on the basis of population. Havana, with the largest representation, sent eight delegates; Puerto Principe, with the smallest, sent two. Leonard Wood called the convention's first meeting to order and made a short opening statement, the chief significance of which was that it ended the long discussion about the convention's order of business.[1]

Wood had suggested to Root back in August that the wording be changed in the order which created the constitutional convention. This order directed the convention to write a constitution for Cuba, and "as a part thereof" to agree upon the nature of future relations between Cuba and the United States. Since August, the Military Governor had repeatedly requested that the convention be allowed to consider the constitution and the question of Cuban-American relations as two separate matters.[2] To tie the two together, he argued, looked to the Cubans like a form of coercion, and had "given all the rabid anti-Americans a chance to howl from one end of the Island to the other."[3]

To reassure the Cubans, Root finally assented, and when Wood opened the convention he made the change of instructions quite clear. It would be their duty, he told the delegates, first to frame a constitution for Cuba, and only "when that has been done," to

150

agree upon future relations with the United States. Wood did not make clear what the role of the United States would be in determining these mutual relations. When the delegates, he said, had formulated the relations "which, in your opinion, ought to exist between Cuba and the United States," the United States government would "doubtless take such action on its part as shall lead to a final and authoritative agreement."[4] With this vague declaration, the convention began its work.

In accord with the new understanding, the delegates directed their attention solely toward the Cuban constitution during the early weeks of the convention's sessions. They were allowed to proceed in this task substantially without interference, and made steady, though slow, progress. There was no attempt on the part of the American authorities to present the delegates with a "model" constitution such as Wood had suggested during the summer.[5] Rather, the attitude of the military government was indicated in Root's annual report for 1901:

I do not fully agree with the wisdom of some of the provisions of this constitution [wrote the Secretary of War]; but it provides for a republican form of government; it was adopted after long and patient consideration and discussion; it represents the views of the delegates elected by the people of Cuba; and it contains no features which would justify the assertion that a government organized under it will not be one to which the United States may properly transfer the obligation for the protection of life and property under international law, assumed in the Treaty of Paris.[6]

The United States government, however, was not prepared to take such a tolerant position toward the second issue before the convention, that of Cuba's future relations with the United States. The Secretary of War, it is true, had promised the Cubans much in his trail-blazing annual report of November, 1899. When the new Cuban government was established, Root had said then, "the relations which exist between it and the United States will be matter for free and uncontrolled agreement between the two parties." This implied that the United States would give the Cubans their independence without exacting any reservations or prior commitments, and settle for the best bargain it could make afterwards. But the convention was not long in session before it became clear that the administration expected some very specific guarantees on the score of "relations." The question was whether or not the delegates would freely concede all that was desired, and if they would not, what ought to be done.

In the opening days of 1901, Leonard Wood sought the answers to some of these questions. He had a long private conference with a group of delegates headed by Domingo Méndez Capote, who had resigned the presidency of the Cuban Assembly to join Brooke's cabinet, and who had quit with the rest of that cabinet when Wood took office as Governor. Méndez Capote and his friends were living reminders to Wood that seven of the convention's thirty-one regular delegates, plus three of the alternates, had once been members of the Cuban Assembly. The Méndez Capote group, Wood reported, was "touchy" on the subject of granting naval stations to the United States, but Wood doubted that they would put up really serious opposition on that point. Instead, he feared some trouble on the general issue of Cuban foreign relations, and suggested to Root that the convention might be persuaded to adopt a declaration that "no foreign negotiations in any way affecting matters of interest to the United States shall be entered into without our full consent and approval."

For the present, the General said, he had told the delegates that there was little chance of getting the proposed Cuban constitution before the current session of Congress. He had suggested to them, as a feeler, that the President might temporarily authorize the partial adoption of the constitution, while the military governor remained in office with an absolute veto power. But Méndez Capote and his "radical" friends received this suggestion coldly. They proposed in return that the Americans select one of three alternatives: the President could call a special session of Congress to consider the Cuban question; the constitution could be put into effect provisionally, while the United States Army stood by, but did *not* interfere in government; or the President could submit the constitution to the next session of Congress in December, 1901, but in that case should immediately announce a definite date for the election of the officers of the new government.[7]

These, Wood told Root, were the radicals' propositions; "the conservatives will agree to anything we prefer." But he urged Root to do all he could, as quickly as possible, to get tariff concessions for Cuban products. Such tariff favors, he said, would "do more than all other things combined" to reduce tensions and secure favorable action by the convention, even if they were granted with the understanding that they would not be continued after independence.[8]

A few days later in January, Elihu Root moved to resolve at least some of the uncertainties with which the Cuban situation was plagued. He hoped, he wrote Wood, that the Cubans would not make tariff concessions a condition of taking proper action on the subject of American relations. He would rather see the whole subject of the tariff postponed until the convention had done its work. The main thing was for the convention to finish its task quickly, and to submit the results to the President. The Cubans should understand that "we desire as soon as possible to be relieved from the burden and annoyance of their government." Then, in a rare loss of self-control, Root unburdened himself of the strain and irritation to which the Cuban problem had so long subjected him:

I am getting pretty tired of having Congress on the one hand put us under the independence of Cuba resolutions, and Foraker franchise resolutions and resolutions of hostile inquiry and criticism, and on the other hand shirk all responsibility; and I do not relish the prospect of having the Cuban Constitution and proposals as to our relations just too late for Congress to act, compelling us to go on and govern for another year with the Cubans howling at us to do something and the democratic press abusing us because we do not do something, and with the certainty that we will be met by a denial of our lawful authority if we undertake to do anything, and with a possibility of a change for the worse in Cuban conditions.

Root had obviously decided to get out of Cuba completely, and in a subsequent paragraph he rejected Wood's favorite scheme of keeping the military governor in office for a time with an absolute veto power. Such a division of power between Cubans and Americans was unsafe, Root thought. Instead, "matters should be shaped so that we can make a clean cut between the military government and the new Cuban government, turn over the administration and get out."

As for the future relations of Cuba with the United States, Root told Wood: "Of course, you are taking special care not to permit anyone with whom you talk to have the opportunity to say that you are making demands, or even official suggestions. It seems to me important that the convention shall be required either to take the initiative in stating what they want the relations to be, or to distinctly refuse it." Wood might, however, use one incentive to influence the delegates. Root suggested that, in talking with them as individuals, Wood "disabuse their minds of the idea that they are certain of being protected by the United States no matter what they do or refuse to do."[9]

On January 11, only two days later, the Secretary of War gave evidence of planning to take the initiative himself on the subject of relations. In a letter to Secretary of State John Hay, he wrote:

Will you turn over in your mind, until our next meeting, the advisability of requiring the incorporation into the fundamental law of Cuba of provisions to the following effect:

1. That in transferring the control of Cuba to the Government established under the new Constitution the United States reserves and retains the right of intervention for the preservation of Cuban independence and the maintenance of a stable government, adequately protecting life, property and individual liberty.

2. That no government organized under the Constitution shall be deemed to have authority to enter into any treaty or engagement with any foreign power which may tend to impair or interfere with the independence of Cuba, or to confer upon such foreign power any special right or privilege without the consent of the United States, and that the United States shall be entitled to be a party, in the first instance, to any negotiations having in view any such provision.

3. . . . The United States may acquire and hold the title to land, and maintain naval stations at certain specified points.

4. That all acts of the Military Governor, and all rights acquired thereunder, shall be valid and be maintained and protected.

Root recalled to Hay the long discussions in the past over the effect of Great Britain's retaining a right of intervention in Egypt; he had an impression, he said, that "some good authorities were of the opinion that it would enable England to retire and still maintain her moral control." He requested that the State Department make a study of the subject, for it was important now to "reach sound conclusions upon the scope and effect which the reservation of a right of intervention in Cuba would have."[10]

While Root was formulating future relations with Cuba in increasingly specific terms, Wood wrote to several Congressional leaders urging lower tariff rates for Cuban products. The results were discouraging for the General. Senators Lodge and Platt agreed, in their replies, that nothing could then be done. Since Cuba was foreign territory, all tariff reductions extended to her must be generalized to everyone growing the same products, under the "most favored nation" clause which was written into all American commercial treaties. This clause would not apply if a reciprocal trade treaty existed between the two countries, but such a treaty could not be made until there was a government in Cuba with which to negotiate it. In short, no tariff arrangements could be made before the constitutional convention had finished its work.

Senator Platt suggested in his letter that this very situation, if used correctly, was one way to force the convention to act quickly and in the right way.[11] Senator Lodge was more explicit. "The hope of Cuba," he wrote Wood, "lies in annexation which would give her immediate entrance into our markets," and the Senator found it "amazing" that the Cubans did not realize it. But at least they should be made to understand that "they will get no reduction on their products unless the provisions of their constitution are absolutely satisfactory to the United States."[12]

By February, Congress was becoming restive over the failure of the convention to declare itself on the subject of relations, and on February 5, Senator Platt declared himself to Root:

Talking the matter over with the republican members of the Committee on Relations with Cuba, we think that it would be advisable, without much delay, to formulate a resolution authorizing the President to discontinue the military occupation of Cuba whenever certain things shall have been agreed to and incorporated into the constitution of Cuba, making it certain that results which we deem essential are assured. Of course the difficulty is to formulate the conditions in such a resolution, and I want to talk with you about it, and also with the President.

The proposed resolution, Platt explained, would state the essential conditions which must be formally agreed to by the Cubans before the occupation could end. It would be referred to Platt's Committee on Relations with Cuba, and added to the current army appropriation bill as an amendment. "It would at least be a notice to Cuba," Platt wrote, "which I think it is high time to give as to what the United States is going to insist on."[13]

This plan of action was the product of a meeting of the Republican members of Platt's committee, which had been held two days before at the Washington home of Senator William E. Chandler of New Hampshire. One of the highlights of the meeting was Chandler's suggestion that the United States should demand $100,000,000 in four per cent bonds from the Cubans as part payment of the costs of the Spanish War! Senator Spooner of Wisconsin had immediately opposed the idea, protesting that the United States could not ask money for freeing Cuba. Chandler retorted that the Americans need not insist upon actual payment of the huge sum, but could use the provision for bargaining purposes—something to give up in return for Cuban concessions. This strategy, however, met with little favor, and was rejected by the meeting. Instead, the senators turned their attention toward the imposition of a debt limitation on the future Cuban government, which they feared might contract greater debts than it could repay.[14]

In the next few days work went ahead rapidly on defining what the United States would demand from the Cubans. On February 7, Platt's committee conferred with Root and McKinley,[15] and on February 9, the Secretary of War informed Wood in detail of the position which the administration had decided to take. His message read less like a letter of instruction than a legal brief, full of precedents and arguments for the action to be taken. Root began by quoting the Teller Resolution and all of the relevant articles of the Treaty of Paris, which made peace with Spain. He followed this with a long historical summary of American-Cuban relations, designed to prove that it was the fixed policy of the United States to allow no foreign power but Spain to exercise control in Cuba. From all this, he concluded that the United States had both a moral responsibility for the future performance of the Cuban government, and a substantial national interest in the maintenance of that government free of foreign control and internal disorder. It was necessary to guarantee these things "for our own protection," Root said: "It would be a most lame and impotent conclusion if, after all the expenditure of blood and treasure by the people of the

United States for the freedom of Cuba, and by the people of Cuba for the same object, we should . . . be placed in a worse condition in regard to our own interests than we were while Spain was in possession, and the people of Cuba should be deprived of that protection and aid from the United States which is necessary for the maintenance of their independence."

After this long preamble, Root came to the core of his message. "The people of Cuba," he stated flatly, "should desire to have incorporated in her fundamental law, provisions in substance as follows." What followed was a refined version of the provisions Root had suggested to Hay a month earlier. The Cuban government must not make any treaty which would impair its independence, or confer any special right or privilege upon a foreign power without the consent of the United States. It must formally grant the United States the right to intervene internally in Cuba for the preservation of independence, life, and property, and must lease the United States lands for naval stations which would facilitate such intervention. It must validate all the acts of the previous military government and all legal rights acquired under it. To these provisions of Root's was added the one formulated by Platt's committee at Chandler's house, that the Cuban government must not contract debts beyond its normal ability to pay. The final determination of all these requirements would rest with Congress, Root warned, but Wood was to be guided by Root's instructions until Congress had acted.[16]

On February 12 the Cuban convention at last chose a committee to take up the subject of relations with the United States.[17] Three days later, in a conference which took place during the course of a railroad journey from Havana to Batabanó on the South Coast, the General confronted this committee with Elihu Root's instructions. Wood had summoned the committee to the unusual meeting at the last minute, and one American correspondent charged that the Military Governor had dragged the delegates across the island in this fashion in order to keep the meeting from interfering with an alligator hunt which he had planned in the South.[18] Whatever the cause, Wood took the Cubans on the train trip and told them of the provisions contained in Root's letter, pointing out that Congress might desire additional conditions when it acted on the matter. Although the Cubans objected to the articles concerning the right of intervention and the leasing of naval stations, Wood reported, he thought really serious opposition unlikely in regard to the right of intervention, and had told the committee that this article could not be modified.[19]

Root approved of what Wood had told the committee, but was somewhat uneasy about his methods of telling them. He had been informed by a "private source," he cabled Wood, that the committee had been offended at being summoned on the journey to Batabanó and might be less reasonable as a result. It seem unlikely, Root concluded, but had better be looked into.[20] Wood replied at once that there was "absolutely no truth in it." The committee had thoroughly enjoyed the trip, and reports to the contrary were spread only by some Americans who were eager to defeat the proposed provisions.[21]

On February 21, Wood sent an official letter to Dr. Diego Tamayo, the president of the convention's Committee on Relations, formally submitting the proposals of which the committee had been verbally informed the week before.[22] On the same day, the Secretary of War informed Wood that it was too late for the Cuban constitution to reach the present Congress before adjournment. Whether or not an extra session would be called, Root said, would depend on what provisions the convention submitted in regard to relations with the United States.[23]

At this point the American public began to realize that the Cuban situation was coming to a head. The Literary Digest reported: "Almost in a day, last week, the rather academic newspaper discussion of the provisions of the new Cuban constitution gave way to animated questionings as to whether it would be safe for the United States and safe for Cuba to let the latter start out alone upon the perilous seas of national sovereignty."[24]

In Elihu Root's opinion, everything was going well at home in regard to the Cuban settlement. The great thing was to get the country interested, for "Congress will never pay any attention to anything until it has to. Public opinion will not form on any question until discussion commences." So far, Root felt, the administration had accomplished much in arousing support for its program. "More good, sound, sensible, public opinion has formed regarding American relations with Cuba during the past three weeks than had formed during the preceding two years," the Secretary declared. Everything was "getting into beautiful shape" for the United States to stand firm on the "reasonable propositions which concern our interests and the real interests of Cuba." Soon, Root concluded, "the gentlemen who have gone to the Convention with the idea that they are all there is of it" would have "discovered their mistake."

Root was doubtful, however, of the expediency of adding a provision suggested by Wood, which would compel the Cubans to continue the American sanitation and sewerage programs after the occupation had ended.[25] Because "any sanitary control involves so great an infringement of the independence and internal government of Cuba," it would be clearly inconsistent with the Teller Resolution, and the executive could not properly demand it. But Congress might do so, and Root had brought the proposal to the attention of the President and of Senators Platt and Spooner.[26] These gentlemen apparently approved of Wood's idea, for it appeared as Article 5 in the final version of the Platt Amendment.

While Root found matters progressing well in the United States, Wood became aware of mounting difficulties in Cuba. The delegates to the convention had been shocked by the conditions demanded by the Americans. Although they had suspected that something specific might be required of them, the reality surpassed their worst fears. The chief hope left to them was that the American Congress might refuse to support the demands of the executive branch.[27]

As February drew toward its close, Wood complained increasingly of unnamed American "agitators" who tried to influence the convention delegates to resist the administration's proposals. He complained even more of the timidity of the Cuban delegates, who feared future political ruin if they proposed a basis of relations too favorable to the United States. Some delegates, Wood reported, had suggested to him that the convention might find it easier to yield to an American demand than to make voluntary offers, since in the former case little blame could attach to them personally.[28]

While he claimed to be on good terms with the Cuban Committee on Relations, the Governor scored "the moral cowardice of

all these men, even as good ones as Tamayo." They would agree to
the American position in private, he charged, but in public they
would say nothing. In Wood's opinion, the delegates' chief preoccupation was to keep their political record clear for the future, but
they "say they are willing to accept pretty much whatever we propose if the United States insists on it." Some of them, however,
had tried to maintain that the constitutional convention was not
really empowered to agree on relations with the United States, and
were "attempting to wiggle out in any way." To these, the government must show "the strong hand of authority."[28]

The reluctance of the delegates to declare themselves may well
have been enhanced by the tone of public discussion in Cuba. On
February 24 both political parties held meetings in Havana to com-
memorate the sixth anniversary of the 1895 revolution. While
the National and Republican party meetings both featured anti-
American speeches, it was the Republicans who showed the greatest fervor. One patriotic orator told his audience that Cuba must
be a sovereign nation and that "sovereignty lay in the machetes of
its inhabitants." The more prominent politicians of all persuasions
took a moderate line, but the subject of relations was clearly becoming politically dangerous.[30]

On February 27 the convention in secret session received and
approved the report of its Committee on Relations. The committee had tried valiantly to find a middle course between either accepting or rejecting the American proposals outright, and in the
end it took up a bargaining posture. They had expected, the committee reported, that their task would be an easy one, since all
Cuban patriots desired the closest friendship with the United
States, and there was no conflict between the legitimate interests of
the two countries. But no sooner had the committee been formed,
than the Military Governor had told them of the desires of the
Secretary of War. This represented a change in their original understanding of their task, the committee complained; the convention was instructed to formulate freely what kind of relations ought,
in its opinion, to exist between Cuba and the United States, but
now they were faced with specific proposals upon which to act.

Nevertheless, the convention must still do as it thought best.
While the Root proposals embodied only the opinions of the exe-

CUBA.—"One calls for the other."
—*The Philadelphia North American*
Reprinted in *Literary Digest,* March 2, 1901.

cutive branch of the United States government, this alone made them worthy of serious study. "But our power is left intact to accept or not," the committee concluded boldly. The delegates agreed with Root that the independence of Cuba must be absolutely guaranteed, and thought therefore that some of his stipulations were unacceptable, "just because they violate the independence and sovereignty of Cuba." The constitution which the convention had just created was sufficient to insure Cuba's independence, and there was no reason for apprehension about the future behavior of the Cubans, since they had behaved so well in the past.

In order to strengthen the confidence of the United States in the new Cuba, however, the committee was prepared to recommend a set of counterproposals which the future governmental authorities of the Republic of Cuba should adopt, if they thought proper. According to these proposals, the government of Cuba should undertake not to enter into any treaty with a foreign power which would tend to impair Cuban independence, or permit the introduction of foreign authority into any part of Cuba. Cuba should never permit her territory to be used as a hostile base against the United States, or any other foreign nation. The new government should accept in full all the obligations contained in the Treaty of Paris and now borne by United States, particularly those concerning the protection of life and property. The Cuban government should validate all the acts of the military government, as well as those rights acquired under it which were in conformity with the Foraker Amendment. And finally, the two countries ought to make a reciprocal trade agreement to promote the freer exchange of their natural and manufactured products.[31]

By adopting this report, the convention took up a position very different from that desired in Washington. Most notably, it refused to agree to the United States' right of intervention in Cuba, to grant naval stations, or to limit the capacity of the Cuban government to contract debts. On the other hand, it included the tariff issue in that of relations, while the Americans wished this question postponed until later. Furthermore, instead of writing the terms of relations into the constitution, the convention merely agreed to recommend such terms to the future government, which would still have full freedom to accept or reject them. The convention had finally declared itself, and it was obvious that the United States would not get the settlement it wanted through any free offer of the Cubans.

In Washington the preparations for coercing the convention were already far advanced. The Congressional resolution which Platt had discussed with Root, and which was to specify the minimum conditions necessary to end the occupation, took shape in the same week that the Cubans made their stand. The sub-committee which wrote this, the so-called Platt Amendment, consisted of Senators Orville H. Platt of Connecticut, John C. Spooner of Wisconsin, Hernando de Soto Money of Mississippi, and Henry M. Teller of Colorado, and worked closely with Root and McKinley. On February 25, 1901, Senator Platt introduced the finished resolution in the Senate, as an amendment to the current army appropriation bill.

According to Platt's resolution, the President was authorized to end the military occupation of Cuba

As soon as a government shall have been established in said island under a constitution which, either as a part thereof or in an ordinance appended thereto, shall define the future relations of the United States with Cuba, substantially as follows:

I. That the government of Cuba shall never enter into any treaty or other compact with any foreign power or powers which will impair or tend to impair the independence of Cuba, nor in any manner authorize or permit any foreign power or powers to obtain by colonization or for military or naval purposes or otherwise, lodgement in or control over any portions of said island.

II. That said government shall not assume or contract any public debt, to pay the interest upon which, and to make reasonable sinking fund provision for the ultimate discharge of which, the ordinary revenues of the island, after defraying the current expenses of government, shall be inadequate.

III. That the government of Cuba consents that the United States may exercise the right to intervene for the preservation of Cuban independence, the maintenance of a government adequate for the protection of life, property, and individual liberty, and for discharging the obligations with respect to Cuba imposed by the treaty of Paris on the United States, now to be assumed and undertaken by the government of Cuba.

IV. That all acts of the United States in Cuba during its military occupancy thereof are ratified and validated, and all lawful rights acquired thereunder shall be maintained and protected.

V. The government of Cuba will execute, and as far as necessary extend, the plans already devised or other plans to be mutually agreed upon, for the sanitation of the cities of the island, to the end that a recurrence of epidemic and infectious diseases may be prevented, thereby assuring protection to the people and commerce of Cuba, as well as to the commerce of the southern ports of the United States and the people residing therein.

VI. That the Isle of Pines shall be omitted from the proposed constitutional boundaries of Cuba, the title thereto being left to future adjustment by treaty.

VII. That to enable the United States to maintain the independence of Cuba, and to protect the people thereof, as well as for its own defense, the government of Cuba will sell or lease to the United States lands necessary for coaling or naval stations at certain specified points, to be agreed upon with the President of the United States.

VIII. That by way of further assurances the government of Cuba will embody the foregoing provisions in a permanent treaty with the United States.[32]

The terms of the Platt Amendment represented the pooled thinking of a number of men. Almost two years earlier, James Harrison Wilson had sketched out the provisions concerning the right of intervention and the grant of naval stations. Leonard Wood had suggested the article on sanitation, at which Wilson had also hinted strongly in his proposed treaty of 1899. The limitation of Cuba's treaty-making powers was Elihu Root's idea. It was Root, too, who conceived of putting the finished agreement not merely in a treaty, but in the Cuban constitution itself, as well as into the laws of the United States. The article limiting Cuba's capacity to go into debt originated with the Platt Committee, as did that reserving to the United States a future claim to the Isle of Pines, which was added toward the last. As Senator Platt said, "I am scarcely entitled to the credit of having my name attached" to the final amendment, for it was drafted in consultation with many others, who had drawn their ideas from a wide variety of sources.[33]

The press reaction to the Platt Amendment was divided, with Democratic newspapers generally condemning it as a betrayal of the Cubans, and most Republican organs steadfastly defending it as necessary for Cuba's welfare. There was a surprising amount of agreement, however, about the essential nature of the amendment. The *Springfield Republican,* which opposed it, called the Platt Amendment "a protectorate boldly outlined and insisted upon." The *Brooklyn Eagle* admitted freely that it was "in fact a protectorate," but maintained that it was "as necessary as it is considerate." And some editors complained that it did not go far enough, but permitted the Cubans a dangerous degree of freedom.[34]

The Senate debate on the Platt Amendment occurred on February 26 and 27. Leading the Democratic opposition was Senator John T. Morgan of Alabama, the man who had given the Cuban Commission such short shrift back in December of 1898. In his major speech, Morgan argued that the content of the Platt Amendment was properly matter for diplomatic negotiation between two existing governments, and could not justly be imposed as a precondition to creating a Cuban government. In Morgan's opinion, the terms of the amendment clearly infringed Cuban sovereignty, and should be substantially changed or dropped entirely. The Alabama Senator also called for immediate free trade with Cuba.[35]

On the following day the attack continued. Senators James K. Jones, an Arkansas Democrat, and Joseph B. Foraker of Ohio, who still opposed the administration's Cuban policy, attempted unsuccessfully to modify the terms of Article Three, which granted the United States the right of intervention. Both men introduced motions to delete "the maintenance of a government adequate for the protection of life, property, and individual liberty" as a valid ground for intervention,[36] hoping in this way to limit intervention to purely external matters. With considerable foresight, Foraker prophesied that any attempt to insure Cuba's internal stability by the threat of intervention would be self-defeating. Instead, the Senator thought, it would become a weapon of the minority against the majority in Cuba, tempting the losing party in each election to raise such a furor as to necessitate American intervention, and thus undo the result of the election.[37] The opposition concluded with speeches by a half-dozen Democratic orators, including the formidable Senator Benjamin R. Tillman of South Carolina.

The attack on the amendment, however earnest, was relatively brief, and then the proponents of the measure had their turn. Senator Money, a Democratic member of Platt's sub-committee with an independent voting record, spoke for the amendment with limited enthusiasm. Money defended most of the provisions as necessary and proper: the limitation of Cuba's treaty-making and debt-contracting powers, as well as the grant of naval stations, were necessary insurance against the risk of foreign intervention in Cuba. But he did not like the form of the right of intervention in Article Three, and admitted that it seemed to impair Cuban independence. Nevertheless, he felt it preferable to the alternative of leaving the army in control of Cuba for another year. The main thing was to get the troops out of Cuba, Money said, and though he himself was paired, he advised his fellow Senators to vote for the bill: "I could not get all I wanted; the gentlemen on the other side could not get all they wanted; and we met each other in a spirit of concession. . . ."[38]

The surprise of the debate came from Senator George Hoar of

Massachusetts, a leading anti-imperialist, who found the amendment "eminently wise and satisfactory" and gave it his unqualified endorsement.[39] Senator Teller also spoke for the measure, although he disliked Article Three, and regretted that something better could not have been achieved.[40] But according to his biographer, Teller had not intended much more than local self-government for Cuba anyway, and was not seriously disappointed with the outcome.[41]

Considering the importance of the issue, the Senate debate on the Platt Amendment was relatively short, partly because the session was in its closing days and every one was hurrying to get through. The final vote came on February 27, when the amendment was carried unchanged in a strict party vote. All forty-three yeas came from Republicans, while of the twenty nays, seventeen were cast by Democrats and Populists, and the remaining three by Republicans. Senator Foraker, who had opposed the bill, voted for it in the end, while Senator Teller, who spoke in its favor, voted against it.[42]

In the House, with its greater discipline, the amendment was allowed only cursory discussion. The administration majority voted on March 1 to consider the appropriation bill and the Senate amendments to it in gross, and allowed only two hours debate for the whole. At the end of the allotted time the Platt Amendment was adopted with the rest of the bill, by a vote of 161 to 137, again divided along party lines.[43] On the following day, March 2, the whole was signed by President McKinley and became law.

In spite of the solidarity of the Democratic vote against the Platt Amendment, the Democrats were widely charged with having made only token resistance rather than a real fight on the issue. The *New York Tribune* declared that Senate Democrats had been "soothed into acquiescence" by a generous River and Harbor Bill and other special appropriations. Of the $50,000,000 to be appropriated for rivers and harbors, over half was to go to the South and West. In addition, Congress had voted $5,000,000 of Federal money to aid the forthcoming St. Louis Fair, and incidentally to please Missouri's influential Senator Francis M. Cockrell, the *Tribune* claimed, while Senator Tillman's native South Carolina got funds in support of the Charleston Exposition and money for public construction elsewhere.[44] According to one *Tribune* story, Senator William Allen of Nebraska had received a telegram from William Jennings Bryan urging him to rally the Senate Democrats for an all-out battle, even at the risk of losing the River and Harbor Bill. Allen duly made the attempt, the *Tribune* said, but Democratic leaders, especially Tillman and Cockrell, refused to make the fight.[45]

Even this, however, does not explain the support given the Platt Amendment by such firm anti-imperialists as Senator Hoar, or the limited opposition presented by men like Foraker. The real explanation seems rather to lie in a general recognition that the amendment represented a true compromise. It promised to give the Cubans real internal self-government and at least the semblance of independence, to end the dangers and vexations of United States rule, and at the same time to safeguard American interests in the island as thoroughly as anyone could reasonably desire. Besides, no one could find an alternative that had any reasonable chance of acceptance in both Cuba and the United States; the Platt Amendment seemed to represent at once the least that the McKinley administration was willing to take, and the most that Cuba could be expected to give.

In the opinion of Senator Platt, it was also the most that Congress could be expected to give. "Personally," he wrote a few months later, "I was in favor of very much more stringent measures requiring much more as to our future relations, but in legislation you have got to consider the preponderance of public sentiment." A harsher settlement would not only have aroused even more Cuban resistance, but it would have created "a party in the United States and in Congress giving aid and comfort to the Cuban radicals." As matters stood, the United States had gotten enough concessions to preserve a sufficiently effective position in Cuba. "It is easy to say that we ought to insist on more," Platt concluded, but "it was impossible to pass through Congress anything more than we did."[46]

Cuba Reluctantly
Accepts the Platt Amendment

In Havana Leonard Wood had anxiously attempted to estimate in advance the Cuban reaction to Congress' action. Just before he transmitted the Platt Amendment to the Cuban constitutional convention, he informed Root that the "intelligent classes" were satisfied, and predicted that there would be no serious popular excitement in Cuba over the amendment. However, he suggested moving in a naval squadron from Florida as a safety measure, and admitted uncertainty as to the probable action of the convention. "Extreme element has used every effort to induce Convention to dissolve and go home," he cabled. "If this is done we have in any case the complete constitution."[1]

On receiving this message, Root wrote his subordinate another letter of instructions. The members of the convention, he told Wood, should understand that "they cannot escape their responsibility by a refusal to act," in which case the American authorities would simply convene another convention. Whatever they did, there was absolutely no possibility of the Cubans maneuvering free of their dilemma. "Under the act of Congress they never can have any further government in Cuba, except the intervening Government of the United States, until they have acted." Root showed impatience at Wood's statement that "we have in any case the complete constitution"; it could not go into effect, he insisted, until the question of relations had been settled. The American people were solidly behind the Platt Amendment, and the Cubans should realize it. If they accepted it gracefully they would create "a sense of kindliness" in the United States, but opposition would create bad feeling and make it more difficult to get tariff concessions in the future.[2]

In spite of Root's threats and Wood's cautious optimism, the news of the Platt Amendment aroused a storm of excitement in Cuba. Havana was in turmoil on the night of March 2. A torchlight procession delivered a petition of protest to Wood at the Governor's Palace, and another crowd of demonstrators sought out the convention delegates and urged them to stand firm in their opposition to the American demands. Similar demonstrations occurred on the following night.[3] Outside the capital, municipal governments throughout the island poured out a flood of protest messages and resolutions, while public meetings were epidemic. On the night of March 5 speakers told a procession in Santiago that if the United States held to its demands, the Cubans must go to war once more.[4]

In many ways the situation appeared similar to the crisis of the previous December, but in his dispatches to Washington Wood maintained a tone of determined optimism. He described the Havana torchlight procession of March 2 as composed of "about three thousand persons in line, two thousand boys following" and its temper as "most friendly."[5] The Governor played down the importance of such popular protests: "The people of Cuba lend themselves readily to all sorts of demonstrations and parades, and little significance should be attached to them."[6] On March 8 he reported "everything quiet throughout island," and two weeks later was cabling, "tranquillity island complete."[7]

But in spite of his simulated calm, the Governor was obviously worried about the Cuban reaction. On March 4, he recommended to Root that the convention be adjourned temporarily, and the delegates return home. This would give them a chance to think things over away from the pressure of the Havana crowds. The attitude of the convention in declining to recommend the desired relations, Wood thought, was due largely to outside influences. Especially pernicious to Wood were some American agitators who, he reported, had assured the delegates before the passage of the

Platt Amendment that the American Congress would not support the President's demands. Wood charged that one result of this advice had been the convention's own version of "relations," adopted on February 27, which had been hurried through in order to head off the Platt Amendment by disagreeing with it in advance.[8] Some members of the convention still thought that if they rejected the amendment Congress would call a special session to reconsider it. As the days passed, Wood grew increasingly doubtful of the intentions of the delegates. On March 6 he had been confident that they would accept the Platt Amendment; on the 20th, he cabled Root: "Can you indicate our action in case Convention should refuse to accept Platt Amendment?"[9]

Most of the articles of the amendment were objectionable to the Cubans, but the most unpalatable of all was Article Three, which provided for the right of intervention by the United States. The "radicals" in the convention maintained that this clause destroyed Cuba's independence in advance by making it possible for the United States to meddle at will in her internal affairs. But Root insisted that Article Three gave the United States "no right which she does not already possess and which she would not exercise." It did not imply ordinary and habitual meddling in Cuban affairs, he wrote Wood late in March; the contemplated intervention would be exercised only if absolutely necessary, and for such major causes as "actual failure or imminent danger" in Cuban government.[10] Wood replied with a request that Root embody such an assurance in a formal statement which he could show to the Cubans.[11] The Secretary of War cabled the desired statement on April 2. He authorized Wood to say officially that, in the view of the President, intervention was "not synonymous with the intermeddling or interference with the affairs of the Cuban government," but meant only the formal action of the United States to preserve Cuban independence or to maintain the protection of life, liberty, and property in Cuba.[12]

Whatever the delegates thought of this statement, it had no visible effect on the Cuban press and public. The Havana press especially made increasingly violent attacks upon the Platt Amendment, which reached their climax in a famous cartoon printed on the front page of *La Discusión* on Good Friday, 1901. The cartoon, entitled "The Cuban Calvary," showed a figure representing "the Cuban people" crucified between two thieves, who bore the faces of Leonard Wood and William McKinley. To complete the allusion, Senator Orville Platt (the cartoonist mistakenly showed Senator Thomas Platt of New York) stood by in the guise of a Roman soldier, holding a spear on the point of which was impaled a sponge labelled "Platt Amendment." When Wood saw this cartoon, he had both the editor and the cartoonist arrested immediately, but thought better of it and ordered them released the following day.[13]

By this time the strain of the situation was telling on Cubans and Americans alike. "The nervous members of the Convention are becoming thin," Wood wrote; "old friendships are broken up and the groups are rearranging themselves constantly." The General added, with a touch of sympathy, that "they have been lied to so systematically for generations that one can in a way understand their condition." Nevertheless, he kept pressure on the delegates to accept the amendment. Senators Cockrell of Missouri and Redfield Proctor of Vermont visited Cuba in this period, and told the Cubans, at Wood's urging, that they would get harsher terms from the next Congress than they had from the present one. The Platt Amendment was the most favorable settlement possible, the Senators said, and the Cubans were jeopardizing it by their delay.[14]

On April 11, the American press reported that the Cuban convention was debating the merits of sending a commission to Washington to explore the meaning of the controversial clauses of the Platt Amendment.[15] A few days later Wood wrote Root that the commission had actually been appointed, and that its president, Domingo Méndez Capote, wanted advance assurance that it would be received in Washington. Wood strongly urged Root to receive the group. "Purpose of this visit is in reality to accept Platt Amendment," he cabled. He had been told as much by the members of the commission, but "everything depends upon this being unknown." The "apparent purpose" of the commission's trip would be to seek information on disputed points. "Information received will remove doubts and the amendment will be accepted." Wood concluded that "this is Latin method but we are after results."[16]

With the way thus cleared for them, the Cuban commission

arrived in Washington on April 24 accompanied by General Wood, and spent the next three days conferring with government leaders. Most of the work was done at two afternoon conferences with Root, where the Platt Amendment was systematically explored.

According to the Cubans' report, Root began the talks by presenting the case for the American right of intervention. The United States, he declared, did not want to intervene in Cuba and hoped it would never have to. Nevertheless, its right to do so was implicit in the Monroe Doctrine, of which Article Three was merely an explicit extension. While the Monroe Doctrine was not recognized in international law, the Platt Amendment would be, and thus European nations would have no choice but to recognize the American right of intervention in Cuba. If, therefore, the United States were ever forced to intervene for the protection of Cuban independence, no foreign power could take it amiss. The real purpose of Article Three, Root insisted, was not to give the United States any new rights, but to avoid international disputes in exercising the powers she already possessed. The Secretary of War went on to assure the Cubans that the naval stations desired by the United States were to be used only for military defense of both countries, and had no role in internal Cuban affairs.

When Root had finished, Méndez Capote turned the discussion in a different direction, insisting on the urgent need for tariff reciprocity between Cuba and the United States. Root explained once more that reciprocity would have to await the establishment of a Cuban government competent to enter into a reciprocity treaty. He assured the Cubans, however, in McKinley's name as well as his own, that the President would move to negotiate such a treaty as soon as a Cuban government had been established. This promise closed the first afternoon's discussion.[17]

The next day's talks covered much the same ground, and featured further assurances by Root on the subject of Article Three. The most impressive of these was a letter written at Root's request by Senator Platt, who disclaimed any idea of using the right of intervention to establish a United States protectorate over Cuba. Platt declared that the amendment was "carefully worded with the purpose of avoiding any possible thought" that it involved any interference with the real independence of Cuba. For himself, "it seems impossible that such an interpretation can be given to the clause."[18]

As on the previous day, the Cubans appeared most interested in the subject of tariff concessions. In the face of their continued insistence, Root conceded at least the possibility that the Cuban tariff might be modified at once, by authority of the military government, and he promised to see what could be done. The question of the United States tariff, however, would still have to await independence. With this the Cubans had to be content.[19] The behavior of the Cubans throughout their visit indicated that one of their main objectives in coming to Washington was to secure the promise of tariff concessions in return for their approval of the Platt Amendment. In this they were successful, securing commitments from both the President and his Secretary of War.

With the return of the delegates to Cuba, both sides settled down to a several weeks' war of nerves during which the pro-administration forces carried on vigorous propaganda in favor of the Platt Amendment. Senator Albert J. Beveridge of Indiana, a leading expansionist spokesman, wrote an article for the *North American Review* in which he reduced the American case to its barest essentials. It was simply unreasonable, the Senator said, to assume that the Teller Resolution meant the unconditional abandonment of Cuba by the United States. But if this *was* the meaning of the resolution, the only thing to do was to call it a mistake and forget about it. The United States could neither ignore its own interests in Cuba, nor allow the Cubans to drift into the state of revolution, tyranny, and anarchy which Beveridge considered normal to Latin American republics.[20]

Senator Platt himself wrote a magazine article at this time, defending his policy in somewhat more diplomatic terms than Beveridge had used. But he charged that the Cuban constitutional convention had failed to do its duty, making it necessary for Congress to show it what was required by means of the Platt Amendment. After repeating most of the same reassurances and explanations which Root had given the Cubans, Platt attempted the knotty task of reconciling the Platt Amendment with the Teller Resolution. The key to his argument was the interpretation of "pacification." In the Teller Resolution, the United States disclaimed control of Cuba "except for the pacification thereof." But "pacification," said the resourceful senator, was a long-term process, and must be considered very broadly. So considered, the Platt Amendment was a *part* of the pacification of Cuba, and thus in perfect harmony with the Teller Resolution. Any contrary interpretation of the resolution led to an absurdity: "That we should assert in the same sentence our right and duty to put an end to abhorrent conditions in the island of Cuba, and also abandon our right to insist upon stability and peace thereafter, is inconceivable." Furthermore, Platt declared that the amendment made Cuba more independent rather than less, since under it Cuban independence was guaranteed by the United States. "Cuba needs a real not a paper independence, and this the United States alone can assure her."[21]

In Cuba the political discussion of the Platt Amendment was accompanied by considerable backstage maneuvering. The Cuban political picture was much confused by the equivocal positions taken by two of the principal leaders, Máximo Gómez and Tomás Estrada Palma. Gómez, to Cubans the very embodiment of the revolution, had been quoted by the American press in February as saying that if the Americans left the island, the Cubans would be fighting among themselves within two months. According to these reports, Gómez said that he did not wish to be president, and that the country was in no condition to be handed over to the Cubans for self-government.[22] When this story appeared in print, the old general indignantly denied it in writing. But Wood cabled Root: "No importance should be attached to Gómez's letter which he assures me personally is simply to retain his hold on the radical element." In March, during the crisis over the Platt Amendment, Gómez told Wood that "his word of honor is given that there will be no trouble in this country whatever comes."[23]

Actually, Wood reported, Gómez came to see him on February 26, and urged that the United States military government should remain in control of Cuba for the present. Gómez intended that Tomás Estrada Palma should be president when the Cuban government was formed, while he and the army would make Estrada Palma's administration strong and stable. But it would take eighteen months or two years to prepare for this properly, Gómez thought, and in the meantime, the United States should stay in control. Wood gleefully estimated that Gómez and Estrada Palma "swing ten times the influence of the Convention."[24]

Tomás Estrada Palma, whom Gómez wished to make President of Cuba, had spent the revolutionary years in the United States as Foreign Delegate of the Cuban Republic. Before 1895 he had maintained a school for the sons of wealthy Cubans at Central Valley, New York. In 1899 he resigned his office and moved back to Central Valley, where he remained as a private citizen during the period of the American occupation. In spite of his long absence from Cuba, Estrada Palma retained great political influence there, and he became the first President of the Cuban Republic in 1902.

During the debate over the Platt Amendment, Estrada Palma stated his position in a letter to Gonzalo de Quesada, who had worked closely with him in the United States and was then a delegate in the Cuban constitutional convention. While he deplored the dictatorial tone of the amendment, he advised Quesada strongly against rejecting it. The United States, he said, had a right to some guarantee of order in Cuba. He himself had told American political leaders, before the passage of the War Resolutions, that United States intervention in the Cuban Revolution would give them a base from which to insure future internal peace there. In his opinion, the Platt Amendment was a fair compromise of United States and Cuban interests.[25]

The fact is that Estrada Palma hoped eventually to see the annexation of Cuba to the United States. He wished this to happen only after Cuba had gained its independence, however, and as the result of a free choice by the Cuban people.[26] Given this point of view, the importance of the Platt Amendment was considerably decreased, and Estrada Palma's acceptance of it becomes understandable. Whether or not Gómez shared the hope for annexation, the attitude of Gómez and Estrada Palma at this time greatly weakened the Cuban nationalists, since it deprived them of the leadership and prestige of the two most important surviving revolutionary leaders.

A complicating factor on the American side was the bitter opposition raised against the Platt Amendment by the small but vocal anti-imperialist press. Leonard Wood regarded these American newspapers as one of the chief sources of his troubles. "The persistent misrepresentations of papers like the New York *Evening Post* and even the *New York Herald*," he told Root, were to blame for the lingering Cuban belief that the next American Congress would repudiate the Platt Amendment if the Cubans refused to accept it.[27]

It was the *Evening Post* in particular which drew Wood's wrath. This newspaper had been edited for a generation by the vitriolic and anti-expansionist E. L. Godkin, and while Godkin had retired at the end of 1899, his influence shaped the course of his successor, Oswald Garrison Villard. Ever since the issue of Cuban-American relations had broken into the open, the *Evening Post* had hammered at the administration's policy in almost daily editorials and news stories. The *Post* editorials early took the position that the government was breaking the pledge contained in the Teller Resolution. One of them stated the problem of the imperialist as follows: "Given a solemn and unmistakeable promise of independence to Cuba, how can I lie out of it and still go to church to thank God that I am not as other men are?"[28] With biting satire, the *Post* declared that "the Army Bill is just the place for an Amendment embodying the demands of the United States upon Cuba, as they are an assertion of stark force." And it charged: "if there is bloodshed in Cuba, the guilt of it will stain the hands of the men who have consented to sign away our fair fame as a truth-loving and honorable people."[29] Finally, the *Post* openly accused McKinley's government of working for Cuban annexation, toward which the Platt Amendment was to be only the first step.[30]

The *Evening Post*'s Cuban correspondent also kept up a steady fire of criticism and ridicule aimed at Leonard Wood. In story after story Wood was pictured as inept, dictatorial, and blundering. One typical story declared that Wood was a failure as a diplomat and an executive, and had made his reputation in Cuba by taking the credit for the work of other men.[31]

Such attacks stretched Wood's temper to the breaking point, and led him increasingly to blame his troubles on their authors. "This political situation is largely due to papers like the *Evening*

Post," he wrote Theodore Roosevelt.[32] Roosevelt, to whom Wood had complained at length about the *Post,* wrote furiously that "the Villards, the Godkins and their like are simply unhung traitors, and are liars, slanderers and scandal mongers to boot."[33] But nothing could silence the offending newspaper, which continued to be the most effective critic of the government's actions in Cuba.

Nothing definite was heard from the Cuban convention until mid-May, when Domingo Méndez Capote came to Wood with a proposition. He could get the convention to adopt the Platt Amendment by a large majority, Méndez Capote said, if Articles Three and Seven could be slightly re-worded. In Méndez Capote's version, Article Three would grant the United States the right to intervene in Cuba to avert a threat from without, or, in case of internal anarchy, to re-establish orderly government "in accordance with the Constitution of the Republic of Cuba." Article Seven would grant the United States naval stations in Cuba "on such conditions that they will only serve the military or naval purposes to which they should be applied." Wood thought these propositions acceptable, and cabled Root for instructions.[34]

The Secretary of War reacted with characteristic caution. While he saw little to object to specifically in the new Cuban proposals, he feared lest any loosening in the original terms should provide the Cubans new room for maneuvering. "I think it would be better for the Convention to use the exact words of the Platt Amendment and add their construction," he told Wood, "rather than to substitute their construction for the words of the law."[35] Wood relayed this decision to the convention, which plunged into new deliberations.

Nine days later the convention's Committee on Relations presented another formula to the delegates. They proposed an appendix to the constitution which should contain not only "the exact words of the Platt Amendment" as Root demanded, but the text of the Teller Resolution and of the Treaty of Paris, as well as long extracts from Root's various explanations and assurances concerning the Platt Amendment. Proclaiming that the quoted "declarations and assertions made by the Secretary of War of the United States constitute an authoritative interpretation of the so-called Platt Amendment," the committee finished by adding further stipulations of its own as to the meaning of the amendment, and suggesting that the negotiations for naval stations should be joined with those on tariff reciprocity.[36]

The New York *Evening Post,* to whom the news had been leaked in advance, reported in high glee that this time the Cubans had "left Secretary Root looking uncommonly foolish": "All his private assurances to the delegates who went to Washington, all his labored explanations of the intent of the Platt Amendment, they have incorporated in the majority report and propose to make a part of the binding agreement between Cuba and the United States!"[37]

On May 28, the convention adopted the proposed appendix to the constitution by a vote of 15 to 14, and Wood reported that its action had "produced a general feeling of relief."[38] This satisfaction was short-lived, however, for Root immediately cabled Wood that he did not regard the form in which the convention had adopted the Platt Amendment as one which would authorize the withdrawal of the army. In a subsequent letter, the Secretary of War complained that "the acceptance of the Platt amendment is surrounded by such a cloud of words, by way of recitals and explanations, that it is difficult to tell what the real meaning is." Furthermore, Root charged, the use of statements made by him in private conversations was an impropriety, and some of the "explanations," particularly the mention of reciprocity negotiations, actually changed the meaning of the amendment.[39]

The Cubans were again stalemated by Root's determination. The rejection of this latest proposal, Wood said, caused "considerable excitement" in Havana, and he deplored the inability of the Cubans to appreciate that "no one can interpret the scope of the Platt amendment except Congress."[40] But the Cubans were at last convinced that there was no way out. Root had succeeded in convincing them that a refusal to accept the American demands simply insured the continuation of the American occupation. After staving off the inevitable for two weeks more, the delegates adopted the Platt Amendment without modification on June 12, by a vote of 16 to 11, with 4 not voting.[41]

Four months later, Wood wrote a private last word on the subject of Cuban relations: "There is, of course, little or no independence left Cuba under the Platt Amendment."[42]

15

The Drive for Cuban Reforms

With the end of the crisis over the Platt Amendment, Leonard Wood and his military government were free to resume their systematic efforts to change Cuba internally through a general program of reforms. This reforming zeal, evident throughout the entire period of the occupation, produced many results of permanent importance for Cuba. Beginning modestly with General Brooke's programs for sanitation and rehabilitation, the drive for internal change reached its peak under General Wood, who placed great faith in the ability of the American authorities to make over the island in a few years. When he replaced Brooke as military governor, Wood was already determined to teach the Cubans new ways; his principal criticisms of his predecessor were that Brooke had allowed the Cubans too free a hand in running their own affairs, and that the former regime had been much too cautious in instituting basic reforms. A few months after taking office, the new governor wrote McKinley that "we are dealing with a race that has steadily been going down for a hundred years and into which we have got to infuse new life, new principles and new methods of doing things."[1] It proved harder to fulfill this ambitious design than Wood had anticipated. His efforts to do so brought both solid achievement and sharp controversy, some of which has not yet ended.

The first and most basic of Wood's reform programs was the

establishment of an adequate public school system. That which had existed under Spanish rule had had serious shortcomings. The pupils were taught, not in schools, but in the homes of the teachers, who could provide only the scantiest books and equipment. Learning was largely by rote, and the principal textbook was the catechism. The teachers, whose appointment by the government tended to be made on political grounds, eked out their meager salaries by charging the pupils fees, a practice which excluded the children of the poorer classes. This so-called "system" could accommodate barely a tenth of the school-age children of Cuba, and was a major reason for the 66 per cent adult illiteracy revealed by the census of 1899. In December of 1899, only 21,000 children were enrolled in schools, and even fewer actually attended.[2]

General Brooke had made a first step toward attacking this problem in the closing weeks of his rule, when he published a basic school law and appointed a superintendent of schools. The latter, Alexis E. Frye, was Brooke's chief bequest to Wood on the school problem. Frye was a Harvard graduate of independent means, who had applied to Root for a commission to do educational work in the former Spanish possessions. Impressed with his evident zeal, Root sent him to Brooke in Cuba, along with a letter advising Brooke to include him in any educational program which the military government might undertake there.[3] Frye had just begun his new duties when Wood became governor.

Working without pay, the new superintendent of schools attacked his job with the energy of a fanatic. In the first three months of 1900, he established 2600 new schools in Cuba, with a paper enrollment of over 125,000 children. Abandoned buildings, old Spanish army barracks, warehouses, and former homes were pressed into service as schoolhouses. Wood made available the funds to buy school supplies and furniture for 100,000 pupils, and began the construction of permanent school buildings.[4]

In spite of these impressive achievements, friction soon developed between Wood and Frye. Frye's enthusiasm often ran away with him, and dozens of hastily organized schools were set up in the early days of the program and then left without materials, guidance, or proper teachers. In March of 1900, Wood called a temporary halt to the founding of new schools until it was possible to put those already established on a firmer footing, and to secure qualified teachers and adequate supplies. This offended the impetuous Frye, and from then on his relations with the iron-handed governor were stormy.[5] The causes of their differences proliferated, Wood eventually charging the educator with spreading "the most intense radicalism as to the future relations between Cuba and the United States."[6] In a reorganization of the school administration, Lieutenant Matthew E. Hanna of Wood's staff emerged in the newly created post of commissioner of public schools, a position to which the superintendent of schools was made subordinate. By-passed and outranked, Frye finished out the year in his job, but resigned in January, 1901.

From the start the military government modelled its Cuban school system closely upon that of the United States. Wood replaced Brooke's school law with one written by Hanna, and based on the laws of the state of Ohio. The new school equipment was bought in the United States. Textbooks were obtained simply by translating existing American texts into Spanish, with no attempt to make them relevant to the experience of Cuban children.[7] There was even talk in the United States of manning the new schools with American teachers, but Wood refused to consider this. Pointing out the folly of flooding the island with "American teachers ignorant of the language and customs of the people, and foreign in religion and sentiment," the governor added that "such a course of action would have led at once to the charge that we were trying to Americanize the children."[8]

Instead, it was the teachers who were to be "Americanized." In the summer of 1900, Harvard University raised enough money through voluntary contributions to bring nearly 1300 Cuban teachers to Cambridge for a summer's instruction in American teaching methods. The following year similar summer sessions were organized at several places in Cuba, while selected groups were again sent to the United States. Shortly before the end of the occupation, Lieutenant Hanna negotiated a long-term contract with a New York normal school providing for the training in the United States of thirty Cuban teachers a year. After the occupation ended, however, the new Cuban Republic declined to carry out this contract, and it became a dead letter.

By the end of 1901 free public education was a reality in Cuba. With an average daily attendance of 140,000 pupils, the school system reached most children, though by no means all of them. Furthermore, the moribund University of Havana had been rejuvenated, and the island's private schools up-graded through a system of government inspection.[9] Of all the programs of the American military government, it was probably this educational effort which was received with the greatest enthusiasm by the Cubans themselves, which they most readily understood, and to which they gave the most active cooperation.

Along with the new schools, Wood gave top priority to an overhaul of the Cuban judicial system. Cuban justice had long since developed a luxuriant bureaucracy and a dizzying intricacy of procedure which made difficult, if not impossible, the efficient dispensing of justice. At each of the endless steps which constituted a legal case, the payment of a fee was necessary, and lawsuits tended to become financial endurance contests in which the wealthier litigant simply outlasted his opponent.

Starting with the premise that "the law is excellent, the procedure alone is bad," Wood undertook measures to clean up and speed up the administration of justice. A board of prison pardons examined the inmates of the prisons and released many who had never come to trial or had already been over-punished. A permanent system of prison inspection inaugurated an attack on the shocking conditions found in many of the penal institutions. A system of police courts was established throughout Cuba to give quick summary judgment in minor cases, and thus clear off the press of work which had choked the old courts almost to a standstill. A new law defined the crime of perjury, and provided for its punishment. Penniless defendants were provided with legal counsel at public expense. There was a large-scale removal of inefficient or untrustworthy judges, in an attempt to raise both the level of the Cuban bench and the Cuban public's opinion of it. The courts themselves were overhauled, and court employees put on fixed salaries rather than being supported by the pernicious fee system.[10]

If the legal reforms had stopped at this, the opposition to them would have been limited largely to that which sprang from the natural conservatism of the legal profession, and from the vested interest which some of its members had in the old system. But American attempts to graft Anglo-Saxon legal concepts onto an alien tradition of Roman law at first confused the Cubans, and finally created a strong hostility within much of the Cuban bar.

The most important of the transplants were the jury system and the writ of *habeas corpus*. The former was a failure from the first. A unique fruit of the English common law, it was a mystery even to Cuban lawyers. Wood's own Secretary of Justice explained to his superior that he thought it would be better to select paid lawyers "to assist the judge" than to leave it to laymen selected at random.[11] As for the public, Wood's biographer writes, "they declared frankly that they were not going to act as judges to convict their friends, and generally let them off."[12] Root admitted the failure of the experiment late in 1901, when he reported that the functioning of the jury system was still unsatisfactory.[13]

The introduction of the writ of *habeas corpus* also met resistance. A somewhat parallel writ had already existed under Spanish law, but the Spanish version was merely an appeal to the courts and contained no certainty of action. The American military judge advocate proposed the adoption of *habeas corpus* as early as Brooke's regime, but Brooke's Secretary of Justice declared flatly that such a writ was not adapted to Spanish law. The advent of Wood brought a new Cuban secretary, whose attempt to draft a decree for the use of *habeas corpus* failed to provide for the actual delivery of the body of the prisoner, but was again merely an appeal, subject to proceedings and delays. The final decree was not issued until October, 1900, and then had to be written by the American legal authorities in order to get the desired result.[14]

"Nothing more idiotic can be imagined," Wood had written in 1899, "than the attempt to establish a liberal government under Spanish laws."[15] The difficulty was that the Cubans knew and understood Spanish law, and regarded it as a part of their heritage.

Another of the Wood reforms overhauled the system of local government, the basic unit of which was the municipality. Here the military governor undertook a two-fold campaign to reduce the number and diversity of the municipalities, while at the same time tightening up their extremely casual administrative procedures and accounting practices. Of the 138 municipalities which existed in 1899, 56 had been abolished by the end of the occupation, while the haphazard aggregation of large and small units had been standardized into more uniform administrative divisions, each containing at least 12,000 people. Wood reduced the number and pay of the municipal officials, made them responsible for their finances, and steadily reduced their dependence on the central government for revenue.

The military government held its first municipal elections in June, 1900. The new elected officials tended to be less tractable than the former appointed ones had been, and there soon appeared a good deal of friction between municipal and central authorities. The problem of local finances became a particularly sore point, as Wood drastically cut grants to municipalities from the central treasury, while at the same time abolishing the local consumption taxes which had provided much of the municipal revenues. When some cities ran their budgets into the red, Wood instituted a central inspection system and carried on a running battle with the mayor and councils of Havana, Santiago, Cienfuegos, and other of the larger towns, which was not yet resolved when the occupation ended.[16]

The difficulties of Wood's municipal reform program were due in part to a wide divergence in the views of Cubans and Americans as to what municipal government should properly be. In the Cuban system, the municipalities were simply the lowest level in an integrated unitary government. They had traditionally been directly subject to the central authority and largely dependent upon it. Thus the American ideal of independent local self-government fell in Cuba on an alien soil. In the eyes of one commentator, "The basic weakness ... lay in the attempt to engraft the Anglo-Saxon principle of local self-government on an Iberian system to which it was wholly foreign. It is doubtful whether in the brief period allowed for experimentation and development such a radical change was wise."[17]

During the year 1901 the governor obtained the settlement of the troubled church-land question inherited from the Spanish regime by the American military government. In the course of the nineteenth century, the Spanish government had assumed control of large amounts of Cuban property owned by the Roman Catholic Church, and had taken over many *censos,* or land mortgages, which the church held. The church, in turn, maintained for many years a legal effort to recover its property. In time a *modus vivendi* was reached, under which, in return for its sequestered lands, the church in Cuba received large annual payments from the Spanish government. The American military government, when it assumed power, had not continued these payments, but it still held the assets turned over to it by Spain, including those which formerly belonged to the church. When the church protested and demanded compensation for its property, the military government gave jurisdiction in the matter to two special Cuban commissions, one for each of the two bishoprics into which Cuba was divided. In due time these commissions found that the church had valid claims. The whole affair presented a knotty problem, however. The precise extent of the church's claims had long been in dispute, and furthermore the settlement of this dispute required an excursion into the thorny field of church-state relations which might stir up passions in the United States as well as in Cuba.

Working through his Cuban negotiators, Wood eventually reached agreement with the church authorities. The church would again receive its rents, at an agreed rate. But in return, the church gave to the future Republic of Cuba an option which allowed it to buy up all the property in question at a price of just over $2,000,000. At the same time the military government, itself paying the church almost $1,000,000 took up the *censos* at fifty cents on the dollar, and gave them to the debtors at the same price. Since the Roman Catholic Church was one of the largest landlords and money-lenders in Cuba, this settlement eased the situation of a large group of rural tenants and debtors, and made new land available for purchase in the future.[18]

Perhaps the most successful of all the military government's programs was its attack on tropical diseases. Brooke had placed great emphasis on the sanitation of the island, and this had somewhat improved health conditions. But one of the worst killers, yellow fever, had been little affected by the sanitation campaign, though it was commonly supposed at the time to be a filth-generated disease. In 1901 a Yellow Fever Commission came to Cuba under the authority of the Surgeon General of the Army. This group, whose mission was to discover the causes of yellow fever, was headed by Major Walter Reed of the Army, and included both Cuban and American doctors. The commission soon centered its attention on the theories of a Cuban doctor, Carlos Finlay, who believed that the yellow fever organisms were transmitted by a type of mosquito common to the area. After an exhaustive series of tests, Finlay's theory was found to be correct. At last it was possible to take the proper precautions against the dread disease, a discovery which Wood called "worth the cost of the war," and large areas of the world became safer to live in as a result.[19]

The conquest of yellow fever, the brightest chapter in the history of the American occupation of Cuba, must properly be credited to the joint efforts of the medical profession of Cuba and the Surgeon General's Bureau of the United States Army. General Wood played a praiseworthy, if secondary, role in the achievement. His own medical training enabled him to see the importance of the work of the yellow fever commission, and he gave it consistent and generous support.

Besides the actions already described, the American military government in Cuba built roads, dredged harbors, strung telegraph wires, paved streets, and installed sewers, and in general carried on a comprehensive program of public works. In all of these varied activities, the American military government of Cuba secured lasting benefits for the island, while Leonard Wood revealed impressive administrative ability, and worked for reforms which were in many cases sorely needed. Yet there is another side to this reform program, which helps to explain both its nature and its limitations. Wood worked in Cuba with a dual purpose: to improve the condition of the island, and at the same time to prepare it for union with the United States. Back in 1899, Wood's plan to enlist Cuban regiments into the army of occupation had the avowed object of Americanizing Cuban youth. The plan was never adopted, but its object, the Americanization of Cuba, remained one of the governor's basic goals, and is visible in the background of many of his reforms.

As a result, the new ways urged on the Cubans by the American authorities were at times insufficiently rooted in the Cubans' own customs and traditions. It was of course natural that, sur-

"I wish the Americans would get out."
—*The St. Paul Pioneer Press*
Reprinted in *Literary Digest,* April 20, 1901.

rounded with problems, the Americans should seize on solutions which were familiar to them, whether or not they harmonized with local customs. Furthermore, Wood and most of his contemporaries shared a boundless faith in the superiority and universality of American institutions. They tended to forget that the strength of such institutions grew from their foundation in local conditions, traditions, and experience, an advantage that disappeared with their transplantation to a new area. Finally, Wood's methods were essentially autocratic, and stressed compulsion rather than persuasion in pushing Cuba along the new course.

It was always a source of sorrow to Wood that it was so hard to impose the desired changes on the Cubans, and that they never shared his passion to change their ways. "There has been as a rule little public spirit displayed by the citizens of the different municipalities," Wood wrote in his official report for 1900. "There have been very few instances of organization by the citizens with the purpose of local improvements."[20] In private correspondence he was equally disappointed in the Cubans. "You saw, while you were here, that whatever is done has got to be done largely under American direction," he wrote Root.[21] To McKinley he reported that "the great mass of public opinion is perfectly inert," and that "it is hard to get them out of old ruts and old grooves."[22] In instituting reforms, the occupation was successful; in Americanizing the Cubans, it was not.[23]

16

American Economic Policy Toward Cuba

While the Platt Amendment defined the basic shape of future Cuban-American relations, it by no means represented the total United States policy toward Cuba. The occupation also created a well-defined body of economic policy, which dealt with both the internal economy of Cuba and with her external economic relations with the United States. Internally, the military government under General Wood fostered the fuller development of the island through American investment and enterprise. Externally, the long-awaited program of tariff reciprocity would play a vital economic role with major political implications.

Leonard Wood and Elihu Root were eager to improve the economic condition of Cuba for obvious reasons of expediency, and because of an undoubted interest in the welfare of the Cubans. But they had another reason as well. As Wood wrote to Root in the autumn of 1901, "we shall sometime own or at least must always control the destinies of Cuba." Wood himself had not lost faith in the inevitability of Cuba's ultimate annexation. In spite of the Platt Amendment, he concluded that, "All Americans and all Cubans who look ahead know that the Island is going to be part of the United States and it is as much to our interest as it is to theirs to place the Island upon its feet."[1]

But this was easier said than done. The economic situation in Cuba was unhealthy during the occupation. The recovery from the

189

war years was necessarily slow. In addition, the agricultural rehabilitation program, so much discussed during 1899, was not implemented, although Wood's regime did take a few steps toward agricultural relief. In 1900 the Governor had $100,000 worth of work cattle bought in Mexico, and resold at cost to small farmers in some of the hardest hit Cuban districts. In the same year the military government distributed some simple agricultural implements to the poor.[2] But beyond these small-scale beginnings, Wood did little for the direct aid of agriculture. He explicitly rejected Wilson's plan of extending small government loans to needy farmers. "There has been considerable thoughtless talk in Cuba about making loans to aid agriculturalists," the Governor reported in 1902. "It is not believed that any such policy is either wise or desirable." The real cause of the credit shortage, he argued, was the uncertainty of finding profitable markets for Cuban crops, and the answer was not government loans, but tariff reciprocity with the United States.[3]

In the meantime, Cuban agriculture was left to make the best of the situation. Tasker Bliss reported in 1900 that "the economic situation of Cuba ... can not be regarded as favorable." There was a very large unfavorable balance of trade, Bliss explained, while current production of two of Cuba's principal crops, sugar and cattle, was still only a fraction of the prewar norms.[4]

Perfecto Lacoste, the Secretary of Agriculture, Commerce, and Industry, came close to an open attack on Wood's attitude in an official report written in the spring of 1901. He declared that Cuban planters had tried repeatedly to get the government to help them in their struggle to rebuild, but "though it is true that something has been accomplished in the way of reconstruction, it is due exclusively to the personal efforts of the planters." Lacoste complained that there was not a single credit institution in Cuba to fill the needs of the planters, and concluded that "up to the present time nothing has ever been done toward the improvement of our agricultural situation" by the military government.[5]

But Leonard Wood saw relief in another direction than government paternalism. He had placed his hope for external aid in tariff reciprocity with the United States; internally, salvation was to come from American investment and development. Shortly after becoming Governor, Wood defined a stable government in Cuba as one under which money could be borrowed at a reasonable rate of interest, and capital was willing to invest in the island.[6] He told Senator Aldrich early in 1901 that as long as he worked under such handicaps as the Foraker Law, "which prohibits all enterprises of any magnitude being carried through on a secure footing, you can readily see the production of prosperity, tranquillity and happiness is not the easiest task in the world."[7] Wood soon regarded the Foraker Amendment as a major obstacle to progress, writing Root that it "must be revoked if possible," because it kept money out of the country and made investors uncertain.[8]

In Wood's opinion, the most pressing need for American development lay in the Cuban railroad system. In 1899 this covered the western end of the island with a fairly adequate network of tracks, but the larger part of Cuba, everything east of the city of Santa Clara, contained only a scattering of short and disconnected lines. The other forms of internal transportation were rudimentary; the roads were wretched at best, and in the rainy season became little better than rivers of mud. The cost of taking bulk crops to market overland from eastern Cuba was prohibitive. Early in 1900, however, there appeared the prospect that the eastern half of the island might get its own railroad net.

Sir William Van Horne, the famous railroad-builder, had recently retired from the presidency of the Canadian Pacific Railroad. In February of 1900, he began a vacation in Cuba in the company of an American businessman, George B. Hopkins. The trip was purely for pleasure, but as the two men travelled about the island they were struck by the bad service and high fares of the existing railroads, and the need for a line in eastern Cuba. They soon conceived the idea of forming a company to build a railroad from Santa Clara, where the western roads ended, to Santiago. From this "spinal" road, short branches would reach to the ports on the north coast. When the two left Cuba they headed for New York, where Van Horne caught the interest of such prominent business figures as James J. Hill, General G. M. Dodge, Thomas Fortune Ryan, and Levi P. Morton. The result was the formation, under a New Jersey charter, of the Cuba Company to carry out the project.[9]

The promoters lost no time in seeking backing in Washington. Van Horne, who was a business associate of Russell Alger, the ex-Secretary of War, in a Canadian wood-pulp enterprise,[10] made overtures to Elihu Root through General Dodge. Hopkins, who knew Senator Spooner of Wisconsin, wrote him a letter which described the company's prospects in glowing terms. The proposed railroad would open up a rich new country, Hopkins said, and create a lucrative traffic within a few years. It would also greatly increase American influence in Cuba, and stimulate further American investment there. "Commercial interests now and must always favor annexation," Hopkins told Spooner. After a few years of favorable conditions in Cuba, "commercial interests will have become so powerful that they can dictate and will dictate the final policy of the whole people."[11]

Within a few months, the Cuba Company's energetic managers had begun the surveys for their railroad, and were busily acquiring right-of-way property. They were immediately faced, however, with a serious legal obstacle. Since the Foraker Amendment forbade the military government to grant concessions or franchises of any kind, the new railroad could not get the necessary governmental authority to bridge rivers, cross public roads, and the like. Senator Platt made plans to secure the modification of the Foraker Amendment by Congress, but he had to abandon the attempt in the face of the uproar caused by the Cuban postal scandals of 1900.[12] General Wood was a strong partisan of the Cuba Company from the first, and he appealed to Elihu Root for a solution to the problem, as did General Dodge. After some thought, Root hit on the device of issuing revocable permits to the company for the necessary intrusions on the public domain, and trusting to the Cubans to accept the completed railroad as a *fait accompli* after independence. In addition, Wood was authorized to use the power of eminent domain to condemn lands for the railroad.[13]

Thinking it wise to forestall possible trouble with Congress, Wood wrote Senator Foraker late in 1900, asking if the Senator would object to the construction of the railroad under the revocable permits. While tactfully praising the past good effects of the Foraker Amendment in preventing the exploitation of Cuba, Wood nevertheless insisted that the Van Horne railroad was necessary to

Cuba's development, and suggested that the time had come for the repeal of the troublesome law.[14] Foraker readily agreed to the revocable permits, but refused to allow his resolution to be repealed. The Cuba Company would have to take its chances, Foraker said, on getting a regular franchise when the independent government was set up.[15] This was good enough for the Van Horne group, and work went ahead rapidly. The new railroad began to carry traffic in December, 1902. For the first time in Cuban history, there existed effective land communication between Santiago and the West, and bulk crops could go economically to market from the interior of the eastern provinces.[16]

In the closing months of the occupation, Wood turned his attention to the established railroads. At the end of the war, most of the Cuban roads had been bought up by British investors at bargain prices. The new owners charged what Wood regarded as excessively high rates, and he was eager to increase the profits of the hard-pressed planters by cutting their freight costs. After getting permission from both Root and McKinley, the Governor named a railroad commission to make a study of rates, and on January 3, 1902, he published a schedule of maximum freight rates on sugar.[17] This schedule was only temporary, pending the completion of a permanent railroad law. Such a law was later drawn up in accordance with the advice of, among others, Sir William Van Horne and General G. M. Dodge, the builders of the new competing line.[18]

Wood intended his railroad program both to help the Cuban planters and to further American investment. His Civil Report for 1900 had contained an open bid for the latter, painting Cuba as the new land of opportunity. "I can not imagine a better country for young men with moderate capital," the Governor declared. "The island, under a stable government, has wonderful possibilities."[19]

The other half of Wood's recovery program, tariff reciprocity, had implications which went far beyond the interests of the Cuban planters. General Wilson had made the future economic relationship between the United States and Cuba fundamental to his planning, and had early predicted that the establishment of powerful economic ties would produce more certain results than could be obtained by a purely political policy. Elihu Root had echoed Wilson's call for tariff reciprocity between the United States and Cuba in his annual report for 1899. In this report, Root concluded that the Cuban economy was at the mercy of the American sugar market, and expressed his faith that the United States would "deal generously" with Cuba when the time came to make permanent tariff arrangements.[20]

The Cubans had pushed hard for tariff concessions throughout the negotiations over the Platt Amendment. As a result the McKinley administration, including the President himself, had firmly committed itself to work for reciprocity with Cuba if the Cubans accepted the amendment. Thus reciprocity had been a consideration in the government's Cuban policy almost from first to last, figuring both as a binding force to tie Cuba more tightly to the United States, and as an inducement to reconcile the Cubans to the American policy.

General Wood, an early convert to the cause of reciprocity, gave expression to both of these motives in the opening months of 1901. He wrote to Theodore Roosevelt: "Trade relations will shortly draw the two countries together and place them not only upon a footing of commercial friendship and confidence, but, I believe, also upon a political one."[21] And he advised Senator Nelson Aldrich of Rhode Island that, if the United States wanted to "hold" the Cubans, it "must show them that the protection of the United States carries with it some practical benefits," the most obvious of which would be large American tariff concessions.[22]

With the acceptance of the Platt Amendment by the Cuban constitutional convention and the imminent independence of Cuba, Root and Wood prepared to carry through the reciprocity arrangements which they had so long urged in America and promised in Cuba. This was a formidable task, for reciprocity could be implemented only through the favorable action of a Congress dominated by Republican protectionists. The situation called for a carefully planned campaign, which Leonard Wood opened in the autumn of 1901. His first move was to send circular letters to the mayors of all Cuban municipalities and the entire membership of the Cuban judiciary, asking the recipient to determine the views of the people of his area on the reduction of United States import duties on sugar and tobacco, and to forward a summary of them to the Military Governor.[23]

Cuban planters were still feeling the effects of the loss of capital which they had suffered during the war years, and their troubles were compounded by a steady decline in the world price of sugar. This combination of circumstances made the economic future look black, and planters and workers alike had pinned their hopes of salvation on securing a preferential position in the American market. As he had intended, Wood's circular letters gave the signal for a deluge of messages, not only from mayors and judges, but from planters' and merchants' organizations, political parties, and private citizens, all pleading for a reduction of United States tariffs on Cuban products.

Though varying in content, these missives agreed on essentials. A petition of the General Society of Merchants and Business Men of Cuba dramatically described the economic crisis facing Cuba, declared that only swift relief could save the situation, and appealed for tariff concessions in the name of economic survival.[24] Another approach was that of a Matanzas judge, who said bluntly that, having made a dependency of Cuba through the Platt Amendment, the United States had thereby assumed the duty of seeing that the Cubans maintained a civilized standard of living.[25] But whatever arguments they used, the Cubans were unanimous in calling for reciprocity. During September and October, Wood diligently forwarded all of these appeals to Washington, very content with the impressive display of Cuban opinion which he had evoked. The beginning of Wood's publicity campaign nearly coincided with a much larger event which threw everything into momentary confusion. On September 14, 1901, President William McKinley died from the effects of an assassin's bullet, after a week of apparent recovery from the wound. Although a cautious and noncommittal leader, McKinley had had a powerful influence with Congress and great perseverance in getting what he wanted. During his last year of life, the President had let Root handle the Cuban situation with little interference, and had committed himself to the whole Root program, reciprocity included.

McKinley's successor, Theodore Roosevelt, was cool toward tariff reciprocity in principle, particularly in any form that would expose American farmers to foreign competition. "I wish that Cuba grew steel and glass," he wrote, "as I should much rather see us reduce duties on these than on agricultural products." But the new President was as firmly committed as McKinley to the Cuban policies of Root and Wood, and he regarded tariff concessions to the Cubans as falling into a special category in which the action was justified by the unusual factors present.[26]

If there were any doubts about where he stood, Roosevelt removed them in his first annual message to Congress, written less than three months after he assumed the Presidency. In the case of Cuba, he told Congress, there were "weighty reasons of morality and national interest" for granting tariff reciprocity. Cuba had consented to occupy a unique position in regard to the United States, and now the United States was "bound by every consideration of honor and expediency" to guard the Cubans' material well-being.[27] Roosevelt stated his position with characteristic vigor; the real question was whether he would show McKinley's skill in handling Congress.

The unexpected change of presidents did not long interrupt the War Department's campaign for Cuban reciprocity. In November, Wood sent to Washington a delegation of nine prominent Cubans, whose mission was to urge reciprocity on Congress and the public. This group addressed a series of petitions to President Roosevelt and the President of the Senate, asking for a mutual reduction in import duties of 50 per cent on all Cuban-American trade.[28] At the end of November, Root issued his annual report, which contained a strongly worded argument for Cuban reciprocity.[29] Wood's report for 1901, which followed in a few days, called for a 50 per cent reduction in the duties on Cuban sugar.[30] Wood also put Tasker Bliss, the head of the Cuban Customs Service, to work drawing up a draft for a reciprocity bill which would embody the concessions that the Cubans most needed.[31]

Thus, in the space of a single week, the President, the Secretary of War, and the Military Governor of Cuba all called for Cuban reciprocity in the most solemn official utterances. A vigorous propaganda campaign already emanated from Cuba. Now a new ally appeared in a group of Americans who had a large financial interest in the Cuban sugar industry. The chief spokesman for this group was Edwin F. Atkins of Boston, himself perhaps the largest single owner of Cuban sugar properties, and chairman of the Associated American Interests in Cuba. In an article which appeared in the December, 1901, *North American Review,* Atkins used an impressive array of statistics to draw a dark picture of the plight of the Cuban sugar industry. The material interests of Cuba, he said, were largely in the hands of foreigners—Spaniards, Americans, Englishmen, and Germans—who owned directly, or indirectly through mortgages, about three-fourths of the value of all Cuban property. Since these people would have no vote or direct representation in the Cuban government, Atkins declared, the United States was morally obligated to see that their interests were protected. In addition, the failure of Cuba's sugar trade would cripple her government revenues and thus wreck the program of internal reconstruction which the Americans had begun. Worse yet, a really bad depression would imperil the political stability of the island.[32]

All these warnings and exhortations, however, failed to impress the bitterest enemies of Cuban reciprocity, those who grew sugar in the United States. The beet sugar industry especially wielded great political influence, and was inflexibly opposed to encouraging Cuban competition. The beet growers could claim with some justice that the federal government itself had encouraged them to grow sugar beets, and thus had a responsibility toward their well-being. The American sugar beet industry had begun on a large scale in 1897, when the United States Department of Agriculture began a program of importing European beet seeds and sending them free to farmers. Besides distributing the seeds, the Department publicized the merits of the new crop and supplied information about its cultivation. The industry caught on quickly in large areas of the upper Midwest, the Rocky Mountain region, and the Pacific Coast, where the most efficient growers soon made handsome profits. While beet sugar was still an infant industry in 1902, it had already attracted substantial investments, and had caught the imagination of thousands of American farmers.[33]

The House Ways and Means Committee began hearings January 15, 1902, on the administration's proposed bill for Cuban reciprocity. The hearings, which lasted two weeks, gave a clear indication of the powerful opposition the bill would face. Witnesses favoring reciprocity included Edwin F. Atkins, Colonel Tasker Bliss, and representatives of the Cuban Sugar Planters' Association, the United States Export Association, the National Sugar Refining Company, and several New York importer's groups. Opposition to reciprocity was led by H. T. Oxnard, president of the American Beet Sugar Association, and included spokesmen for the American Cane Growers' Association, the Hawaiian Sugar Planters' Association, and other beet and cane producers' groups, the League of American Producers, and several bodies representing the American tobacco industry.[34]

Although the testimony of the witnesses ranged over a wide area, both sides concentrated their emphasis on a few main points. The proponents of reciprocity argued that the United States had assumed a moral commitment to work for the welfare of the Cubans, that economic prosperity was a condition necessary to order and stability in Cuba, and that Cuban reciprocity would insure a greatly enlarged market in Cuba for American exports. They denied that reciprocity would harm American sugar growers, who produced only a fraction of the national needs and who would retain their priority in the home market.

The opponents of reciprocity argued that American farmers needed protection from cheap tropical competition. They said that reciprocity would, at the very least, curtail the expansion of domestic beet sugar growing, which if encouraged would mean prosperity for a large segment of American agriculture. These witnesses complained that the entire cost of Cuban reciprocity would be borne by the American sugar and tobacco industries, and declared that any government relief program for Cuba should be financed out of general taxation rather than by impoverishing a few selected interests. Their most telling point, however, was the charge that the American "refining trust" had already bought up existing Cuban sugar supplies, and that reciprocity was really a scheme to bring the refiners cheap raw materials and huge profits, without really improving the position of the Cuban planter who had lost control of his product. If they could convince the public that reciprocity was for the benefit, not of the Cuban people, but of an American monopoly, their fight was as good as won.[35] One of

Wood's principal tasks in the following months was to gather evidence to contradict this claim.

While the House hearings were under way, Wood sent Root an alarming forecast of the future: "The economic situation here has become serious. I am besieged from morning to night with delegations from all over the Island, and I fear that if we do not get a reasonable reduction of sugar, we shall find it embarrassing to get out of here, as the chaotic business condition, accompanied by a lack of employment, might result in such a condition of affairs as to render our presence here desirable." A tariff cut of 25 per cent should be the absolute minimum, Wood said, and he announced his intention to send a new commission of Cuban planters to Washington in time to testify in the hearings.[36]

The Military Governor took other measures as well. In January he began sending letters to the prominent members of both Houses of Congress, pleading the case for tariff concessions to Cuba. Several congressmen complained to the President that these circular letters represented an improper exercise of influence on the actions of Congress by the executive branch. Root soon called a halt to them, and Wood conceded that "possibly I may have carried the war a little too actively into the enemies' country."[37]

By March it appeared to Root in Washington that the reciprocity bill might well be rejected by Congress. He wrote Wood:

A really serious fight is going on in Congress over the question of making any concessions whatever to Cuba. The Oxnard [beet sugar] lobby has succeeded in creating the impression that it is an attempt to take protection away from the American farmer, who is represented as being on the eve of making an everlasting fortune by raising beets, and that this would be done for the real benefit of the sugar trust, which would simply pocket the amount of the duty without giving any increase of price to the Cuban producer.

The beet sugar people, Root said, claimed to have enough votes in Congress to control the Republican caucus, and thus prevent the reciprocity bill from being reported out. The Secretary of War had no illusions about his program's chances of success. "You will perceive," he concluded, "that the question is not when the thing will be done, but whether it will be done at all."[38]

On March 19 Sereno E. Payne, Congressman from New York and Chairman of the House Committee on Ways and Means, introduced in the House of Representatives a bill providing for tariff reciprocity with Cuba. The Payne bill offered a 20 per cent reduction of import duties on the products of Cuba, providing the Cubans agreed to grant a similar concession to the United States. It was referred to Payne's committee, which reported it out favorably on March 31.[39]

The terms of the Payne bill met considerable public criticism on the ground of being too niggardly. A large segment of the press, representing both political parties, expressed disappointment that the bill offered the Cubans a tariff reduction of only 20 per cent, and several editors suggested that 33 ⅓ per cent would have been fairer.[40] On the other hand, it was only in the face of strong opposition in the Republican caucus that the bill was reported out at all. The opposition Republicans favored an alternate plan by which, rather than cutting the tariff on Cuban sugar, the United States would rebate annually to Cuba 20 per cent of the total duty paid on Cuban sugar.[41]

The House passed the Payne bill on April 18, but only after adding an amendment which abolished the existing high tariff on refined sugar, making the duty the same on raw and refined sugars. This amendment, aimed at the refiners, was the work of a coalition of beet sugar congressmen and anti-trust Democrats. If left in the bill, the amendment would force refiners and protectionists in general to oppose Cuban reciprocity, for it exposed a domestic manufacture to foreign competition. If it were taken out, the Democrats would be convinced that the bill was designed to benefit "the interests" and would vote against it. In either case, the beet sugar interest would gain strong allies in the Senate.[42]

The Senate Committee on Relations with Cuba held hearings on the Payne bill from May 1 to June 16, and finally agreed upon a modified version known as the Platt bill, which embodied further concessions to the opposition. The Platt bill specified that the proposed reduction in tariffs between Cuba and the United States should expire in five years, and that during that time the President of the United States should have the power to terminate the agreement at will if he found evidence that it benefited American refiners rather than Cuban producers. There was no mention, however, of removing the tariff differential in favor of domestically refined sugar.

But the Platt bill was never reported out. A Republican caucus on the measure showed nineteen Republican senators determined to vote against it. Some of these came from beet sugar areas like Michigan, the mountain states, and the far West, while others were opposed in principle to any breach in the nation's tariff walls. The thirty-three Senate Democrats were also opposed to the bill. A few of them represented sugar-growing areas of the South and West; many saw a chance to strike at the hated "monopoly power" which the party had challenged in the last election campaign; and most of them enjoyed discomfiting the hopelessly divided Republicans. The result was a clear majority against the bill, and the Senate Republican leaders reluctantly abandoned hope for it.[43]

At this point President Roosevelt took a hand in the proceedings. On June 13 he sent a special message to Congress, renewing his plea for favorable action on Cuban reciprocity. After repeating his previous arguments in the strongest terms, Roosevelt went on to imply that the United States was going to take an increased interest in the Caribbean area, and must be prepared to pay the price of increasing her influence there.[44] Such interference from the executive branch was promptly attacked by Senator Teller, who now appeared in the role of champion of the Western beet sugar growers. Teller charged that the administration was hand in glove with the refining interests, and struck a damaging blow when an investigation he had sponsored revealed that Wood had used Cuban funds to pay a lobbyist who was simultaneously working for the American Sugar Refining Company. On June 16 Teller introduced a resolution of inquiry, demanding to know how much money the military government of Cuba had spent to promote the reciprocity bill. The resolution was adopted, and Wood eventually admitted having spent $15,626 to send his Cuban commissioners to Washington and for other purposes connected with the bill.[45]

These skirmishes occupied the rest of the session, which adjourned on July 1, 1902. The President's message had no effect on the "beet Republicans," and the reciprocity bill died in committee. The defeat had been complete and crushing; Republican protec-

"Free to do what?"

—*Detroit News*
Reprinted in *Literary Digest,* February 1, 1902.

tionists had apparently wrecked the economic side of the government's Cuban policy.

As if to emphasize the finality of the defeat, on the day before adjournment Senator Stephen B. Elkins of West Virginia called up a resolution which he had introduced earlier, authorizing the admission of Cuba as a state of the union upon her own voluntary application. Although he denied the connection, Elkins clearly believed that the defeat of reciprocity would force Cuba to seek annexation to the United States in order to avoid commercial ruin, and he had opposed the reciprocity bill with that object in mind.[46]

Neither Roosevelt nor Root, however, was ready to give up the fight. During the summer of 1902, Roosevelt had Secretary of State John Hay polish up Bliss's proposed reciprocity treaty and submit it to the new Cuban minister in Washington, Gonzalo de Quesada. The American occupation of Cuba had ended on May 20, 1902, when the Cubans assumed their own government under President Tomás Estrada Palma. The independent government was slow to act on the United States proposal, but finally submitted a counter-proposal on October 28, after which Bliss went to Havana as the American negotiator.

The United States offered Cuba a 20 per cent tariff reduction similar to that which had just been rejected by the Senate, in return for concessions from the Cubans ranging from 20 per cent on most items to 25, 30, and 40 per cent on certain selected categories. Both countries could change their tariff rates at will, with the exception that neither could impose future duties on items currently on the free list. But, whatever the rates, each would give the other an exclusive rate below that scheduled for general use against the rest of the world, and each would have a favored position in the other's markets.

The Cubans were not entirely happy with this proposed agreement. They had hoped for a much larger concession than 20 per cent, and they objected to giving larger concessions in return on the stipulated special categories. Finally, they refused to give any concession whatever on United States tobacco, which competed with their own second largest crop. The last point was the only one which they carried, however, as Bliss refused either to raise the American concessions above 20 per cent, or to lower all the Cuban concessions to that figure. The treaty was signed at Havana on December 11, and Roosevelt submitted it to the Senate on December 17, 1902.[47]

The Senate reached no decision on the Cuban reciprocity treaty during the regular session, which ended on March 4, 1903. But the embattled President, determined to make the reluctant Senators declare themselves one way or the other, called a special session of Congress with the express purpose of considering the Cuban treaty, as well as a canal treaty which had been negotiated with Colombia.[48]

Between the spring of 1902 and the spring of 1903, there had been significant changes in the status of the Cuban reciprocity issue. In March of 1902, the European powers met at Brussels and agreed to end the prevailing system of supporting beet sugar production through the payment of government export bounties.[49] This agreement would not go into effect until September of 1903, but its implications became clearer as time went on, especially in

Cuba. Without the artificial stimulation of the bounties, European beet sugar production could be expected to decline drastically. There was hope that the chronic world over-production of sugar would soon be eased, leading to better prices for the remaining producers. To the more optimistic Cubans, dazzling opportunities brightened the future. Perhaps Great Britain would want a reciprocity treaty, if the United States did not. Perhaps it would be better to avoid any reciprocity arrangement at all which would tie Cuban sugar to one market, and await the possibilities offered by selling dear and buying cheap.

While these golden opportunities were highly conjectural, it was clear that the Cubans had suddenly acquired more economic bargaining power. Cuban sugar had been almost entirely dependent on the American market; now other buyers might appear. During the time that Roosevelt was negotiating his reciprocity treaty, the realization grew in America that its Cuban trade was no longer a fixed prerogative. Manufacturers and exporters knew that the Cubans could be expected to buy where they sold. To the hope that reciprocity might bring an increased Cuban market for American exports had been added a well-grounded fear that the rejection of reciprocity might bring the loss of the existing Cuban market.[50]

The administration, too, had new grounds for anxiety. For one thing, the President feared that Cuba might develop close economic ties with another nation, thereby lessening the influence of the United States. For another, the Cubans showed a tendency to link together the tariff issue and the current negotiations for the cession of naval stations to the United States, making the fulfillment of their own commitment contingent on that of the promises of the administration for tariff relief.[51]

Perhaps most important of all, the American Beet Sugar Association had suddenly dropped its opposition to Cuban reciprocity. The reason for this startling reversal soon leaked out: the sugar beet interests had been bought off by the American Sugar Refining Company, popularly known as the "sugar trust." Determined to secure cheap Cuban sugar, the "sugar trust" had invested heavily in leading beet sugar concerns in the course of the year 1902, thus solidifying all American sugar interests behind its leadership. The "beet Republicans" who had defeated the previous reciprocity bill now found themselves in an embarrassing position. The Michigan delegation in the House of Representatives, which had voted unanimously against reciprocity in the previous session, fell into indignant dissension. Representative Washington Gardner eventually told a laughing House that he and his colleagues had been "sold out," while Joseph W. Fordney asserted that "Mr. Oxnard . . . had sold the factories to the sugar trust."[52]

These new considerations gave the Senate pause. After a week's delay, it recommended the ratification of the Cuban reciprocity treaty on March 13, but with the provision that the treaty must be approved by both Houses of Congress. Since the Senate also made some minor modifications in the treaty, it was necessary to send it back to Havana for re-ratification by the Cubans. Having thus provided itself with ample time to observe how the wind blew, Congress adjourned for the summer.[53]

Roosevelt reconvened Congress on November 9, 1903, calling upon it, in another special message, to approve ratification of the reciprocity treaty.[54] This time the administration forces had the advantage, although opposition to reciprocity was still formidable and the President now feared "that vicious body, the American Protective Tariff League."[55] Threatened with the loss of foreign markets, Eastern Republicans swung into line in favor of the treaty, while Western sugar interests no longer posed a threat. Sereno Payne set the keynote for the new appeal in a speech before the House on November 16. The United States was not getting the trade from Cuba that it had under the reciprocity agreement of 1891–94, Payne said, and now was the time to remedy the situation. Let Cuba become prosperous; let American capital go down and develop the island; establish a preferential tariff agreement; and American businessmen would reap a rich reward. The Cubans would multiply their material demands and their buying capacity, and they would look to the United States to supply their increased needs.

"Under such improved conditions what shall be the future of our imports into Cuba?" Payne asked rhetorically. The answer was calculated to electrify his listeners. The annual exports to Cuba need not be a mere $60,000,000, as in 1902, the orator predicted, nor even $100,000,00, as in the best years before the war. Instead, he quoted Tasker Bliss in prophesying American sales to Cuba of no less than $300,000,000 a year in the near future, if only a tariff agreement were made. "Why, there are millions in this bill to the farmers and manufacturers of the United States," Payne cried triumphantly.[56]

The House of Representatives passed the reciprocity bill on November 19 by an overwhelming majority. The Senate, which began its discussion of the bill on December 7, also voted strongly for reciprocity on December 16. The collapse of the beet sugar lobby, added to the combined pressure of the President, the aroused manufacturers, and those who all along had felt a moral duty toward the Cubans, was enough to carry the day. Even the Democrats were swept with the tide, as half of them voted with the majority.[57]

Although it required a bitter two-year struggle between Congress and the executive branch to achieve it, the Cuban reciprocity treaty was to represent a permanent feature of Cuban-American relations. It never fulfilled the hopes of the exporters; sales of American goods in Cuba grew steadily, but in the long run, not spectacularly.[58] In political terms, however, reciprocity proved to be all that the policymakers had expected of it. By tying Cuba's principal export crop to the American market, and by keeping the marketing conditions subject to its control, the United States government gained an influence in Cuba more enduring than that based on the terms of the Platt Amendment.

Conclusion

On May 20, 1902, the old Governor's Palace at Havana witnessed a ceremony in many ways similar to that which had opened the occupation more than three years before. General Wood stood with his staff in the same big, bare room, along with a number of foreign officers from warships in the harbor. Tomás, Estrada Palma, the newly elected President of Cuba, headed a large group of dignitaries which included the new Cuban Congress and representatives of the insular judiciary. Outside, United States troops again drew up in the Plaza de Armas, while huge crowds jammed the streets of the city. At the stroke of noon, Wood began reading the words that transferred sovereignty to the Cuban Republic, and on flagstaffs about the city the American flag fluttered down.

The United States military government of Cuba had come to an end. For Leonard Wood, there remained only the summing-up: "The work called for and accomplished [he wrote] was the building up of a Republic, by Anglo-Saxons, in a Latin country . . . in short, the establishment, in a little over three years, in a Latin military colony, in one of the most unhealthy countries in the world, of a Republic modelled closely upon the lines of our great Republic."[1]

Thus the Cuban intervention ended, as it had begun, in disagreement about its purposes. To Wood the real object of the intervention was the annexation of the island, if not immediately, then gradually through Americanization and close economic ties. To William McKinley the intervention had seemed necessary to prevent a chronic condition of disorder and destruction in Cuba which was injurious to important American interests. And to many Americans the purpose of the Cuban adventure had been the humanitarian one of ending suffering, anarchy, and death in a closely neighboring area.

This ambiguity of purpose had been largely resolved in fact, if not in theory, by the settlement embodied in the Platt Amendment and the Reciprocity Treaty of 1902. This was done, however, only at the cost of disavowing some earlier national commitments. The Platt Amendment, which imposed controls on Cuba, was quite clearly inconsistent with the Teller Amendment, which renounced such controls. But the Teller Amendment soon seemed inconsistent with almost any rational purpose the United States might have in Cuba. It directly forbade annexation. It also forbade the exercise of future control over Cuba. But if the United States was to end the Cuban chaos for either economic or humanitarian reasons, it could do so only by excercising some control over what happened there. The wording of the War Resolutions had implied that Cuba's ills stemmed solely from Spanish misrule and could be ended simply by the expulsion of Spanish authority, but this assumption was rapidly undermined by growing doubts of the Cubans' ability to rule their island properly after the Spanish had left it. At any rate, to go to war for the purpose of changing the Cuban situation, and at the same time to renounce all influence over that situation, did not appear to be a rational proceeding to the policy-makers of the administration.

The Teller Amendment, and the sentiments which produced it, nevertheless had a beneficial effect: they restrained the headlong annexationists from forcing any conclusive action until the nature of the situation could emerge clearly. When it did so, the administration could see that there were significant limitations on its freedom of action in Cuba. The first of these was that already imposed by the altruistic and idealistic thinking of many Americans. This element proved too strong to be openly flouted without a degree of political embarrassment. American leaders had also to consider the attitude of the Cubans themselves. The late revolution against

Spain was sufficient proof that the Cuban people were capable of a formidable protest when aroused. The Philippine Insurrection served to remind the nation that such revolts were all too possible It also introduced another political factor. The unhappy events in the Philippines had greatly depleted the reservoir of tolerance in America for colonial setbacks. Both the McKinley administration and its opponents believed that an insurrection in Cuba, coming on top of the Philippine Insurrection, would threaten the Republican expansionist program with political bankruptcy. This factor gained immediacy from the need to make some of the basic decisions about Cuba just prior to the presidential election of 1900.

The delay imposed by circumstances, and the limitations of action which this delay revealed, resulted in the step by step formation of a Cuban policy based on a growing knowledge and experience, rather than an uninformed a priori decision like that which led to the annexation of the Philippines.

It should be kept in mind, however, that the views of the Cuban situation held by even the best-informed Americans were strongly colored by the racism which was rampant at the time throughout the western world. The chief figures of national politics and of the occupation were no more immune from such influences than were the mass of Americans. The imperialists among them argued that the peoples of the former Spanish empire were inherently incapable of stable self-government, and that it was therefore a national duty to extend good government to them. The anti-imperialists argued that such peoples could not make worthy citizens of the United States, and thus should not be assimilated at all. The real point is that both sides assumed the innate inferiority of tropical peoples, while drawing opposite conclusions from the assumption.[2]

This added weight to the already grave doubts about the Cubans' ability for self-government. General Wilson revealed a good deal in trying to calm the fears of his fellow countrymen: "When it is remembered that the whites are to the colored in Cuba as two to one, while in the Philippines they are not more than one to fifty, the political and sociological inferiority of the Filipinos will be apparent to all."[3] In his attempts to reassure Americans about Cuba, Wilson repeatedly declared that white domination was as solidly established in Cuba as in the southern United States.

The prevalent racism, moreover, was not directed solely at nonwhites, but at any ethnic group beyond the Anglo-Saxon pale. White Latin-Americans were also considered inferior to Anglo-Saxons, though perhaps less so than Negroes. The New York *Evening Post* based a part of its anti-annexation propaganda on the argument that Cuba was inhabited by a "mongrel race" which was unfit to share the benefits of United States citizenship.[4] General Ludlow thought that the Cubans were "not as we. They are Latin, and belong to a dying race" which was incapable of stable self-government.[5] Leonard Wood described them as "a race that has been steadily going down for a hundred years."[6] Elihu Root declared late in life that "all of the Latin Americans have a genius for misrepresentation."[7] Theodore Roosevelt richly exhibited this larger racism. He not only expressed contempt for the Filipinos, calling them "Malay bandits" and "Chinese halfbreeds,"[8] but described the wholly white government of Colombia as "the Bogota lot of jack rabbits."[9] Such attitudes were re-inforced by the wave of anti-Catholicism which crested to a peak during the 1890's in organizations like the American Protective Association. These biases, held by both imperialists and anti-imperialists, would weigh heavily in any estimate of Cuban capabilities.

In general, it was the executive branch of the government which took the lead in creating the new Cuban policy. The War Department played by far the most significant role, with the personnel of the military occupation in the forefront, and Elihu Root making many of the pivotal decisions.

Congress also played an important part in the process, though primarily of a limiting rather than a positive nature. Not only did the legislative branch exercise an effective veto over executive policy, but from time to time it abruptly modified that policy, notably through the Teller and Foraker Resolutions. Even when Congress did nothing at all, the threat of what it might do acted as a constant brake on the actions of the executive. The executive, on its side, secured Congressional adoption of its own permanent policy through the Platt Amendment and the Reciprocity Treaty of 1902.

It is less easy to define the role of economic factors in the drama. As has been shown, important economic interests were involved at every stage of the Cuban story. When a runaway Congress finally forced President McKinley to intervene in Cuba, it was to such interests that he strove to give first priority in his thinking, though purely political considerations often intervened. The economic realities of the situation all along imposed a frame of reference within which any settlement would have to be worked out, and the final settlement embodied economic as well as political arrangements.

Why, then, does "Big Business" not loom up more commandingly from the pages of this work? Essentially, because the necessary decisions were made, not by businessmen, but by soldiers, politicians, and civil servants. If these decision-makers sought to satisfy the desires of the business community—and obviously they did—they tried even harder to satisfy the voting public. If economic interests defined many of the broad goals to be sought, political necessities forced the specific choices of method and technique which make the Cuban settlement uniquely significant. The business world had been divided, to say the least, on the question of going to war over Cuba in the first place. Such episodes as that of the Foraker Resolution, in which Congress temporarily impeded the penetration of Cuba by United States capital, indicate that even when the voice of business was reasonably united, it was not the only one heard at the seats of power. Indeed, in regard to reaching the specific terms of the final settlement, it is clear that political factors were of more immediate importance than any other. While American business interests soon got all they wanted in Cuba, they did so under a settlement shaped by many forces, prominent among which were the clash of domestic party politics and the demands of the oft-forgotten Cuban people.

The effects of the Cuban settlement were not limited to Cuba, but helped to set the stage for a new interpretation of the Monroe Doctrine as well. The Monroe Doctrine had begun life as a formal opposition by the United States to European intervention in American affairs. After 1900, it quickly metamorphosed into a justification *for* United States intervention in Latin-American affairs. The Platt Amendment played an important role in that metamorphosis, and in the accompanying shift to an interventionist policy on the part of the United States.[10]

In the first place, the invasion and occupation of Cuba was itself a precedent-setting intervention by the United States in a Latin-American country, while the Platt Amendment guaranteed to the United States a right to further interventions in Cuba if she should desire them. In exacting this right of intervention, however, Congress made little mention of the Monroe Doctrine. It is true that during the Senate debate on the Platt Amendment, Senator Hoar referred to it as "a proper and necessary stipulation for the application of the Monroe Doctrine," but this remark brought vigorous attacks from Senators Jones of Arkansas and Morgan of Alabama.

"This Monroe Doctrine never had anything to do with a proposition like this, the maintenance of a government adequate to the protection of life, property and individual liberty in any one of the American states. It has no connection with that," Morgan stated positively. Senator Hoar hedged and retreated, and there the matter rested.[11]

It was rather Senator Tillman who best illustrated the real connection between the passage of the Platt Amendment and the reshaping of the Monroe Doctrine, though Tillman never mentioned the doctrine at all. In the same debate, he referred to the recent entry of a German warship into a Dominican port to collect a citizen's claim. "Now," he said, "if Cuba is a kind of ward in chancery of the United States—and I think it is—we would not tolerate any European nation going there and undertaking to browbeat or to rob that people; but I can see a great deal of reason and justice in the contention that we are under some obligations to European powers to have Cuba not do such things to their citizens as will embroil her with them."[12]

In short, if the United States refused to allow European nations to enforce their rights in Cuba, then it must itself assume the responsibility for seeing that such rights were not violated there. The denial of European intervention thus involved a potential need for United States intervention. If a parallel line of reasoning were applied to the Monroe Doctrine, which forbade European intervention in all of Latin America, it would lead to the assumption by the United States of a potential right of intervention anywhere in the hemisphere. Neither Tillman nor the other senators drew the parallel, but it was to be given expression three years later in Theodore Roosevelt's famous corollary.

If Congress would not openly tie the Platt Amendment to the Monroe Doctrine, Elihu Root did not hesitate to do so. When the committee of the Cuban constitutional convention came to Washington to confer about the Platt Amendment, Root told them that "Clause 3 is the Monroe Doctrine, but with international force." The intervention article, he said, gave the United States no rights which she did not already possess; through the Monroe Doctrine and its applications, she had for three-quarters of a century proclaimed a right before the world to intervene in Cuba. But the doctrine, being a unilateral proclamation, was not recognized in international law, while, as an agreement between two nations, the Platt Amendment would be. "Because of it," Root claimed, "European nations will not dispute the intervention of the United States in defense of the independence of Cuba."[13] The United States, in other words, would have a clear right to intervene in Cuba in order to prevent intervention from any other source. Thus Root, starting from a different position than Congress, also bridged the gap between the idea of non-intervention in Latin America by European powers and the new policy of intervention by the United States.

That tireless expansionist, Senator Beveridge, also saw the possibilities of extending the Platt Amendment beyond Cuban soil. The amendment had not only settled the Cuban question, he wrote soon after its passage, but had also paved the way for American control of other areas: "No man can now deny that the Republic may be suzerain whenever the interests of the American people or the peace of the world may make that form of control convenient."[14]

The passage of the Platt Amendment and the discussion attendent upon it had supplied a precedent, a technique, and a rhetorical defense mechanism for a general American policy of intervention. But in 1901 the man who was to make the major formal statement of that policy had not yet espoused it. Theodore Roosevelt wrote in July: "If any South American State misbehaves towards any European country, let the European country spank it."[15]

Roosevelt, however, was essentially a man of action, and when, in 1904, he wished to act, the tool was ready to his hand. He had only to add a last ingredient, an "international police power," and to synthesize the whole in the Roosevelt Corollary. "Chronic wrong-doing," he wrote, "or an impotence which results in a general loosening of the ties of civilized society, may in America, as elsewhere, ultimately require intervention by some civilized nation, and in the western hemisphere the adherence of the United States to the Monroe Doctrine may force the United States, however reluctantly, in flagrant cases of such wrong-doing or impotence, to the exercise of an international police power."[16]

Whether or not the Platt Amendment was in any part derived from the Monroe Doctrine, it provided an example and a line of reasoning which needed only to be applied to the doctrine to produce the Roosevelt Corollary. The spirit of the times insured that the application would be made.

In its purely Cuban context, the Platt Amendment represented a middle course between altruism and annexationism. It was a realistic compromise designed to award to each side its minimum demands. The United States allowed the Cubans nationhood and internal self-government; it demanded from them special protection for its own interests in Cuba. In the years after 1902, however, the nature of this compromise was warped by a shift in the United States' interpretation of its right of intervention. Elihu Root had declared in 1901 that United States intervention under the Platt Amendment "was not synonymous with the intermeddling or interference with the affairs of the Cuban Government."[17] But as time passed, the threat of intervention was increasingly used to coerce the Cuban government, and in fact for "intermeddling" in Cuban affairs. Root, who for years watched and privately deplored the widening applications of the right of intervention, denounced the trend as a violation of the government's original intent, and denied that it was inherent in the wording of the famous Article Three.[18]

It should also be noted that the second part of the permanent settlement, the commercial tie represented by the Reciprocity Treaty of 1902, was carried through in response to the demands of the Cuban public. It is true that American policy-makers had envisaged such an agreement as a part of their own program. But they found their original support for it in Cuba, not the United States, and it was only with the greatest difficulty that Cuban reciprocity survived the early assaults of Congress. The Americans who conceived the treaty believed it to be genuinely beneficial to both parties, Cuban as well as American, and in 1902 most Cubans would probably have agreed.

The Cuban program formulated from 1898 to 1902 was to show an impressive durability in an age of rapid change. The Platt Amendment, abrogated in 1934, was the first of its elements to disappear. The other two elements, continuing Cuban-American trade agreements and the American economic penetration of Cuba, survived for a generation longer, only to fall prey to the Castro revolution. By that time the original settlement had long since become obsolete, and the program of general Caribbean expansion which it initiated had passed its zenith and moved toward liquidation. In Haiti, in the Dominican Republic, in Nicaraugua, the Marines had come and gone, while United States domination in Cuba appeared ended. But if the Cuban policy of Root and McKinley, of Wilson and Wood and Roosevelt, had had its day, that day was surely a long and full one.

Reference Matter

Notes

Chapter 1

1 The description of the transfer of government is derived from the *Civil Report of Major General John R. Brooke, Military Governor, Island of Cuba* (Washington, 1900), pp. 6–7, and the *New York Tribune,* January 2, 1899.

2 For an analysis of the Cuban economy in this period, see Ramiro Guerra y Sánchez and others, editors, *Historia de la Nación Cubana* (Havana, 1952), VII, book 4.

3 For a sugar planter's description, see Edwin F. Atkins, *Sixty Years in Cuba* (Cambridge, 1926), Chapters XII–XVIII.

4 For discussions of the Cuban Revolution from special points of view, see Atkins, *Sixty Years in Cuba;* Frederick Funston, *Memories of Two Wars* (New York, 1911); Horatio S. Rubens, *Liberty, the Story of Cuba* (New York, 1932); and Walter Millis, *The Martial Spirit* (Cambridge, 1931).

5 Ernest May, *Imperial Democracy* (New York, 1961), p. 71. See also Joseph E. Wisan, *The Cuban Crisis as Reflected in the New York Press* (New York, 1934), and Marcus M. Wilkerson, *Public Opinion and the Spanish-American War* (Baton Rouge, 1932).

6 *Congressional Record,* 54th Congress, 1st Session, XXVIII, 2256–57, 3541, 3627–28.

7 *Ibid.,* 55th Congress, 1st Session, XXX, 1186.

8 See John Basset Moore, "Cuban Belligerency," *The Forum,* XXI (May, 1896), 288–95.

9 Richard Olney to Enrique Dupuy de Lôme, April 4, 1896, *Foreign Relations of the United States, 1896* (Washington, 1897), pp. 540–44.

10 Atkins, *Sixty Years in Cuba,* pp. 208 ff.

11 *Foreign Relations of the United States, 1896,* pp. xxx–xxxvi.

12 James D. Richardson, *A Compilation of the Messages and Papers of the Presidents* (Washington, 1899), X, 126–36.

13 *Foreign Relations of the United States, 1896,* p. xxxii.

14 Woodford to McKinley, March 17, 1898, *Foreign Relations of the United States, 1898* (Washington, 1901), pp. 685–88.

15 *New York Tribune,* February 20, 27, and 28, 1897.

16 *Ibid.,* May 25, 1897; and *New York World,* May 24, 1897.

17 The Cuban silver dollar was stabilized in 1899 by the United States Military Government at $.60 United States gold. See Robert P. Porter, *Industrial Cuba* (New York, 1899), p. 196.

18 Emeterio S. Santovenia and Joaquín Llaverías, eds., *Actas de las Asambleas de Representantes y del Consejo de Gobierno Durante la Guerra de Independencia* (Havana, 1932), III, 68–70.

19 *Ibid.,* pp. 76–77.

20 *Ibid.,* p. 115.

21 *Ibid.,* p. 116; for a discussion of these contracts, see Herminio Portell Vilá, *Historia de Cuba en sus relaciones con los Estados Unidos y España* (Havana, 1939), III, 348–61.

22 *New York Journal,* March 12, 1898.

23 *Ibid.,* March 13, 1898.

24 *Ibid.,* March 18, 1898.

Chapter 2

1 For a standard account of these events, see French Ensor Chadwick, *Relations of the United States and Spain, Diplomacy* (New York, 1909), pp. 538–50.

2 See Wisan, *The Cuban Crisis . . . in the New York Press,* p. 181.

3 *New York World,* March 1, 1898.

4 New York *Evening Post,* February 25, 1898.

5 *Congressional Record,* 55th Congress, 2nd Session, XXXI, 2916–19.

6 *New York Journal,* March 22, 1898.

7 *New York Tribune,* April 10, 1898.

8 *New York Tribune,* April 6, 1898.

9 Platt to John H. Flagg, April 7, 1898, printed in Louis A. Coolidge, *An Old Fashioned Senator, Orville H. Platt* (New York, 1910), p. 278.

10 Richardson, *Messages and Papers of the Presidents,* X, 139–47.

11 Woodford to McKinley, March 30, 1898. *Foreign Relations of the United States, 1898,* p. 720.

12 Woodford to McKinley, March 18, 1898. *Ibid.,* p. 689.

13 Richardson, *Messages and Papers of the Presidents,* X, 147–50.

14 *Congressional Record,* XXXI, 3811.

15 *Ibid.*, p. 3989.
16 *Ibid.*, pp. 3988–93.
17 *New York Tribune*, April 17, 1898.
18 *Congressional Record*, XXXI, 3293, 3776.
19 *Ibid.*, pp. 3777–80.
20 *Ibid.*, p. 3948.
21 *Ibid.*, p. 3988.
22 *Ibid.*
23 *Congressional Record*, 53d Congress, 2nd Session, XXVI, 1578.
24 See Elmer Ellis, *Henry Moore Teller, Defender of the West* (Caldwell, Idaho, 1941), especially pp. 307–9.
25 Rubens, *Liberty, the Story of Cuba*, pp. 341–42.
26 *Congressional Record*, XXXI, 3684–85.
27 Secretary of the Exterior to Tomás Estrada Palma, May 12, 1898, *Actas de las Asambleas de Representantes*, IV, 61–63.
28 *Ibid.*, pp. 64–65.
29 *New York Tribune*, August 20, 1904; Manuel Luciano Díaz, *The Republic of Cuba, a brief sketch compiled for distribution at the Louisiana Purchase Exposition, Saint Louis, Mo., U.S.A.* (Department of Agriculture, Industry and Commerce, Havana, undated pamphlet), pp. 92–93.
30 *New York Tribune*, August 20, 1904.
31 Squiers to Secretary of State John Hay, September 9, 1904, and attached memorandum, Despatches from U. S. Ministers to Cuba, 1902–1906, National Archives.
32 Charles G. Dawes, *A Journal of the McKinley Years* (Chicago, 1950), p. 154; John Basset Moore to Charles E. Chapman, March 15, 1925, printed in Charles E. Chapman, *A History of the Cuban Republic* (New York, 1927), pp. 643–45.
33 *Congressional Record*, XXXI, 3842.
34 *Ibid.*, p. 4031.
35 *Ibid.*, p. 3890.
36 *Ibid.*, pp. 4017–41, 4062.
37 Reid to McKinley, April 19, 1898, printed in Royal Cortissoz, *The Life of Whitelaw Reid* (New York, 1921), II, 222–23.
38 Undated memorandum dictated by Platt, printed in Coolidge, *An Old Fashioned Senator*, pp. 281–82.

Chapter 3

1 García to Tomás Estrada Palma, June 27, 1898, printed in *Boletín del Archivo Nacional*, Havana, 1936 (Año XXXV), p. 110.

2 Admiral William T. Sampson to Secretary to the Navy, June 12, 1898. Adjutant General of the Army, *Correspondence Relating to the War With Spain* (Washington, 1902), I, 40.

3 French Ensor Chadwick, *The Relations of the United States and Spain, The Spanish-American War* (New York, 1911), II, 23–26.

4 García to Estrada Palma, June 27, 1898, *Boletín del Archivo Nacional,* 1936, pp. 108–112.

5 General Shafter to Adjutant General of the Army, June 25, 1898, *Correspondence Relating to the War With Spain,* I, 53–54; John Black Atkins, *The War In Cuba* (London, 1899), p. 108.

6 Chadwick, *The Spanish-American War,* II, 69, 75; Atkins, *The War In Cuba,* p. 114.

7 General Shafter to Adjutant General of the Army, July 4, 1898, *Correspondence Relating to the War With Spain,* I, 87; same to same, July 10, 1898, *ibid.,* p. 122.

8 General Shafter to Adjutant General of the Army, July 23, 1898, *ibid.,* pp. 174–75; Shafter to Secretary of War, July 29, 1898, *ibid.,* p. 185.

9 General Lawton to Adjutant General of the Army, August 16, 1898, *ibid.,* p. 230.

10 General Shafter to Adjutant General of the Army, August 16, 1898, *ibid.,* pp. 231–32.

11 Adjutant General of the Army to General Lawton, August 16, 1898, *ibid.,* p. 231.

12 Newspaper interview, *New York Times,* June 24, 1899.

13 Atkins, *The War In Cuba,* p. 100.

14 *New York World,* July 14, 1898.

15 See Chadwick, *The Spanish-American War,* II, 44, 69, 95; and Atkins, *The War In Cuba,* pp. 98, 289. For a Cuban view, see Miguel Varona Guerrero, *La Guerra de Independencia de Cuba, 1895–1898* (Havana, 1946), III, 1627 ff.

16 Atkins, *The War In Cuba,* p. 98.

17 *Ibid.,* pp. 288–89.

18 *New York Tribune,* December 19, 1898.

19 *New York World,* July 20, 1898.

20 *New York Tribune,* August 7, 1898.

21 *Literary Digest,* XVII (July 30, 1898), 123.

22 New York *Evening Post,* August 19, 1898.

23 *New York Tribune,* August 19, 1898.

Chapter 4

1 *Foreign Relations of the United States, 1898,* pp. 824–25.

2 Rubens, *Liberty,* pp. 380–81.

3 *Congressional Record,* 55th Congress, 2nd Session, XXXI, 3779–80.

4 For relevant correspondence between the administration and the American Peace Commissioners, see *Foreign Relations of the United States, 1898,* pp. 924–39.

5 *Ibid.,* pp. 831–40.

6 Robert P. Porter, *Life of William McKinley, Soldier, Lawyer, Statesman, with a biographical sketch of Garret A. Hobart* (Cleveland, 1896).

7 Robert P. Porter, *Report on the Commercial and Industrial Condition of the Island of Cuba* (Washington, 1898), p. 3.

8 Robert P. Porter, *Special Report on the Revenue and Customs Tariff of Cuba* (Washington, 1898), pp. 12–15.

9 Porter, *Report on Commercial and Industrial Conditions . . . of Cuba,* pp. 4–5.

10 Porter, *Special Report on Revenue and Customs tariff of Cuba,* p. 21.

11 *Ibid.,* p. 19.

12 Porter, *Industrial Cuba,* pp. 32–46.

13 Robert P. Porter, "The Future of Cuba," *North American Review,* CLXVIII, No. 509 (April, 1899), 418–23.

14 Porter, *Industrial Cuba,* p. 204.

15 *New York Tribune,* February 20, 1899; Albert G. Robinson, "Cuban Self-Government," *The Independent,* LII (December 13, 1900), 2970.

16 Secretary of the Exterior to Tomás Estrada Palma, May 12, 1898, *Actas de las Asambleas de Representantes,* IV, 61–63.

17 *Ibid.,* V. 45–46.

18 Rubens, *Liberty,* pp. 392–93.

19 *Ibid.,* p. 389; "Report of the Commission Sent to Washington, February 25, 1899," *Actas de las Asambleas de Representantes,* V, 152–54.

20 *Actas de las Asambleas de Representantes,* V, 152–53.

21 Porter, *Industrial Cuba,* pp. 204–10.

22 *Congressional Record,* 56th Congress, 2nd Session, XXXIV, 3041–42; *Actas de las Asambleas de Representantes,* V, 158–59.

23 García to Morgan, undated, *Actas de las Asambleas de Representantes,* V, 160–65.

24 *New York Tribune,* December 12 and 14, 1898.

25 *Actas de las Asambleas de Representantes,* V, 157.

26 *Foreign Relations of the United States, 1898,* pp. lxvi–lxvii.

27 *London Chronicle,* December 7, 1898.

28 *London Daily Telegraph,* December 7, 1898.

29 *London Standard,* December 7, 1898.

30 *New York Sun,* December 8 and 14, 1898; General James Harrison Wilson, *Under the Old Flag* (New York, 1912), II, 470–71.
31 See Earl S. Pomeroy, "The American Colonial Office," *Mississippi Valley Historical Review,* XXX (1944), 521–32.

Chapter 5

1 *Civil Report of General John R. Brooke,* pp. 6–7; *New York Tribune,* December 30, 1898.
2 *New York Tribune,* December 13, 14, 1898.
3 *Civil Report of General John R. Brooke,* pp. 6–7.
4 *New York Tribune,* December 30, 1898.
5 Teller to McKinley, December 30, 1898, McKinley Papers, Library of Congress.
6 *Civil Report of General John R. Brooke,* pp. 6–7.
7 *Ibid.,* p. 7.
8 McKinley to Brooke, December 22, 1898, copy in McKinley Papers, Library of Congress.
9 *Civil Report of General John R. Brooke,* p. 8.
10 Report of Pablo Desvernine, Secretary of Finance, October 1, 1899, in *Civil Report of General John R. Brooke,* pp. 232–33.
11 Report of Domingo Méndez Capote, Secretary of State and Government, September 16, 1899, in *ibid.,* pp. 174–81.
12 The original structure of the civil administration under the American Military Government is described in *Civil Report of Brigadier General Leonard Wood, Military Governor of Cuba, for the period from December 20, 1899, to December 31, 1900* (Washington, 1901), I, 3–5.
13 *Annual Reports of the Secretary of War, 1899–1903* (Washington, 1904), pp. 16–17.
14 *Ibid.,* pp. 16–17, 22; *New York Tribune,* March 9, 1899.
15 *Civil Report of General Leonard Wood . . . from December 20, 1899, to December 31, 1900,* I, 3–5.
16 Special Report of General James H. Wilson, September 7, 1899, in *Civil Report of General John R. Brooke,* I, 330.
17 *Actas de las Asambleas de Representantes,* V, 62–63; *Civil Report of General Leonard Wood . . . from December 20, 1899, to December 31, 1900,* I, 8.
18 See William Harding Carter, *The Life of Lieutenant General Chaffee* (Chicago, 1917), and Frederick Palmer, *Bliss, Peacemaker* (New York, 1934).

19 George W. Cullum, *Biographical Register of the Officers and Graduates of the U. S. Military Academy* (Boston and New York, 1891), III, 19–20; IV, *Supplement, 1890–1900* (Cambridge, 1901), 144–45.

20 *Ibid.,* II, 671–72; IV, 105.

21 See Wilson, *Under the Old Flag,* Vol. II.

22 See Hermann Hagedorn, *Leonard Wood,* Vol. I (New York, 1931).

23 New York *Evening Post,* August 16, 1898.

24 *New York Tribune,* May 28, 1899.

25 See *ibid.,* August 18 and September 17, 1899; and New York *Evening Post,* August 18, 1898.

26 Report of Estes G. Rathbone, Director General of Posts, August 28, 1899, in *Civil Report of General John R. Brooke,* p. 414.

27 Report of Colonel Tasker H. Bliss, August 1, 1899, in *ibid.,* p. 372. See also Palmer, *Bliss, Peacemaker,* Chapter VII.

28 Porter, *Industrial Cuba,* Chapter X; Charles J. Allison to William McKinley, November 30, 1898, William McKinley Papers, Library of Congress.

29 Special Report of General William Ludlow, September 15, 1899, in *Civil Report of General John R. Brooke,* p. 360.

30 Wood to McKinley, November 27, 1898, McKinley Papers, Library of Congress.

31 Special Report of General Leonard Wood, September 20, 1899, in *Civil Report of General John R. Brooke,* p. 367.

32 Special Report of General James H. Wilson, September 7, 1899, p. 19, in Records Relating to the United States Military Government of Cuba, National Archives of the United States.

33 W. G. Beal to Edwin F. Atkins, September 12, 1898, cited in Atkins, *Sixty Years in Cuba,* p. 289.

34 For an eyewitness account, see Franklin Matthews, *The New-Born Cuba* (New York, 1899), pp. 127–34.

35 The relief program is summarized in *Annual Reports of the Secretary of War, 1899–1903,* pp. 18–19.

Chapter 6

1 "Memorandum dictated by General Leonard Wood in January, 1899," copy in Elihu Root Papers, Library of Congress.

2 See Rubens, *Liberty,* pp. 382–83.

3 Chaffee to Wood, January 10, 1899, copy in Leonard Wood Papers, Library of Congress.

4 Chaffee to Wood, January 10, 1899, Leonard Wood Papers, Library of Congress.

5 *Civil Report of General John R. Brooke,* p. 6. See also Matthews, *The New-Born Cuba,* pp. 37–38.

6 *New York Tribune,* January 4, 1899; Rafael Martínez Ortiz, *Cuba, los Primeros Años de Independencia* (Havana, 1911), I, 33.

7 Máximo Gómez to the Executive Committee of the Cuban Assembly, January 6, 1899, in *Actas de las Asambleas de Representantes,* VI, 34–35.

8 Executive Committee of the Cuban Assembly to Máximo Gómez, January 11, 1899, *ibid.,* pp. 35–37.

9 "Special Report on the Commissioner's visit to General Gómez, and in relation to the payment and disbanding of the Cuban Army, by Robert P. Porter," included in Robert P. Porter, *Reports on the Commercial and Industrial Condition of Cuba* (Washington, 1899).

10 Gómez to McKinley, March 4, 1899, printed in Ramón Infiesta, *Máximo Gómez* (Havana, 1937), pp. 226–28.

11 *Civil Report of General Leonard Wood . . . from December 20, 1899, to December 31, 1900,* I, 62–65.

12 "Special Report on the Commissioner's visit to General Gómez," included in Porter, *Reports on Commercial and Industrial Condition of Cuba.*

13 *Ibid.*

14 *New York Tribune,* February 10, 1899.

15 Domingo Méndez Capote to José Miguel Gómez and others, February 14, 1899, printed in *Actas de las Asambleas de Representantes,* V, 65.

16 *New York Tribune,* February 12, 1899; Portell Vilá, *Historia de Cuba,* IV, 35.

17 Adams to Elizabeth Cameron, February 26, 1899, in Worthington C. Ford, *Letters of Henry Adams* (Boston and New York, 1938), II, 220.

18 *New York Tribune,* February 25, 1899.

19 *Civil Report of General John R. Brooke,* p. 16.

20 *Ibid.,* p. 16; *Actas de las Asambleas de Representantes,* V, 101–22.

21 *Actas de las Asambleas de Representantes,* V, 87–97.

22 Pánfilo D. Camacho, *Estrada Palma, el Gobernante Honrado* (Havana, 1938), pp. 150–51.

23 *Actas de las Asambleas de Representantes,* V, 102.

24 *Civil Report of General John R. Brooke,* p. 16; unsigned cable (copy), White House to Brooke, March 13, 1899, William McKinley Papers, Library of Congress.

25 Brooke to Alger, March 14, 1899, copy in *ibid.*

26 Brooke to Adjutant General of the Army, March 14, 1899, copy in *ibid.*
27 George Cortelyou to Russell Alger, March 15, 1899, copy in William McKinley Papers, Library of Congress.
28 Brooke to McKinley, March 17, 1899, copy in *ibid.*
29 Adjutant General of the Army to Brooke, March 17, 1899, copy in *ibid.*
30 Headquarters, Division of Cuba, to all Departmental Headquarters, March 18, 1899, Records of the United States Military Government of Cuba, National Archives of the United States.
31 Brigadier General Carpenter to Division Headquarters, March 19, 1899; Major General Ludlow to Division Headquarters, March 19, 1899; Major General Lee to Division Headquarters, March 20, 1899; Major General Bates to Division Headquarters, March 20, 1899; Brigadier General Williston to Division Headquarters, March 19, 1899; Major General Wood to Division Headquarters, March 20, 1899; Major General Wilson to Division Headquarters, March 19, 1899; copies in *ibid.*
32 *Actas de las Asambleas de Representantes,* V, 138–44.
33 *Ibid.,* p. 145.
34 *Civil Report of General John R. Brooke,* pp. 16–17; *Actas de las Asambleas de Representantes,* V, 146–47.
35 *Civil Report of General John R. Brooke,* pp. 16–17.
36 Brooke to McKinley, May 17, 1899, McKinley Papers, Library of Congress.
37 Alger to McKinley, May 17, 1899, in *ibid.*
38 Brooke to General H. C. Corbin, May 24, 1899, copy in *ibid.*
39 *New York Tribune,* May 28, 29, and 30, 1899.
40 Report of Colonel Edward Moale to Adjutant General, Division of Cuba, September 7, 1899; Moale to Adjutant General, Division of Cuba, July 4, 1899; both in Records of the U.S. Military Government of Cuba, National Archives of the United States.
41 Report of Major Frank H. Edwards, to Adjutant General, Division of Cuba, July 27, 1899, in *ibid.*
42 *New York Times,* June 7, 1899.
43 *Civil Report of General John R. Brooke,* p. 17.

Chapter 7

1 *New York World,* July 20, 1898.
2 Matthews, *The New-Born Cuba,* Chapter IX. See also the later statement of Herbert G. Squiers to John Hay, September 17, 1904, Despatches from U. S. Ministers to Cuba, National Archives.

3 Telegram, General H. C. Corbin to Brooke, December 23, 1898, Records of the U.S. Military Government of Cuba, National Archives.

4 The complete article is inserted in the *Congressional Record,* 55th Congress, 3rd Session, XXXII, 2807.

5 Joseph Benson Foraker, *Notes of a Busy Life* (Cincinnati, 1916), II, 40–41.

6 *Congressional Record,* XXXII, 2572.

7 *Ibid.,* p. 2807.

8 *Ibid.*

9 *Ibid.,* p. 2810.

10 *Ibid.,* pp. 2809–10.

11 *Ibid.,* p. 2811.

12 *Ibid.,* p. 2812.

13 *Congressional Record,* XXXII, 20.

14 Ellis, *Henry Moore Teller, Defender of the West,* p. 314.

15 *Congressional Record,* XXXII, 325–27.

16 *Ibid.,* p. 1385.

17 Sewell to McKinley, April 15, 1899, William McKinley Papers, Library of Congress.

18 Henry Adams to Elizabeth Cameron, January 22, 1899, printed in Ford, *Letters of Henry Adams,* II, 206.

19 Wilson, *Under the Old Flag,* II, 482–83.

20 Brooke to General H. C. Corbin, Adjutant General of the Army, May 24, 1899, copy in William McKinley Papers, Library of Congress.

21 Porter, *Industrial Cuba,* p. 63.

22 A. E. Mestro to Wood, October 16, 1898, Leonard Wood Papers, Library of Congress.

23 "Memorandum dictated by General Leonard Wood in January, 1899," copy in Elihu Root Papers, Library of Congress.

24 Wood to Roosevelt, February 18, 1899, Theodore Roosevelt Papers, Library of Congress.

25 Wood to McKinley, April 27, 1899, William McKinley Papers, Library of Congress.

26 Leonard Wood, "The Existing Conditions and Needs in Cuba," *North American Review,* CLXVIII (May, 1899), 593.

27 *New York Times,* June 24, 1899.

28 Hagedorn, *Leonard Wood,* I, 144.

29 Lodge to Wilson, May 4, 1898, and June 2, 1898, James H. Wilson Papers, Library of Congress.

30 Lodge to Wilson, September 14, 1898; Roosevelt to Colonel J. H.

Dorst, August 7, 1899; both in James Harrison Wilson Papers, Library of Congress.

31 *New York Times,* December 20, 1898.

32 *Ibid.,* December 21, 1898; Wilson, *Under the Old Flag,* II, 467–70.

33 Albert G. Robinson, *Cuba and the Intervention* (New York, 1905), p. 106; Porter, *Industrial Cuba,* pp. 198–99.

34 Wilson to Adjutant General, Division of Cuba, May 9, 1899, Records of the U.S. Military Government of Cuba, National Archives.

35 *New York Tribune,* January 26, 1899; General J. P. Sanger to Wilson, November 4, 1899, James Harrison Wilson Papers, Library of Congress.

36 Brooke to General H. C. Corbin, May 24, 1899, copy in William McKinley Papers, Library of Congress. Also Brooke's memorandum on Wilson's letter to the Adjutant General, Division of Cuba, May 9, 1899, filed with the letter in the Records of the U.S. Military Government of Cuba, National Archives.

37 Wilson to Foraker, May 12, 1899, copy in James Harrison Wilson Papers, Library of Congress.

38 The most complete expositions of these ideas are in James H. Wilson, *An Address on Our Trade Relations With the Tropics* (Pamphlet: Boston, 1901), pp. 10–20; and *Our Relations With Cuba, An Address delivered by General James H. Wilson at the request of the Commercial Club of Chicago at the Auditorium Hotel on the Evening of October 25, 1902* (Pamphlet: Wilmington, Delaware, 1902), pp. 30–34.

39 Foraker to Wilson, May 22, 1899, James H. Wilson Papers, Library of Congress.

40 "Report of Major General James H. Wilson, June 20, 1899," quoted in Hagedorn, *Leonard Wood,* I, 421.

41 Wilson to Roosevelt, July 5, 1899, Theodore Roosevelt Papers, Library of Congress.

42 Roosevelt to Wilson, July 12, 1899, copy in *ibid.*

43 Henry Adams to Elizabeth Cameron, February 19, 1899, printed in Ford, *Letters of Henry Adams,* II, 218–19.

Chapter 8

1 Brooke to General H. C. Corbin, May 24, 1899, copy in William McKinley Papers, Library of Congress.

2 Wilson, *Under the Old Flag,* II, 490.

3 *Ibid.*

4 Ludlow to Wilson, June 18, 1899, James H. Wilson Papers, Library of Congress.

5 Wilson, *Under the Old Flag,* pp. 490–91.

6 Roosevelt to Lodge, April 27, 1899, copy in Theodore Roosevelt Papers, Library of Congress.

7 Roosevelt to Hay, July 1, 1899, Leonard Wood Papers, Library of Congress.

8 Roosevelt to Wood, March 1, 1899, copy in Theodore Roosevelt Papers, Library of Congress.

9 Roosevelt to Wood, July 10, 1899, copy in *ibid.*

10 Foraker to Wilson, March 5, 1899, James H. Wilson Papers, Library of Congress.

11 Roosevelt to Wood, March 8, 1899, copy in Theodore Roosevelt Papers, Library of Congress.

12 Frye to Wilson, March 20, 1899, James H. Wilson Papers, Library of Congress.

13 Alger to McKinley, July 31, 1899, William McKinley Papers, Library of Congress.

14 Brooke to McKinley, April 3, 1899, in *ibid.*

15 Wood to Roosevelt, July 12, 1899, Theodore Roosevelt Papers, Library of Congress.

16 Roosevelt to Lodge, July 21, 1899, copy in *ibid.*

17 Roosevelt to Wood, August 9, 1899, Leonard Wood Papers, Library of Congress; Roosevelt to Root, September 4, 1899, copy in Theodore Roosevelt Papers, Library of Congress.

18 Wood to Roosevelt, August 24, 1899, Theodore Roosevelt Papers, Library of Congress.

19 *New York Times,* June 29, 1899.

20 Wilson to Roosevelt, July 31, 1899, Theodore Roosevelt Papers, Library of Congress.

21 Roosevelt to Wilson, August 5, 1899, copy in *ibid.*

22 Foraker to Wilson, July 24, 1899, James H. Wilson Papers, Library of Congress.

23 Smith to Wilson, August 28, 1899, James H. Wilson Papers, Library of Congress.

24 Sanger to Wilson, November 4, 1899; Sanger to Wilson, April 4, 1900; both in James H. Wilson Papers, Library of Congress.

25 *Civil Report of General John R. Brooke,* p. 13.

26 Wood to Roosevelt, August 18, 1899, Theodore Roosevelt Papers, Library of Congress.

27 McKinley to Root, August 19, 1899, copy in William McKinley Papers, Library of Congress.

28 Root to McKinley, August 17, 1899, William McKinley Papers, Library of Congress.
29 Brooke to McKinley, September 5, 1899, copy in *ibid.*

Chapter 9

1 See Ellis P. Oberholtzer, *A History of the United States Since the Civil War* (New York, 1937), V, 557–61; and Philip C. Jessup, *Elihu Root* (New York, 1938), I, 220–21 ff.
2 Henry Adams to Elizabeth Cameron, February 19, 1899, in Ford, *Letters of Henry Adams,* II, 218–19.
3 *New York Tribune,* April 15, 1899.
4 This story, while substantially that reported at the time by the press, is based on a confidential interview given by Alger to Henry C. Campbell on March 4, 1900, and printed after Alger's death in the *Milwaukee Journal,* January 24, 1907.
5 Roosevelt to Wilson, July 25, 1899, copy in Theodore Roosevelt Papers, Library of Congress.
6 From a speech by Root before the New York County Lawyer's Association, March 13, 1915, printed in Robert Bacon and James Brown Scott, editors, *Addresses on Government and Citizenship by Elihu Root* (Cambridge, 1916), pp. 503–04.
7 Roosevelt to Wood, August 9, 1899, in Leonard Wood Papers, Library of Congress.
8 Foraker to Wilson, August 16, 1899, James Harrison Wilson Papers, Library of Congress.
9 *Report on the Census of Cuba* (Washington, 1900), p. 9.
10 Presidential Proclamation of August 17, 1899, printed in *ibid.,* pp. 10–11.
11 Headquarters, Division of Cuba, to all Department Commanders, August 18, 1899, *Civil Report of General John R. Brooke,* p. 359.
12 "Special Report of Brigadier General Leonard Wood, September 20, 1899," *ibid.,* pp. 368–69.
13 "Special Report of Brigadier General William Ludlow, September 15, 1899," *ibid.,* pp. 361–62.
14 "Special Report of Brigadier General James H. Wilson, September 7, 1899," *ibid.,* pp. 333–42.
15 "Annual Report of Brigadier General Fitzhugh Lee, August 15, 1899," *Annual Reports of the War Department for the Fiscal Year Ended June 30, 1899,* Report of the Major General Commanding the Army, Part I (Washington, 1899), p. 213.
16 "Special Report of Brigadier General Fitzhugh Lee, September 19, 1899," *Civil Report of General John R. Brooke,* p. 344.

17 Lee to Wilson, October 19, 1899, James H. Wilson Papers, Library of Congress.
18 *Civil Report of General John R. Brooke,* p. 15.
19 Brooke to McKinley, September 26, 1899, William McKinley Papers, Library of Congress.
20 Root to Roosevelt, September 11, 1899, copy in Elihu Root Papers, Library of Congress.
21 Roosevelt to Wood, October 9, 1899, Leonard Wood Papers, Library of Congress.
22 Wood to McKinley, September 26, 1899, William McKinley Papers, Library of Congress.
23 Wilson to Roosevelt, September 8, 1899, Theodore Roosevelt Papers, Library of Congress; Wilson to Lodge, November 1, 1899, copy in James H. Wilson Papers, Library of Congress.
24 Wilson to Root, November 3, 1899, copy in James H. Wilson Papers, Library of Congress, and memorandum written on same.
25 New York *Evening Post,* November 17, 1899.
26 Foraker to Wilson, November 20, 1899, James H. Wilson Papers, Library of Congress.

Chapter 10

1 Lee to Wilson, October 19, 1899, James H. Wilson Papers, Library of Congress.
2 Rubens, *Liberty,* p. 422; Manuel Hárquez Sterling, *Proceso Histórico de la Enmienda Platt* (Havana, 1941), pp. 53–54.
3 New York *Evening Post,* November 9, 1899.
4 *La Discusión* (Havana), November 4, 1899.
5 *Ibid.,* November 14, 1899.
6 *La Patria* (Havana), November 5, November 8, and November 18, 1899; *La Tarde* (Havana), November 26, 1899; *Cuba y América,* November 5, 1899.
7 Foraker to Wilson, November 20, 1899, James H. Wilson Papers, Library of Congress.
8 Henry B. Thompson to Wilson, November 20, 1899, in *ibid.*
9 *New York Tribune,* November 25, 1899.
10 Unfavorable endorsement by Brooke, November 27, 1899, on letter, Wood to Adjutant General of the Army, November 11, 1899, recommending reduction of troops in Cuba, in Records of the United States Military Government of Cuba, National Archives.
11 Civil Governor of Santa Clara Province to Secretary of State and Government, November 30, 1899, and December 1, 1899; Civil

Governor of Havana Province to Secretary of State and Government, November 29, 1899; Civil Governor of Matanzas Province to Secretary of State and Government, December 1, 1899; Secretary of State and Government to General Brooke, December 1, 2, and 5, 1899; and numerous individual messages and telegrams, all in *ibid.*

12 Burt A. Miller to Major Charles R. Miller, November 28, 1899, William McKinley Papers, Library of Congress.

13 Root to Rathbone, November 28, 1899, Elihu Root Papers, Library of Congress.

14 Rathbone to Root, December 4, 1899, in *ibid.*

15 *New York Tribune,* November 29, 1899.

16 *Ibid.,* November 30, 1899.

17 Jessup, *Elihu Root,* I, 286–87.

18 *Chicago Inter-Ocean,* November 20, 1899.

19 *Chicago Times-Herald,* November 22, 1899.

20 *St. Paul Pioneer Press,* December 3, 1899.

21 *Kansas City Star,* November 11, 1899.

22 *Boston Herald,* November 12, 1899.

23 See *St. Louis Star,* October 12, 1899; *New Haven Leader,* September 25, 1899; *Cleveland Leader,* November 15, 1899; *Memphis Scimitar,* November 29, 1899; *Dallas News,* December 12, 1899; *Boise Statesman,* December 1, 1899; and *Portland Oregonian,* October 12, 1899.

24 *New York Tribune,* December 2, 1899.

25 *Annual Reports of the Secretary of War, 1899–1903,* pp. 41–44.

26 *New York Tribune,* December 4, 1899.

27 *Ibid.*

28 Wood to Roosevelt, December 3, 1899, Theodore Roosevelt Papers, Library of Congress.

29 Annual Message of the President, December 5, 1899, in *Foreign Relations of the United States, 1899* (Washington, 1901), pp. xxviii–xxix.

30 New York *Evening Post,* December 5, 1899.

31 Ludlow to Root, November 16, 1899, Elihu Root Papers, Library of Congress.

32 Augustus P. Gardner to Wilson, January 3, 1900, and Foraker to Wilson, February 5, 1900, both in James H. Wilson Papers, Library of Congress.

33 *New York Sun,* December 14, 1899.

34 Root to Roosevelt, December 18, 1899, copy in Elihu Root Papers, Library of Congress.
35 "Final Report of Major General John R. Brooke, December 20, 1899," in *Civil Report of General John R. Brooke*, pp. 427–29.
36 New York *Evening Post*, December 21, 1899.

Chapter 11

1 Wood to Root, December 22, 1899, copy in Leonard Wood Papers, Library of Congress.
2 Wood to Root, December 30, 1899, copy in *ibid.*
3 Annual Reports of the War Department for the Fiscal Year ended June 30, 1901, *Civil Report of General Leonard Wood for the period from January 1 to December 31, 1901* (Washington, 1902), I, 21.
4 Rubens, *Liberty*, 397–98.
5 Wood to Root, December 30, 1899, copy in Leonard Wood Papers, Library of Congress.
6 Gómez to Wood, December 30, 1899, in *ibid.*
7 Wood to Root, December 30, 1899, copy in *ibid.*
8 Martínez Ortiz, *Cuba, los Primeros Años de Independencia*, I, 113–14.
9 Foraker to Wilson, December 15, 1899, James H. Wilson Papers, Library of Congress.
10 Wilson to Goldwyn Smith, December 27, 1899, copy in *ibid.*
11 Comparison of a coded cable, Wood to Horatio Rubens, January 1, 1900, with its decoded text as transmitted by Rubens to Root, January 2, 1900, reveals that "Wheeling" was the code name for General Wilson. Both messages in Elihu Root Papers, Library of Congress.
12 Wood to Root, December 22, 1899, copy in Leonard Wood Papers, Library of Congress.
13 See Special Report of General Wilson, September 7, 1899, in *Civil Report of General John R. Brooke*, pp. 337–38, and interview with Wood, *New York Times*, June 24, 1899.
14 Wood to Rubens, January 1, 1900; Rubens to Root, January 2, 1900; both in Elihu Root Papers, Library of Congress.
15 Wilson to Whitelaw Reid, August 3, 1900, James H. Wilson Papers, Library of Congress.
16 Root to Wood, January 27, 1900, copy in Elihu Root Papers, Library of Congress.

17 Root to Paul Dana, January 16, 1900, printed in Jessup, *Elihu Root*, I, 305.

18 Wood to Root, February 23, 1900, Elihu Root Papers, Library of Congress.

19 Root to Wood, February 28, 1900, Leonard Wood Papers, Library of Congress.

20 *Report on the Census of Cuba*, p. 14.

21 *Annual Reports of the Secretary of War, 1899–1903*, p. 107.

22 *Civil Report of General Leonard Wood for 1900*, I, Part 1, p. 36.

23 *Ibid.*, pp. 36 ff.

24 Wood to McKinley, February 6, 1900, copy in Leonard Wood Papers, Library of Congress.

25 Wood to Root, February 6, 1900, Elihu Root Papers, Library of Congress.

26 Wood to Root, February 16, 1900, in *ibid.*

27 Wood to Root, January 13, 1900, in *ibid.*

28 Senate Document 177, 56th Congress, 1st Session.

29 *Congressional Record*, 56th Congress, 1st Session, XXXIII, 1287, 4696.

30 Richard Olney, "The Growth of Our Foreign Policy," *Atlantic Monthly*, LXXXV (March, 1900), 289–301.

31 Wilson to Whitelaw Reid, August 3, 1900, James H. Wilson Papers, Library of Congress.

32 Reid to Wilson, February 13, 1900, and March 7, 1900, James H. Wilson Papers, Library of Congress.

33 Reid to Wilson, March 7, 1900, in *ibid.*

Chapter 12

1 Wood to Root, March 26, 1900, Elihu Root Papers, Library of Congress.

2 Wilson, *Under the Old Flag*, II, 498–510.

3 *New York Tribune*, March 5, 1900.

4 Wood to Root, March 26, 1900, Elihu Root Papers, Library of Congress.

5 Wood to Root, April 27, 1900, in *ibid.*; see also Chapman, *History of the Cuban Republic*, pp. 128–29.

6 For a full account of the Dady case, see Robinson, *Cuba and the Intervention*, pp. 152–56.

7 Wood to Root, January 13, 1900, Elihu Root Papers, Library of Congress.

8 Wood to Root, February 7, 1900, in *ibid.*

9 Root to Wood, February 1, 1900, in *ibid*.

10 *Annual Reports of the Secretary of War, 1899–1903,* p. 78.

11 Wood to McKinley, February 25, 1900, copy in Leonard Wood Papers, Library of Congress.

12 James E. Runcie, "American Misgovernment in Cuba," *North American Review,* CLXX (February, 1900), 284.

13 Wood to Root, February 8, 1900, Leonard Wood Papers, Library of Congress.

14 Root to Wood, February 13, 1900, in *ibid*.

15 Brooke to Adjutant General of the Army, February 15, 1900; Root to Wood, February 21, 1900; copies in *ibid*.

16 Wood to Root, May 1 and June 9, 1900, Elihu Root Papers, Library of Congress.

17 Root to Wood, March 24, 1900; copy in *ibid.;* Jessup, *Elihu Root,* I, 290–92.

18 Wood to Root, May 5, 1900, Elihu Root Papers, Library of Congress.

19 *Ibid*.

20 Root to Wood, May 9, 1900, Leonard Wood Papers, Library of Congress.

21 Joseph L. Bristow, *Fraud and Politics at the Turn of the Century* (New York, 1952), p. 100. See Chapters XV and XVI for Bristow's description of the postal frauds.

22 See *Literary Digest,* XX, No. 22, pp. 655–56.

23 *Congressional Record,* 56th Congress, 1st Session, XXXIII, 5591–96.

24 *Ibid.,* pp. 5885–94.

25 Platt to Wood, June 1, 1900, Leonard Wood Papers, Library of Congress.

26 Root to Wood, June 2, 1900, copy in Elihu Root Papers, Library of Congress.

27 *Civil Report of General Leonard Wood for 1900,* I, Part 1, p. 52.

28 Rodrígues to McKinley, June 21, 1900, copy in William McKinley Papers, Library of Congress.

29 Root to Wood, June 20, 1900, copy in Elihu Root Papers, Library of Congress.

30 A. T. Mahan, *The Interest of America in Sea Power* (Boston, 1897), p. 313.

31 Root to Wood, June 20, 1900, copy in Elihu Root Papers, Library of Congress.

32 Wood to Root, June 3, 1900, in *ibid.*
33 Wood to Root, June 18, 1900, in *ibid.*
34 Wood to Root, June 21, 1900, copy in Leonard Wood Papers, Library of Congress.
35 Wood to Root, July 7, 1900, copy in *ibid.*
36 Wood to Root, July 6, 1900, copy in *ibid.*
37 Wood to Roosevelt, July 7, 1900, copy in *ibid.*
38 Wood to Lodge, August 8, 1900, copy in *ibid.*
39 Wood to Roosevelt, April 20, 1900, Theodore Roosevelt Papers, Library of Congress.
40 Wood to Root, July 6, 1900, copy in Leonard Wood Papers, Library of Congress.
41 *Annual Reports of the Secretary of War, 1899–1903,* p. 108.
42 Allison to Wilson, July 21, 1900, James H. Wilson Papers, Library of Congress.
43 Wood to Lodge, August 8, 1900, copy in Leonard Wood Papers, Library of Congress.
44 Wilson to Allison, May 27, 1900, James H. Wilson Papers, Library of Congress.
45 Wood to Root, June 27, 1900, Elihu Root Papers, Library of Congress.
46 *Annual Reports of the Secretary of War, 1899–1903,* p. 79.
47 *Ibid.*
48 Wood to Root, June 8, 1900, Elihu Root Papers, Library of Congress.
49 Wood to Root, August 6, 1900, in *ibid.*
50 Wood to Root, August 13, 1900, in *ibid.*
51 Wood to McKinley, August 31, 1900, copy in Leonard Wood Papers, Library of Congress.
52 Wood to Root, September 26, 1900, Elihu Root Papers, Library of Congress.
53 Albert Shaw to Roosevelt, December 15, 1899; Lodge to Roosevelt, December 13, 1899; Lodge to Roosevelt, December 29, 1899; all in Theodore Roosevelt Papers, Library of Congress.
54 Republican National Committee to McKinley, June 29, 1900, William McKinley Papers, Library of Congress.
55 Wood to Root, August 6, 1900, Elihu Root Papers, Library of Congress.
56 Wood to Roosevelt, August 13, 1900; Hanna to Roosevelt, August 28, 1900; Theodore Roosevelt Papers, Library of Congress.
57 Rubens, *Liberty,* p. 400.

Chapter 13

1 *Annual Reports of the Secretary of War, 1899–1903*, pp. 108–09.
2 Wood to Root, August 6, 1900, and September 8, 1900, Elihu Root Papers, Library of Congress; Wood to Root, September 14, 1900, copy in Leonard Wood Papers, Library of Congress.
3 Wood to Root, September 14, 1900, copy in *ibid*.
4 *Annual Reports of the Secretary of War, 1899–1903*, p. 109.
5 For an account of the constitutional convention by one of the delegates, see Martínez Ortiz, *Cuba, los Primeros Años de Independencia*, I, 174–315.
6 *Ibid.*, p. 192.
7 It is not clear why the last two alternatives should be mutually exclusive.
8 Wood to Root, January 4, 1901, Elihu Root Papers, Library of Congress.
9 Root to Wood, January 9, 1901, Leonard Wood Papers, Library of Congress.
10 Root to John Hay, January 11, 1901, Elihu Root Papers, Library of Congress.
11 Orville H. Platt to Wood, January 18, 1901, Leonard Wood Papers, Library of Congress.
12 Henry Cabot Lodge to Wood, January 15, 1901, in *ibid*.
13 Platt to Root, February 5, 1901, Elihu Root Papers, Library of Congress.
14 Leon Burr Richardson, *William E. Chandler, Republican* (New York, 1940), pp. 604–5.
15 *New York Sun*, February 8, 1901.
16 Root to Wood, February 9, 1901, Leonard Wood Papers, Library of Congress.
17 Wood to Root, February 12, 1901, Elihu Root Papers, Library of Congress.
18 Albert G. Robinson, "Cuba's Cause of Offense," *The Independent*, LIII (March 21, 1901), 671.
19 Wood to Root, February 19, 1901, Elihu Root Papers, Library of Congress.
20 Root to Wood, February 25, 1901, copy in *ibid*.
21 Wood to Root, February 25, 1901, in *ibid*.
22 Wood to Diego Tamayo, February 21, 1901, copy in *ibid*.
23 Root to Wood, February 21, 1901, copy in *ibid*.
24 *Literary Digest*, XXII (February 9, 1901), 152.
25 Wood to Root, February 19, 1901, Elihu Root Papers, Library of Congress.

26 Root to Wood, February 23, 1901, Leonard Wood Papers, Library of Congress.
27 See Martínez Ortiz, *Cuba, los Primeros Años de Independencia,* I, 272, and Lepoldo Horrego Estuch, *Juan Gualberto Gómez* (Havana, 1954), pp. 151 ff.
28 Wood to Root, February 24, 1901, Elihu Root Papers, Library of Congress.
29 Wood to Root, February 27, 1901, in *ibid.*
30 *New York Sun,* February 25, 1901. See also Horrego Estuch, *Juan Gualberto Gómez,* pp. 154–55.
31 "Report on the Relations which ought to Exist between Cuba and the United States, presented by the respective Committee, February 26–27, 1901," copy in Elihu Root Papers, Library of Congress.
32 *Congressional Record,* 56th Congress, 2nd Session, XXXIV, 2954.
33 Platt to Wood, April 21, 1901, Leonard Wood Papers, Library of Congress. For other discussions of the origins of the Platt Amendment, see Jessup, *Elihu Root,* I, 310–11; Leland H. Jenks, *Our Cuban Colony* (New York, 1928), p. 321; and Hagedorn, *Leonard Wood,* I, 421–23.
34 *Literary Digest,* XXII (March 9, 1901), 273–74.
35 *Congressional Record,* XXXIV, 3036–42.
36 *Ibid.,* pp. 3145–46, 3150.
37 *Ibid.,* p. 3151.
38 *Ibid.,* pp. 3132–34.
39 Frederick H. Gillet unfortunately casts little light on Hoar's motives for this action in his *George Frisbie Hoar* (Boston, 1934).
40 *Congressional Record,* XXXIV, 3145–46.
41 Ellis, *Henry Moore Teller, Defender of the West,* p. 343.
42 *Congressional Record,* XXXIV, 3151–52.
43 *Ibid.,* pp. 3331–36.
44 *New York Tribune,* March 1 and March 2, 1901. The *Tribune*'s charges were repeated in the New York *Evening Post,* March 4, 1901.
45 *New York Tribune,* March 2, 1901.
46 Platt to Edwin F. Atkins, June 11, 1901, quoted in Coolidge, *An Old Fashioned Senator,* pp. 348–49.

Chapter 14

1 Wood to Root, March 2, 1901, Elihu Root Papers, Library of Congress.
2 Root to Wood, March 2, 1901, Leonard Wood Papers, Library of Congress.

3 *New York Tribune*, March 3, 1901; New York *Evening Post*, March 8, 1901.
4 Wood to Root, March 6, 1901, Elihu Root Papers, Library of Congress; J. R. White to William McKinley, March 6, 1901; William McKinley Papers, Library of Congress.
5 Wood to Root, March 3, 1901, Elihu Root Papers, Library of Congress.
6 Wood to Root, March 4, 1901, in *ibid.*
7 Wood to Root, March 8, 1901, and March 20, 1901, in *ibid.*
8 Wood to Root, March 4, 1901, in *ibid.*
9 Wood to Root, March 6, 1901, and March 20, 1901, in *ibid.*
10 Root to Wood, March 29, 1901, copy in *ibid.*
11 Wood to Root, April 2, 1901, in *ibid.*
12 Root to Wood, April 2, 1901, copy in *ibid.*
13 Wood to Root, April 6, 1901, in *ibid.; La Discusión* (Havana), April 5, 1901.
14 Wood to Root, April 4, 1901, Elihu Root Papers, Library of Congress.
15 See *New York Sun* and New York *Evening Post*, April 11, 1901.
16 Wood to Root, April 15, 1901, Elihu Root Papers, Library of Congress.
17 "Report of the Committee Appointed to confer with the Government of the United States, Giving an Account of the Result of its Labors," copy in Elihu Root Papers, Library of Congress.
18 Platt to Root, April 26, 1901, in *ibid.*
19 "Report of the Committee Appointed to confer with the Government of the United States," copy in *ibid.*
20 Albert J. Beveridge, "Cuba and Congress," *North American Review*, CLXXII (April, 1901), 535.
21 Orville H. Platt, "Solution of the Cuban Problem," *World's Work*, II (May, 1901), 729.
22 See *New York Sun*, February 27, 1901.
23 Wood to Root, March 13, 1901, Elihu Root Papers, Library of Congress.
24 Wood to Root, February 27, 1901, in *ibid.*
25 Camacho, *Estrada Palma*, pp. 176–77; see also Estrada Palma to Andrés Moreno de la Torre, February 1, 1898, quoted in Manuel Sanguily, "Sobre la Genesis de la Enmienda Platt," *Cuba Contemporánea*, Vol. XXX, No. 118 (Havana, October, 1922), p. 123.
26 Camacho, *Estrada Palma*, pp. 176–77.
27 Wood to Root, April 4, 1901, Elihu Root Papers, Library of Congress.

28 New York *Evening Post,* February 1, 1901.

29 *Ibid.,* February 26, 1901.

30 *Ibid.,* April 25, 1901.

31 *Ibid.,* April 17, 1901; see also the Havana dispatches of AGR (Albert G. Robinson) in *ibid.,* February 26, March 7, and March 8, 1901.

32 Wood to Roosevelt, April 2, 1901, Theodore Roosevelt Papers, Library of Congress.

33 Roosevelt to Wood, April 17, 1901, Leonard Wood Papers, Library of Congress.

34 Wood to Root, May 17, 1901, Elihu Root Papers, Library of Congress.

35 Root to Wood, May 17, 1901, copy in *ibid.*

36 Wood to Root, May 26, 1901, in *ibid.*

37 New York *Evening Post,* May 20, 1901.

38 Wood to Root, May 28 and May 29, 1901, Elihu Root Papers, Library of Congress.

39 Root to Wood, May 28, 1901, Leonard Wood Papers, Library of Congress.

40 Wood to Root, June 1, 1901, Elihu Root Papers, Library of Congress.

41 Wood to Root, June 12, 1901, in *ibid.*

42 Wood to Roosevelt, October 28, 1901, copy in Leonard Wood Papers, Library of Congress.

Chapter 15

1 Wood to McKinley, April 12, 1900, copy in Leonard Wood Papers, Library of Congress.

2 *Annual Reports of the Secretary of War, 1899–1903,* pp. 110–11.

3 Root to Brooke, September 22, 1899, copy in Elihu Root Papers, Library of Congress; *Civil Report of General Leonard Wood for 1900,* I, Part 1, p. 6.

4 *Annual Reports of the Secretary of War, 1899–1903,* pp. 110–11; *Civil Report of General Leonard Wood for 1900,* I, Part 1, pp. 94–98.

5 *Civil Report of General Leonard Wood for 1900,* I, Part 1, pp. 124–25. See also Robinson, *Cuba and the Intervention,* pp. 141–42.

6 Wood to Root, January 8, 1901, in Elihu Root Papers, Library of Congress. See also Wood to Root, June 18, 1900, in *ibid.*

7 *Annual Reports of the Secretary of War, 1899–1903,* p. 111; *Civil Report of General Leonard Wood for 1900,* I, Part 1, pp. 97–112.

8 *Civil Report of Brigadier General Leonard Wood, Military Governor of Cuba for the period from January 1 to May 20, 1902* (Washington, 1902), Part 1, pp. 17–18. See also Portell Vilá, *Historia de Cuba,* IV, 118–19, and note 153, Chapter I.

9 *Annual Reports of the Secretary of War, 1899–1903,* pp. 111–12, 180–81; Russell H. Fitzgibbon, *Cuba and the United States, 1900–1935* (Menasha, Wisconsin, 1935), pp. 46–50.

10 *Civil Report of General Leonard Wood for 1900,* I, Part 1, pp. 65–66, 68, 73–74; Fitzgibbon, *Cuba and the United States,* pp. 32–35.

11 Miguel Gener y Rincón, "Report of the Secretary of Justice from July 1st, 1900 to December 31, 1900," p. 9 in *Civil Report of General Leonard Wood for 1900,* VI, Part 1.

12 Hagedorn, *Leonard Wood,* I, 319.

13 *Annual Reports of the Secretary of War, 1899–1903,* p. 181.

14 Major Edgar S. Dudley, "Report of the Judge-Advocate of the Department, Calendar Year 1900," pp. 9–10, in *Civil Report of General Leonard Wood for 1900,* VI, Part 1.

15 Wood to Roosevelt, July 12, 1899, Theodore Roosevelt Papers, Library of Congress.

16 *Civil Report of General Leonard Wood for 1900* I, Part 1, pp. 8–10; *Civil Report of General Lenord Wood for 1901,* I, Part 1, pp. 3–4, 6–7. See also Robinson, *Cuba and the Intervention,* pp. 112 ff, and Fitzgibbon, *Cuba and the United States,* pp. 59–61.

17 Fitzgibbon, *Cuba and the United States,* p. 62.

18 *Annual Reports of the Secretary of War, 1899–1903,* p. 183; *Civil Report of General Leonard Wood for 1900,* I, Part 1, pp. 45–47; Robinson, *Cuba and the Intervention,* pp. 322 ff; Fitzgibbon, *Cuba and the United States,* pp. 36–37.

19 *Civil Report of General Leonard Wood for 1901,* I, Part 1, p. 5; *Civil Report of General Leonard Wood for 1902,* Part 1, pp. 160–63; Hagedorn, *Leonard Wood,* I, 324–28.

20 *Civil Report of General Leonard Wood for 1900,* I, Part 1, p. 9.

21 Wood to Root, April 12, 1900, Elihu Root Papers, Library of Congress.

22 Wood to McKinley, April 12, 1900, copy in Leonard Wood Papers, Library of Congress.

23 For Cuban evaluations of the Wood reforms, see the bitterly hostile view in Portell Vilá, *Historia de Cuba,* IV, 90–136, and the more balanced presentations in Martínes Ortiz, *Los Primeros Años de Independencia,* I, 100–22, 427–38, and Guerra y Sanchez, *Historia de la Nación Cubana,* VII, 47–68.

Chapter 16

1 Wood to Root, October 22, 1901, Elihu Root Papers, Library of Congress.

2 *Annual Reports of the War Department for the Fiscal Year Ended June 30, 1900,* Report of the Military Governor of Cuba, Part 1, p. 75.

3 *Civil Report of General Leonard Wood for 1902,* Part 1, p. 13.

4 Report of Major Tasker H. Bliss, August 6, 1900, *Annual Reports of the War Department for the Fiscal Year Ended June 30, 1900,* I, Part II, part 3, pp. 150–53.

5 Report of the Department of Agriculture, Commerce, and Industry, March 15, 1901, in *ibid.,* Part 4, pp. 4–9.

6 Wood to Root, January 13, 1900, Elihu Root Papers, Library of Congress.

7 Wood to Senator Nelson Aldrich, January 12, 1901, copy in Leonard Wood Papers, Library of Congress.

8 Wood to Root, December 22, 1900, Elihu Root Papers, Library of Congress.

9 George B. Hopkins to Senator John C. Spooner, March 14, 1900, John C. Spooner Papers, Library of Congress.

10 See *New York Sun,* December 8, 1898.

11 Hopkins to Spooner, March 14, 1900, John C. Spooner Papers, Library of Congress.

12 Platt to Wood, June 1, 1900, Leonard Wood Papers, Library of Congress.

13 Jessup, *Elihu Root,* I, 297.

14 Wood to Foraker, December 21, 1900, copy in Elihu Root Papers, Library of Congress.

15 Foraker to Wood, January 7, 1901, Leonard Wood Papers, Library of Congress.

16 For further discussion of the Cuba Company, see Jessup, *Elihu Root,* I, 296–98.

17 Wood to Root, November 4, 1901, Elihu Root Papers, Library of Congress; *Civil Report of General Leonard Wood for 1902,* I, Part 1, p. 25.

18 *Ibid.,* p. 28.

19 *Annual Reports of the War Department for the Fiscal Year Ending June 30, 1900,* Report of the Military Governor of Cuba, Part 1, p. 76.

20 *Annual Reports of the Secretary of War, 1899–1903,* pp. 43–44.

21 Wood to Roosevelt, May 9, 1901, Theodore Roosevelt Papers, Library of Congress.

22 Wood to Aldrich, January 12, 1901, copy in Leonard Wood Papers, Library of Congress.

23 Wood to Colonel Scott, September 27, 1901, with sample letter enclosed, in Records of the United States Military Government of Cuba, National Archives of the United States.

24 "Petition of the General Society of Merchants and Business Men of the Island of Cuba to the Honorable Theodore Roosevelt, President of the United States, September 20, 1901," in *ibid.*

25 José Hernández Alverez to Wood, October 8, 1901, in *ibid.*

26 Roosevelt to Nicholas Murray Butler, February 4, 1902, in E. E. Morison, ed., *Letters of Theodore Roosevelt* (Cambridge, 1951), III, 228; Roosevelt to Leonard Wood, November 11, 1901, in *ibid.*, pp. 195–96.

27 Annual Message of the President, December 3, 1901, *Foreign Relations of the United States, 1901* (Washington, 1902), pp. xxxi–xxxii.

28 United States Tariff Commission, *The Effects of the Cuban Reciprocity Treaty of 1902* (Washington, 1929), p. 386.

29 *Annual Reports of the Secretary of War, 1899–1903,* pp. 193–97.

30 *Civil Report of General Leonard Wood for 1901,* I, Part 1, pp. 33–34.

31 Wood to Root, December 17, 1901, Elihu Root Papers, Library of Congress.

32 Edwin F. Atkins, "Cuba's Imminent Bankruptcy," *North American Review,* CLXXIII (December, 1901), 768.

33 See Ray Stannard Baker, "How the Beet-Sugar Industry is Growing," *Review of Reviews,* XXIII (March, 1901), 324–28.

34 See *Reciprocity With Cuba, Hearings before the Committee on Ways and Means, 57th Congress, 1st Session, 1902* (Washington, 1902).

35 For a statement of these arguments, see *ibid.,* and United States Tariff Commission, *The Effects of the Cuban Reciprocity Treaty of 1902,* pp. 392–97.

36 Wood to Root, January 16, 1902, Elihu Root Papers, Library of Congress.

37 Root to Wood, February 7, 1902, copy in *ibid.;* Wood to Root, February 8, 1902, in *ibid.*

38 Root to Wood, March 7, 1902, Leonard Wood Papers, Library of Congress.

39 *Congressional Record,* 57th Congress, 1st Session, XXXV, 3036, 3491.
40 See *Literary Digest,* XXIV (March 29, 1902), 419–20.
41 For a statement of the minority position in the Republican caucus, see *Congressional Record,* XXXV, 4324.
42 *Ibid.,* p. 4419; United States Tariff Commission, *The Effects of the Cuban Reciprocity Treaty of 1902,* pp. 400–07.
43 *Ibid.,* pp. 417–18.
44 *Congressional Record,* XXXV, 6720.
45 *Ibid.,* pp. 4423, 6838; J. Lawrence Laughlin and H. Parker Willis, *Reciprocity* (New York, 1903), pp. 409–10; Senate Document Number 434, 57th Congress, 1st Session.
46 *Congressional Record,* XXXV, 7638–43.
47 *Foreign Relations of the United States, 1903* (Washington, 1904), pp. 375–82; United States Tariff Commission, *The Effects of the Cuban Reciprocity Treaty of 1902,* pp. 27–29.
48 *Congressional Record,* 58th Congress, Special Session, XXXVII, 3.
49 See Laughlin and Willis, *Reciprocity,* pp. 534–39, for the text of the agreement.
50 See *ibid.,* and Jenks, *Our Cuban Colony,* pp. 135–38.
51 Theodore Roosevelt to John Hay, October 23, 1902, in Morison, *Letters of Theodore Roosevelt,* III, 367; same to John Dalzell, February 24, 1903, in *ibid.,* p. 433.
52 *Congressional Record,* XXXVII, 341–42. See also William Dana Orcutt, *Burrows of Michigan and the Republican Party* (New York, 1917), I, 305, and Jenks, *Our Cuban Colony,* p. 138.
53 United States Tariff Commission, *The Effects of the Cuban Reciprocity Treaty of 1902,* p. 29; Special Message of the President, *Congressional Record,* XXXVII, 145.
54 *Ibid.,* pp. 145, 163.
55 Roosevelt to Henry Cabot Lodge, September 30, 1903, in Morison, *Letters of Theodore Roosevelt,* III, 608.
56 *Congressional Record,* XXXVII, 260–64.
57 United States Tariff Commission, *The Effects of the Cuban Reciprocity Treaty of 1902,* p. 30.
58 *Ibid.,* pp. 100–01.

Chapter 17

1 *Civil Report of General Leonard Wood for 1902,* Part 1, p. 271.
2 See James P. Shenton, "Imperialism and Racism," in Donald Sheehan and Harold C. Syrett, editors, *Essays in American Historiography* (New York, 1960).

3 Wilson, *An Address on Our Trade Relations with the Tropics*, p. 18.

4 New York *Evening Post*, February 25, 1898.

5 *Ibid.*, November 17, 1899.

6 Wood to McKinley, April 12, 1900, copy in Leonard Wood Papers, Library of Congress.

7 Root to Philip C. Jessup, November 19, 1924, printed in Jessup, *Elihu Root*, I, 289.

8 Howard K. Beale, *Theodore Roosevelt and the Rise of America to World Power* (Baltimore, 1956), p. 72.

9 Roosevelt to Hay, August 19, 1903, printed in Morison, *Letters of Theodore Roosevelt*, III, 567.

10 The following discussion owes a debt to Dexter Perkins, *The Monroe Doctrine, 1867–1907* (Baltimore, 1937), pp. 398–405.

11 *Congressional Record,* 56th Congress, 2nd Session, XXXIV, 3145–48.

12 *Ibid.*, p. 3151.

13 "Report of the Committee Appointed to confer with the Government of the United States," copy in Elihu Root Papers, Library of Congress.

14 Claude Bowers, *Beveridge and the Progressive Era* (Cambridge, 1932), p. 144.

15 Roosevelt to Hermann Speck von Sternberg, July 12, 1901, in Morison, *Letters of Theodore Roosevelt*, III, 116.

16 Annual Message of the President, December 6, 1904, in *Works of Theodore Roosevelt* (New York, 1925), XVII, 299.

17 Root to Wood, April 2, 1901, copy in Elihu Root Papers, Library of Congress.

18 Jessup, *Elihu Root*, I, 325.

Bibliography

Archival and Manuscript Sources

National Archives of the United States, Division of Interior Department Archives. Records of the United States Military Government of Cuba (Record Group 140).
William McKinley Papers. Library of Congress, Washington, D.C.
Whitelaw Reid Papers. Library of Congress, Washington, D.C.
Theodore Roosevelt Papers. Library of Congress, Washington, D.C.
Elihu Root Papers. Library of Congress, Washington, D.C.
James Harrison Wilson Papers. Library of Congress, Washington, D.C.
Leonard Wood Papers. Library of Congress, Washington, D.C.

Public Documents

Boletín del Archivo Nacional, Año XXXV. Havana, 1936.
Richardson, James D. *A Compilation of the Messages and Papers of the Presidents, 1789–1897*. 10 Vols. Washington, 1899.
Santovenia, Emeterio S., and Llaverías, Joaquín, editors. *Actas de las Asambleas de Representantes y del Consejo de Gobierno Durante la Guerra de Independencia*. 5 Vols. Havana, 1932.
United States *Congressional Record*. 1896–1903.
United States House of Representatives, Committee on Ways and Means. *Miscellaneous House Reports*. Vol. 5, "Reciprocity With Cuba," Report No. 1276. 57th Congress, 1st Session, 1902.
————. *Reciprocity With Cuba, Hearings Before the Committee on Ways and Means*. 57th Congress, 1st Session, 1902.
United States *Senate Documents*. Vol. 28, "The Ethics of the Fight for Cuban Reciprocity," Document No. 434. 57th Congress, 1st Session, 1902.
United States State Department. *Foreign Relations of the United States*. 1897–1903.
United States Treasury Department. Porter, Robert P. *Report on the*

Commercial and Industrial Condition of the Island of Cuba. Washington, 1898.

――――. Porter, Robert P. *Special Report on the Revenue and Customs Tariff of Cuba.* Washington, 1898.

――――. "Special Report of Robert P. Porter on the Commissioner's Visit to General Gómez, and in Relation to the Payment and Disbandment of the Insurgent Army of Cuba," in Robert P. Porter, *Reports on the Commercial and Industrial Condition of Cuba,* Washington, 1889.

United States Tariff Commission. *The Effects of the Cuban Reciprocity Treaty of 1902.* Miscellaneous Series No. 22. Washington, 1929.

United States War Department. Adjutant General of the Army. *Correspondence Relating to the War With Spain.* 2 vols., Washington, 1902.

――――. *Annual Reports of the Secretary of War, 1899–1903.* Washington, 1904.

――――. *Civil Report of Major General John R. Brooke, Military Governor, Island of Cuba.* Washington, 1900.

――――. *Civil Report of Brigadier General Leonard Wood, Military Governor of Cuba, for the period from December 20, 1899, to December 31, 1900.* 12 vols., Washington, 1901.

――――. *Civil Report of Brigadier General Leonard Wood, Military Governor of Cuba, for the period from January 1 to December 31, 1901.* 15 vols., Washington, 1902.

――――. *Civil Report of Brigadier General Leonard Wood, Military Governor of Cuba, for the period from January 1 to May 20, 1902.* Washington, 1902.

――――. Office of the Director, Census of Cuba. *Report on the Census of Cuba, 1899.* Washington, 1900.

Newspapers and Periodicals

New York *Evening Post.*
New York Journal.
New York Sun.
New York Times.
New York Tribune.
Literary Digest.

Articles and Pamphlets

Atkins, Edwin F. "Cuba's Imminent Bankruptcy." *North American Review,* CLXXIII (December, 1901), 768–773.

Beveridge, Albert J. "Cuba and Congress," *North American Review,* CLXXII (April 1901), 535–550.

Bryce, James. "Some Reflections on the State of Cuba." *North American Review,* CLXXIV (April, 1902), 445–456.

"Cuban Reciprocity and Republican Sentiment." *Literary Digest,* XXIV (June 28, 1902), 861.

"Cuba's Future Relations to the United States." *Literary Digest,* XXII (February 9, 1901), 152–53.

"Cuba's Vote Against Annexation." *Literary Digest,* XXI (September 29, 1900), 362–63.

"Further Developments in the Cuban Scandals." *Literary Digest,* XX (June 2, 1900), 655–56.

Harrington, Fred Harvey. "The Anti-Imperialist Movement in the United States, 1898–1900." *Mississippi Valley Historical Review,* XXII (1935), 211–230.

Luciano Díaz, Manuel. *The Republic of Cuba, a brief sketch compiled for distribution at the Louisiana Purchase Exposition, St. Louis, Mo., U.S.A.* (Pamphlet. Department of Agriculture, Industry and Commerce, Havana, n.d.).

McDowell, William O. "The Secret Story of American Interference in Cuba." *Journal of American History,* II (1908), 405–440.

Moore, John Basset. "Cuban Belligerency," *The Forum,* XXI (May, 1896), 288–295.

Olney, Richard. "The Growth of Our Foreign Policy." *Atlantic Monthly,* LXXXV (March, 1900), 289–301.

"Our Demands on Cuba." *Literary Digest,* XXII (March 9, 1901), 273–274.

Platt, Orville H. "Our Relation to the People of Cuba and Porto Rico." *Annals of the American Academy of Political and Social Science,* XVIII (July, 1901), 145–159.

———. "Solution of the Cuban Problem." *World's Work,* II (May, 1901), 729–735.

Pomeroy, Earl S. "The American Colonial Office." *Mississippi Valley Historical Review,* XXX (1944), 521–532.

Porter, Robert P. "The Future of Cuba." *North American Review,* CLXVIII, No. 509 (April, 1899), 418–423.

Robinson, Albert G. "Cuba's Cause of Offense." *The Independent,* LIII (March 21, 1901), 671–74.

———. "Cuban Self-Government." *The Independent,* LII (December 13, 1900), 2968–2971.

———. "Work of the Cuban Convention." *Forum,* XXXI (June, 1901), 401–412.

Rubens, Horatio S. "The Insurgent Government in Cuba." *North American Review*, CLXVI (May, 1898), 560–569.

Runcie, James E. "American Misgovernment in Cuba." *North American Review*, CLXX (February, 1900), 284–294.

Sanguily, Manuel. "Sobre la Genesis de la Enmienda Platt." *Cuba Contemporánea*, XXX (Havana, October, 1922), 119–127.

Shenton, James P. "Imperialism and Racism." Sheehan, Donald, and Syrett, Harold C. (eds.), *Essays in American Historiography* (New York, 1960).

Sumner, William Graham. *The Conquest of the United States by Spain, A lecture before the Phi Beta Kappa Society of Yale University, January 16, 1899*. Boston, 1899.

Taylor, Hannis. "A Review of the Cuban Question." *North American Review*, CLXV (November, 1897), 610–635.

"A Twenty-per-cent. Concession to Cuba." *Literary Digest*, XXIV (March 29, 1902), 419–420.

Wilson, James Harrison. *An Address on Our Trade Relations With the Tropics*. Pamphlet. Boston, 1901.

————. *Our Relations With Cuba, An Address delivered by General James H. Wilson at the request of the Commercial Club of Chicago at the Auditorium Hotel on the evening of October 25, 1902*. Pamphlet. Wilmington, 1902.

Wood, Leonard. "The Existing Conditions and Needs in Cuba." *North American Review*, CLXVII (May, 1899), 593–601.

————. "The Need for Reciprocity With Cuba." *The Independent*, LIII (December 12, 1901), 2927–2929.

Books

Alger, Russell A. *The Spanish-American War*. New York, 1901.

Atkins, Edwin F. *Sixty Years in Cuba*. Cambridge, 1926.

Atkins, John Black. *The War In Cuba*. London, 1899.

Bacon, Robert, and Scott, James Brown, editors. *Addresses on Government and Citizenship by Elihu Root*. Cambridge, 1916.

Baehr, Harry W. *The New York Tribune Since the Civil War*. New York, 1936.

Beale, Howard K. *Theodore Roosevelt and the Rise of America to World Power*. Baltimore, 1956.

Beals, Carleton. *The Crime of Cuba*. New York, 1934.

Bodelson, C. A. *Studies in Mid-Victorian Imperialism*. Copenhagen, 1924.

Bowers, Claude G. *Beveridge and the Progressive Era.* Cambridge, 1932.

Bristow, Joseph L. *Fraud and Politics at the Turn of the Century.* New York, 1952.

Camacho, Pánfilo D. *Estrada Palma, el Gobernante Honrado.* Havana, 1938.

Carter, William Harding. *The Life of Lieutenant General Chaffee.* Chicago, 1917.

Chadwick, French Ensor. *Relations of the United States and Spain, Diplomacy.* New York, 1909.

————. *The Relations of the United States and Spain, The Spanish-American War.* 2 vols. New York, 1911.

Chapman, Charles E. *A History of the Cuban Republic.* New York, 1927.

Coolidge, Louis A. *An Old Fashioned Senator, Orville H. Platt.* New York, 1910.

Cortissoz, Royal. *The Life of Whitelaw Reid.* 2 vols. New York, 1921.

Cullum, George W. *Biographical Register of the Officers and Graduates of the U. S. Military Academy.* 3 vols. Boston and New York, 1891. Also Vol. IV, *Supplement, 1890–1900.* Cambridge, 1901.

Curti, Merle, and Birr, Kendall. *Prelude to Point Four.* Madison, 1954.

Dawes, Charles G. *A Journal of the McKinley Years.* Chicago, 1950.

Dennis, A. L. P. *Adventures in American Diplomacy, 1896–1906.* New York, 1928.

Ellis, Elmer. *Henry Moore Teller, Defender of the West.* Caldwell, Idaho, 1941.

Fitzgibbon, Russell H. *Cuba and the United States, 1900–1935.* Menasha, Wisconsin, 1935.

Foraker, Joseph Benson. *Notes of a Busy Life.* 2 vols. Cincinnati, 1916.

Ford, Worthington Chauncey, editor. *Letters of Henry Adams, 1892–1918.* 2 vols. Boston and New York, 1938.

Funston, Frederick. *Memories of Two Wars.* New York, 1911.

Garraty, John A. *Henry Cabot Lodge, A Biography.* New York, 1953.

Gillet, Frederick H. *George Frisbie Hoar.* Boston and New York, 1934.

Guerra y Sánchez, Ramiro, and others, eds. *Historia de la Nación Cubana.* 7 vols. Havana, 1952.

Guggenheim, Harry F. *The United States and Cuba.* New York, 1934.

Hagedorn, Hermann. *Leonard Wood.* 2 vols. New York, 1931.

Horrego Estuch, Leopoldo. *Juan Gualberto Gómez.* Havana, 1954.

Infiesta, Ramón. *Máximo Gómez.* Havana, 1937.

Jenks, Leland H. *Our Cuban Colony.* New York, 1928.

Jessup, Philip C. *Elihu Root*. 2 vols. New York, 1938.

Kidd, Benjamin. *The Control of the Tropics*. New York, 1898.

Laughlin, J. Laurence, and Willis, H. Parker. *Reciprocity*. New York, 1903.

Lee, Fitzhugh, and Wheeler, Joseph. *Cuba's Struggle Against Spain, with the Causes of American Intervention and a full account of the Spanish-American War, including the Peace Negotiations*. New York, 1899.

Leech, Margaret. *In the Days of McKinley*. New York, 1959.

Lodge, Henry Cabot. *Selections From the Correspondence of Theodore Roosevelt and Henry Cabot Lodge*. 2 vols. New York, 1925.

McCall, Samuel W. *Life of Thomas Brackett Reed*, New York, 1914.

Mahan, A. T. *The Interest of America in Sea Power*. Boston, 1897.

Márquez Sterling, Manual. *Proceso Histórico de la Enmienda Platt, 1897–1934*. Havana, 1941.

Martínez Oritz, Rafael. *Cuba, los Primeros Años de Independencia*. 2 vols. Havana, 1911.

Matthews, Franklin. *The New-Born Cuba*. New York and London, 1899.

May, Ernest. *Imperial Democracy*. New York, 1961.

Miles, Nelson A. *Serving the Republic*. New York, 1911.

Millis, Walter. *The Martial Spirit*. Cambridge, 1931.

Morison, E. E., editor. *The Letters of Theodore Roosevelt*. 5 vols. Cambridge, 1951.

Oberholtzer, Ellis P. *A History of the United States Since the Civil War*. 5 vols. New York, 1937.

Olcott, Charles S. *The Life of William McKinley*. 2 vols. Boston and New York, 1916.

Orcutt, William Dana. *Burrows of Michigan and the Republican Party*. 2 vols. New York, 1917.

Palmer, Frederick. *Bliss, Peacemaker, the Life and Letters of General Tasker Howard Bliss*. New York, 1934.

Perkins, Dexter. *The Monroe Doctrine, 1867–1907*. Baltimore, 1937.

Portell Vilá, Herminio. *Historia de Cuba en sus relacions con los Estados Unidos y España*. 4 vols. Havana, 1937–1941.

Porter, Robert P. *Industrial Cuba*. New York, 1899.

———. *Life of William McKinley, Soldier, Lawyer, Statesman, with a biographical sketch of Garret A. Hobart*. Cleveland, 1896.

Pratt, Julius W. *Expansionists of 1898*. Baltimore, 1936.

Quesada, Gonzala de, and Northrop, Henry D. *The War in Cuba, or the Great Struggle for Freedom*. New York, 1896.

Richardson, Leon Burr. *William E. Chandler, Republican.* New York, 1940.

Robinson, Albert G. *Cuba and the Intervention.* New York, 1905.

Rubens, Horatio S. *Liberty, the Story of Cuba.* New York, 1932.

Souza, B. *Máximo Gómez, El Generalísimo.* Havana, 1936.

Stuart, Graham H. *Latin America and the United States.* New York, 1922.

Thayer, William Roscoe. *Life and Letters of John Hay.* Boston and New York, 1908.

Varona Guerrero, Miguel. *La Guerra de Independencia de Cuba, 1895–1898.* 3 vols. Havana, 1946.

Walters, Everett. *Joseph Benson Foraker.* Columbus, 1948.

Weinberg, Albert K. *Manifest Destiny.* Baltimore, 1935.

Wilkerson, Marcus M. *Public Opinion and the Spanish-American War.* Baton Rouge, 1932.

Wilson, James Harrison. *Under the Old Flag.* 2 vols. New York, 1912.

Wisan, Joseph E. *The Cuban Crisis as Reflected in the New York Press, 1895–1898.* New York, 1934.

Wright, Philip G. *The Cuban Situation and Our Treaty Relations.* Washington, 1931.

Index

255